STIRLING MOSS

Thank you
My thanks to Alan for his friendship and hard work,
and to Viper for all her valuable help with this book.

First published in September 2009

A catalogue record for this book is available
from the British Library

ISBN 978 1 84425 700 3

Library of Congress catalog card no. 2009923210

Haynes North America Inc., 861 Lawrence Drive,
Newbury Park, California 91320, USA.

Published by Haynes Publishing,
Sparkford, Yeovil, Somerset BA22 7JJ, UK
Tel: 01963 442030 Fax: 01963 440001
E-mail: sales@haynes.co.uk
Website: www.haynes.co.uk

Printed and bound in the UK

Editorial Director: Mark Hughes
Designers: Richard Parsons and James Robertson
Editor: Suzanne Arnold
Consultant Editor: Val Pirie

SOURCES
The authors acknowledge that some reference material has been
drawn from *Stirling Moss: My Cars, My Career* by Stirling Moss with
Doug Nye (Patrick Stephens Ltd 1987 and Haynes Publishing 1999)
and *Stirling Moss: The Authorised Biography* by Robert Edwards
(Orion 2001).

ACKNOWLEDGEMENTS
For supplying photographs, the publisher would like to thank LAT
(Kathy Ager, Stephen Carpenter, Emma Champion, Peter Higham
and Zoë Schafer), Karl Ludvigsen, Pete Lyons, Anthony Pritchard
(Tom March Collection), Michael Hammond (Guy Griffiths
Collection), Peter Sachs (Klemantaski Collection), Jens Torner
(Porsche), Daimler-Benz, Brian Moylan and Michael Clark.

CAPTIONS
Front cover: *Monaco GP 1961, Lotus 18/21 (Klemantaski Collection)*
Back cover: *Argentine GP 1955, Mercedes W196; Monaco GP 1956,
Maserati 250F; British GP 1958, Vanwall (Klemantaski Collection)*
Endpapers: *Monaco GP 1955, Mercedes W196; French GP 1958,
Vanwall (Klemantaski Collection)*
Title pages: *British GP 1958, Vanwall (LAT)*
Contents pages: *British GP 1955, Mercedes W196 (Klemantaski
Collection)*
Preface: *British GP 1957 (LAT)*
Introduction: *Le Mans 1955 (Klemantaski Collection)*

STIRLING MOSS

ALL MY RACES

SIR STIRLING MOSS OBE WITH ALAN HENRY

CONTENTS

PREFACE

Because motor racing is such a fast-moving sport, the reader needs to understand that, when racing returned after the war, there were many types of events for all sorts of vehicles taking place all round the world – and many of the rules developed as we went along.

This meant that I was able to compete in all sorts of races, such as Formula 1, Formula 2, Formula 3 and sports car events – from small handicap races at Goodwood to the classic Mille Miglia road race round Italy.

There were days when I might compete in cars as varied as a big Jaguar MkVII saloon and a 500cc Formula 3 car weighing only 500lb. Then there were rallies and even some World Speed Record attempts.

It was a golden era and I was lucky to be born at the right time and into the right family.

I was born on 17 September 1929. My father, Dad, was a dentist, who raced cars at Brooklands and the famous Indianapolis circuit in the USA. My mother, Mum, was an ambulance driver in the Royal Flying Corps during the First World War. Mum and Dad met through their interest in motorsport.

My sister, Pat, was born six years after me and became a champion show jumper and, later, a rally driver, so I suppose it is fair to say that the Mosses were a very competitive bunch.

We had a farm and I was allowed to drive within the grounds but my story really began when Dad allowed me to drive his BMW in a few small competitive motoring events when I was 17. The war was barely over. Petrol, food and many other things were rationed, and biros and nylons were 'Gotta Have' items, along with fresh eggs and Parker 51 pens.

There hadn't been any racing for eight years so, when it started again, all the drivers were from the pre-war era, as were the cars. The following pages tell what happened next.

Sir Stirling Moss OBE

INTRODUCTION

BY ALAN HENRY

There is an infectiously enthusiastic streak about the personality and character of Sir Stirling Moss OBE that utterly belies the fact that he celebrates his 80th birthday in 2009.

Our first work together for this volume took place just after Lewis Hamilton clinched the 2008 World Championship and, having been at Interlagos for that memorable Brazilian Grand Prix, I found myself facing a barrage of questioning about the detail of the event. It did not take long to establish that Stirling knew – or certainly understood and interpreted – far more of the subtleties of that event than I had done.

This compelling interest in contemporary events and need to know about them adds an extra dimension to this remarkable man. Forty-seven years may have passed since his front-line motor racing career ended in the tangled wreckage of a Lotus Formula 1 car against a solid earth bank at Goodwood, but he remains to this day one of the sport's most enduring celebrities.

"I am better known for my name rather than my television face," he told me recently. I would respectfully contradict that view. In this mass-media age when every sportsman is clamouring for his moment of stardom, Moss remains an iconic sporting figure even though he last raced a Grand Prix car in anger so long ago that Lewis Hamilton's father, Anthony, was only 2 at the time.

Moreover, such admiration is not just confined to Britain, but ripples across the globe, as those of us will know who have watched the applause he always attracts in Melbourne, for example, where he has been a hero since winning the Grand Prix at the wheel of a Maserati 250F during Australia's Olympic year way back in 1956.

The fact that Stirling never won the World Championship adds to the allure, giving his story an almost mysterious 'might-have-been' twist to it.

Although he is perfectionist with a rigorous eye for detail, Stirling is also one of the easiest of personalities to get along with. He is convivial. He also manages to be direct and to-the-point without being in any way dismissive. During my career as a motorsport journalist, our paths have crossed from time to time and it has always been a pleasure.

Being invited by him to collaborate in the writing of this volume to celebrate such an important anniversary was deeply flattering. Even more flattering, I might add, than being recruited to drive him to Silverstone for a British Racing Drivers' Club annual general meeting not so many years ago, a journey that elicited a compliment from him about my apparently unflurried driving style – something none of my family nor friends will ever believe!

Millions of words must have been written about Stirling Moss, but this volume, we hope, will put in somewhat sharper perspective not just his extraordinary career as a racing driver but also those epic times in which he raced. If you scan the pages of a 1950s volume of the weekly magazine *Autosport*, you will see what I mean. In the summer months most editions would carry at least one obituary notice of a driver who had been killed in a racing crash somewhere in Europe. Acceptance of this state of affairs simply reflected different times and different attitudes.

As I wrote these words a publication from the FIA, motor racing's international governing body, has landed on my desk. It is called 'Walking Away – how the FIA Institute's work enables drivers to walk away from major impacts' and it features a photograph of Robert Kubica's BMW Sauber exploding into its component parts during his accident in the 2007 Canadian Grand Prix. Kubica was virtually unhurt.

Such levels of driver protection could not have been remotely imagined at the height of Stirling's career. But the whole rationale as to what motor racing is about has changed significantly. To this day Moss is adamant that the risk, the danger, was absolutely integral to the basic challenge during the time he competed. You calculated the risk and drove accordingly. But without the risk of death and injury, that challenge would not have been the same. Or as meaningfully compelling.

Yet study of Stirling's diaries, which he compiled rigorously through his career, reveals another crucial dimension to his life that would astound anyone in today's Formula 1 environment. And that is the sheer normality of it all. The Grand Prix star of that time was far closer to the enthusiast, the man in the street, than his equivalent of 2009. To this day Stirling lives in the same house that he built on a London street in 1961 and he still has an accessible 'phone number that he usually answers.

In his day there were no private jets in which to pamper their highly stressed owners after less than an hour and a half of Grand Prix exertion. No PR people, 'minders' or psychotherapists to mop their fevered brows. Just a world which, to those who remember racing in the 1950s, must have seemed daunting in its sheer size.

He drove in 585 motorsport events between March 1947 and April 1962. Of those, 66 were World Championship Grands Prix, of which he won 16, also starting from pole position on the same number of occasions. Four times he was runner-up in the World Championship, and three times he finished third.

Yet this is only part of a story that seems the more remarkable the longer you examine it. We live in a time when the Formula 1 World Championship utterly dominates the media and the commercial resources available to motorsport. Stirling Moss raced at a time when the textural diversity of international motor racing was of an order that is difficult to grasp. It was fascinating, rich in contrasts and bursting with freedom of spirit. This book offers a taste of that atmosphere.

1947

CUTTING MY TEETH

The grey, post-war period made up my formative years, to a large extent. When the war started I was almost ten and my sister was five but, in a sense, we were lucky because, unlike many others, we were spared the experience of the family being split up.

Before the war, my father, who was a dentist, had met my mother while motor racing. When they were married, in 1927, Dad promised to give up racing. Six years later, he suggested that it would be fun for them to take part in some motoring competitions together. They jointly agreed to start rallying and 'mud-plugging'. This was a competition where the driver endeavours to climb muddy hills with the help of the passenger bouncing up and down and the driver using a 'fiddle brake'. This device, handled correctly, helped the driver to prevent a selected rear wheel spinning and thereby assisted the car to continue up the hill and, hopefully, get a clean climb.

Of course, motoring was put very much on the back burner during the war, although it was going to take a lot more than a world war to suppress my father's imagination and sense of ingenuity. He designed and patented the Morrison shelter, which saved many people's lives during the bombing.

Dad realised that, when the war was over and petrol available to all, really nice cars would again be popular. He therefore bought a very desirable, but completely impractical, 12-cylinder Lagonda drophead coupé – with a cocktail cabinet in the back! – plus a racy-looking Alfa Romeo. Because my father was a dentist, he was allowed a small ration of petrol. He also converted our old Rolls-Royce to run on gas, although, I must admit, it was pretty slow.

A couple of years after the end of the war, I competed in my first car event, which was a hill climb, and Dad let me drive his BMW 328.

By this time my interest in girls had awakened. I was running around in an MG TB and I had met a very nice girl called Sylvia, who was a receptionist for a local dentist. One day Bob Cowan, a fellow who worked on our farm, asked if he could borrow my car to go to buy some cigarettes in town. I agreed to lend it to him in exchange for being allowed to use his flat. I knew my mother was also out in town so I told Bob to take the alternative, shorter, bumpier route to Maidenhead, reasoning that my mother would return by the longer, smoother road. Just my luck, she didn't! She passed Bob in my MG on the way back and demanded to know where I was. I guess she knew, from his face, what I was up to and drove back home at quite a rate of knots. She caught Sylvia and I, and really gave us a dressing-down. There was a huge row and I begged my mother not to tell my father about it – and nothing more was ever said about the affair.

Soon after this, we had our first post-war Continental family holiday in Menton, in the south of France, and I was fortunate enough to be taken to Nice to see the street race along the promenade, which was won by Luigi Villoresi in a Maserati. We later funded the rest of our holiday by selling a spare tyre for £50!

We were on the road again.

LEFT At the Poole Speed Trials during that memorable first season driving my father's BMW 328, a terrific little sports car in which I learned a great deal. Note the lack of a crash helmet: my father would later insist that I wore one even though I thought the notion a bit sissy! (Guy Griffiths Collection)

1 Cullen Cup

Harrow Car Club Trial

BMW 328

2 March 1947, Harrow, Greater London (GB)

Entrant A.E. Moss

The first real motoring I had done was bouncing around the fields on the family farm in a stripped-down Austin Seven that my father had bought for about £15. But I had my eye on a Morgan three-wheeler and, as soon as I was eligible to drive it, I applied for my first driving licence. This was a few months before my 16th birthday, in 1945.

Right from the beginning, my father instilled a sense of incentive in me by making it clear that everything came at a price. To get my hands on the Morgan, I had to give up pretty well everything else I owned.

My father was always extremely supportive of my racing activities but right at the beginning he wasn't quite so understanding. When he heard that I had ordered a Formula 3 racing car, using some of my horse jumping winnings to pay the £50 deposit, he hit the roof. He punished me by taking my Morgan three-wheeler away and made me ride a bike. This certainly made my love life more complicated and less comfortable!

Later, when I moved up to an MG TB, it was the same story. I had to relinquish various other treasured possessions.

However, when my father acquired a BMW 328 from a fellow dentist, Victor Biggs, I managed to persuade him to allow me to compete in various sprints and trials, which gave me an insight into what competition motoring was all about.

The Harrow Car Club Trial was the first such novice event – and I won the Cullen Cup.

2 Retired

Inter-Club Trial

BMW 328

6 April 1947, London (GB)

Organising club North-West London Motor Club **Reason for retirement** Broken half-shaft **Entrant** A.E. Moss

---

I have to confess that, 60 years on, I have only the most sketchy recollection of this event. But the fact that the BMW retired with a broken driveshaft suggests that this was a 'mud-plugging' event because the car was prone to such failures when the mud was too glutinous.

3 1st in class

Junior Car Club Rally

BMW 328

28 June 1947, Eastbourne, Sussex (GB)

Entrant A.E. Moss

This was touted as a rally, but my recollection is that it was more of a gymkhana on the promenade at Eastbourne.

4 7th in class

Brighton Speed Trials

BMW 328

1 September 1947, Brighton, Sussex (GB)

Organising club Brighton & Hove Motor Club **Course length** 1km **Car no** 140 **Entrant** A.E. Moss

---

The Brighton Speed Trials on Madeira Drive, along the seafront, would become a popular feature on the British national racing calendar and endured well into the 1970s. In retrospect, seventh in the sports car class seems a pretty modest achievement.

BELOW *Memories from the Moss album! From left: the Morgan three-wheeler that gave me the initial taste for competition; my MG TB, made in 1940 and one of the last cars to be built before the full effects of the war were felt; my friend Sylvia, who opened my eyes to other attractions.* (Stirling Moss Collection)

5   3rd in class

Poole Speed Trials

BMW 328

6 September 1947, Poole, Dorset (GB)

Course length 0.6 mile approx **Car no** 27 **Entrant** A.E. Moss

This was an event that took place over a winding course of just over half a mile, laid out in the grounds of South Lytchett Manor, near Poole. We removed the rear wheel spats for this event, perhaps thinking that it would save a little bit of weight and improve our performance.

6   Unclassified

Chichester Speed Trials

BMW 328

20 September 1947, Merston Aerodrome, Chichester, West Sussex (GB)

Car no 85 **Entrant** A.E. Moss

This was the final event of my novice year, but I was already thinking about what I might do in the future as far as racing was concerned. One day, on our way home from one of the events with the BMW, my father and I drove past the Cooper garage in Ewell Road, Surbiton, Surrey, where they were building the 500cc single-seater racing cars that would be so successful in the years to come. My father had known Charles Cooper from their days competing at Brooklands before the war. It is not difficult to imagine what I was thinking.

ABOVE *Hard at work during the Brighton Speed Trials, one of the most enjoyable sprint events of the season.*
(Guy Griffiths Collection)

BELOW *My final outing of my first year of competition certainly left me with no doubt as to what I wanted to do next.*
(Guy Griffiths Collection)

1948

SINGLE-SEATER NURSERY

After the BMW was sold, I ordered a brand new Cooper 500 with a JAP engine and a few spares and, in doing so, came up against some fairly serious parental opposition. My father knew enough about racing, from his own experience, to understand just how difficult it would be for me to achieve my aim of making a living as a 'professional racing driver'. He took some time to be won over but, once he had decided to support the idea, his support was wholehearted and unstinting. He even agreed for me to give up work.

Until the end of 1947, I had been working at the Eccleston Hotel in Victoria, waiting at tables, resolving problems with irate guests, acting as telephone operator and even working behind Reception. I had also done a stint in the kitchens of a restaurant called the Palmerston in the City, where we had to serve 1,000 lunches a day. It was pretty gruelling but, for some unfathomable reason, I thought that working in the hotel business would give me plenty of opportunities to go off motor racing at the weekends. How wrong could I be! It did seem, however, that I wasn't destined to have a career in the hotel business.

My motor racing became a bit of a family affair. Because my sister, Pat, was deeply into riding and show jumping, the family owned a two-horse horsebox. The centre division was removed and this allowed my little Cooper to be transported. The old family Rolls-Royce station wagon was pressed into service as a makeshift transporter.

One thing my father did insist on was that, from the start of my racing career, I should wear a crash hat. I told him that it was a bit 'sissy' as none of the really fast drivers like Villoresi, Wimille and Ascari used one. They chose cloth helmets. Anyway, I had to use an enormous black leather-covered device until Herbert Johnson came out with an attractive polo helmet with a peak, and a visor if one wanted it. These helmets cost five guineas, and one more guinea for the optional visor. I liked its style and had mine painted off-white.

I still race using the same kind of helmet today. However, it took me 17 years to talk the FIA into granting me permission to bring out my old racing gear and use it in my historic racing. It came about with my discovering that a waiver could be legally enforced if I added the words 'contributory negligence'. In other words, race organisers could get insurance, even if I was taking part, because I have signed a legal document waiving my rights, and those of my successors, for any claims against them for any reason. To my mind, all these bills of human rights, and so on, are partly to blame for many of the modern restrictions that surround us, like Health and Safety.

To help with the running of my Cooper, I enlisted Don Müller, a German who had worked for BMW before the war and, as a prisoner of war, had come to work for Dad on our farm at Bray-on-Thames, and then decided to stay once peace returned.

Before taking delivery of my car from the Cooper factory, I started trawling through the list of events in which I thought I might compete, and sent away an entry for a hill climb at Shelsley Walsh – one of the most famous venues in the country at the time. In their wisdom, the organisers saw fit to turn it down! However, I was accepted for my first hill climb at Prescott, a week or two later.

LEFT *A flavour of the times! Specially tailored racing car cockpits still lay many years into the future when I began racing my 500cc Cooper-JAP. With my right hand I am steadying myself against the cornering forces while at the same time blocking off the airflow to the engine intake! This is at Silverstone on 2 October.* (LAT)

Prescott Hill Climb

Cooper-JAP 500 MkII

9 May 1948, Prescott, Gloucestershire (GB)

Organising club Bugatti Owners' Club **Course length** 880yds
Best time 51.01s **Car no** 48 **Entrant** S.C. Moss

BELOW *Moving forward to the timing line before my first run at Prescott. My father is puffing nervously on his cigarette as he keeps an eye on my final preparations.* (Guy Griffiths Collection)

This was my very first serious outing in a racing car, my new Cooper 500cc, and it was a close-run thing getting the little car ready in time as we only collected it a week before.

It was pretty clear that I wouldn't have an opportunity to try the car before the event, so I called up Eric Brandon, one of the leading 500cc racers of the time, and asked him whether he would come over to Cippenham, near Maidenhead, Berkshire, to try the car and show me a few things about driving it. Eric, who was a good pal of John Cooper, very graciously said he would, and the exercise took place on roads around an unfinished building estate. Eric told me that the car "was going like a bomb", before climbing out and letting me have a go.

I took off in a cloud of wheelspin but my impromptu test came to a premature end when an elderly lady on a bicycle rode slowly across my bows. I had to take to the dirt to avoid her, in a flurry of stones and general debris. I guess I was lucky there was no permanent damage to the car. And that was as far as my preparation went for the Prescott hill climb.

Other competitors included Lord Strathcarron, John Cooper, Eric Brandon and Clive Lones. I actually set a new class record of 51.01 seconds on my first run, but it was short-lived because Clive Lones hurled his Tiger Kitten Special up the hill in 49.98 seconds. Colin Strang and Eric Brandon also bettered my time by the end of the day. They weren't going to let some whipper-snapper steal their glory!

8 — 1st in class

Stanmer Park Hill Climb

Cooper-JAP 500 MkII

5 June 1948, Brighton, Sussex (GB)

Course length c1,200yds **Best time** 58.78s
Car no 35 **Entrant** S.C. Moss

The Stanmer Park Hill Climb was a new fixture on the calendar and, as my father correctly pointed out, I would be at less of a disadvantage against my more experienced competitors because none of them could claim previous experience at this venue.

Stanmer House, and the surrounding 4,598-acre estate, had been purchased by Brighton Council in 1947 and the sweeping driveways were used to make a most enjoyable event. Eric Brandon again proved the strongest competition and he opened the 500cc class battle with a climb of 61.02 seconds. I then did 60.88 seconds. Eric came back with 59.30 seconds after a change of his car's gearbox. Then I managed a climb of 58.78 seconds, which was enough to take the class and win me my first motorsport trophy. I was ecstatic!

Unfortunately the meeting was abandoned prematurely after Bob Gerard, having set the fastest time of the day, found himself unable to stop after the crossing finishing line and crashed into a tree and some parked racing cars.

9 — 1st

Brough Aerodrome, Heat 3

Cooper-JAP 500 MkII

4 July 1948, Brough, North Yorkshire (GB)

Organising club Blackburn Aircraft Motor Club **Circuit length** 1,144yds **Race speed** 48.9mph **Car no** 44 **Entrant** S.C. Moss

There is a bit of a mystery surrounding this event that I have tried to clear up while writing this book, but I have to admit it now seems lost in the mists of time. According to contemporary reports, I sent the Cooper to Brough by train to save time, and the railway authorities insisted that it could be transported only if its fuel tank was emptied.

The story goes that my father and I had to rush around and buy separate containers, fill them with fuel, and then transport them with us in the train's passenger compartment – something that I have to say sounds pretty dangerous. I recently phoned Ken Gregory, my friend and business manager, to check, but he also had no recollection of our taking the car on the train.

It was raining for this event, my first circuit race, and all rather dreary, but the adrenalin was pumping as I was the new boy trying to show my colours. I was very pleased when I succeeded on this makeshift circuit, which used a combination of perimeter roads and runways.

ABOVE *No, that's not tyre smoke caused by me locking up, but simply the car kicking up a dust trail on the dirty track surface at Stanmer Park, scene of my first class win with the Cooper.* (Guy Griffiths Collection)

10 — 1st

Brough Aerodrome, Final

Cooper-JAP 500 MkII

4 July 1948, Brough, North Yorkshire (GB)

Organising club Blackburn Aircraft Motor Club **Circuit length** 1,144yds **Race speed** 52mph **Car no** 44 **Entrant** S.C. Moss

The rain intensified for the final, but I led throughout to score my second win of the day. *Motor Sport* very kindly described me as the 'complete master of the situation'.

<table>
<tr><td>

11
1st

Brough Aerodrome, Handicap Race

Cooper-JAP 500 MkII

4 July 1948, Brough, North Yorkshire (GB)

Organising club Blackburn Aircraft Motor Club **Circuit length** 1,144yds **Race speed** 51.5mph **Car no** 44 **Entrant** S.C. Moss

</td><td>

12
1st in class

Bouley Bay Hill Climb

Cooper-JAP 500 MkII

15 July 1948, Bouley Bay, Jersey (CI)

RAC British Hill Climb Championship

Organising club Jersey Motor Cycle & Light Car Club **Course length** 1,011yds **Best time** 63.8s **Best speed** 58mph **Car no** 12 **Entrant** S.C. Moss

</td></tr>
</table>

This was my third race that day. Due to lack of entries, the programme at Brough was reorganised to include a special eight-lap handicap race, which earned me my first newspaper headline. 'Brough car race won by back-marker' ran in the following morning's *Daily Mail*. Not quite, perhaps, the exact wording, but you can get the gist of what they were aiming at. At the end of the day, my prize-winnings amounted to the grand sum of £13.

The Bouley Bay international speed hill climb was a round of the prestigious RAC British Hill Climb Championship and, as such, attracted considerable attention. Dennis Poore in his Alfa Romeo managed to beat Raymond Mays in the ERA with a best time overall of 59.2 seconds, but I was pretty satisfied to take almost 6 seconds off the 500 class record, leaving it at 63.8 seconds.

Unfortunately we finished the day facing some pretty serious problems. When we examined the JAP engine after my climb, it was clear that it had suffered a serious internal breakage. The Bouley Bay fixture had taken place on a Thursday so we had to think on our feet if we were going to get the Cooper back to Prescott within 48 hours, in time for my next event on the Sunday.

We duly put Don Müller and the Cooper on the ferry back to Southampton, and my father and I flew to England and collected the parts needed to repair the engine before meeting up with Don. There really was no time to spare and we had to set off for Prescott. My father drove our old Rolls-Royce shooting brake, which was our tow car, while Don and I went to work on the Cooper in the horsebox – stripping an engine is not the easiest of jobs in the best of conditions but even less so if you are confined to the back of a bouncing, swaying horsebox on the move. I am told that Don and I "swore mightily" during the course of the journey – hardly surprising, I guess.

BELOW *Programmes from my albums testify to the wide variety of competitive events that were held all over the country in those exciting and emergent immediate post-war years.* (Stirling Moss Collection)

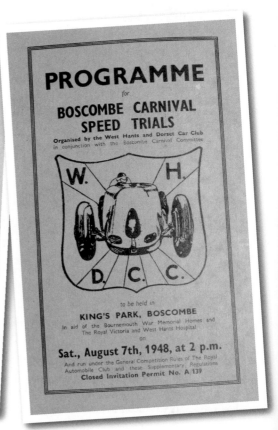

13 1st in class

Prescott Hill Climb

Cooper-JAP 500 MkII

18 July 1948, Prescott, Gloucestershire (GB)

Organising club Bugatti Owners' **Club Course length** 880yds
Best time 49.51s **Car no** 44 **Entrant** S.C. Moss

14 2nd overall

Great Auclum Hill Climb

Cooper-JAP 500 MkII

25 July 1948, Burghfield Common, Berks (GB)

Course length c600yds **Best time** 23.46s **Car no** 72
Entrant S.C. Moss

All the effort we expended proved well worthwhile because the Cooper was ready to run again in time for the start of the meeting at Prescott. I see from my diary that I took part in three timed runs, all under the 50-second mark. The best was 49.51 seconds. Interestingly, I was the only 500 driver to beat 50 seconds.

This was more of a speed trial, or a sprint, if you like, on a very short course on a stretch of private land near Burghfield Common in Berkshire. From the start, the course dived into a dip with a swoop at the bottom, and, after a series of banked corners, dived again through a gate.

Most cars could not get out of second gear. I opted to keep the Prescott gear ratios, which enabled me to pull third gear at a couple of points on the run. I broke the record and set a time that looked good enough to stand as fastest time of the day, but I was pipped right at the end by Ken Wharton in his supercharged special.

15   2nd overall

Boscombe Carnival Speed Trials

Cooper-JAP 500 MkII

7 August 1948, Boscombe, Bournemouth (GB)

Organising club West Hants & Dorset Car Club **Course length** 0.6 mile approx **Best time** 31.4s **Best speed** 46mph **Car no** 58 **Entrant** S.C. Moss

This was quite a quick venue, only about 700 yards long, with two flat-out stretches linked by a hairpin. I set the fastest time in the racing car class but was pipped for the fastest time of the day by Lionel Leonard, a close friend of mine, in a supercharged MG Magnette.

16   4th in class

Brighton Speed Trials

Cooper-JAP 500 MkII

5 September 1948, Brighton, Sussex (GB)

Organising club Brighton & Hove Motor Club **Course length** 1km **Best time** 34.14s **Car no** 75 **Entrant** S.C. Moss

This was my second outing in this flat-out sprint along the seaside promenade at Brighton. Even though my engine was a bit sick on this occasion, it served to convince my father and I that the JAP engine was becoming eclipsed by the rival Norton in terms of power output, so this was something for us to keep in mind for the future.

17   3rd in class

Prescott Hill Climb

Cooper-JAP 500 MkII

12 September 1948, Prescott (GB)

Organising club Bugatti Owners' Club **Course length** 880yds **Best time** 53.67s **Car no** 47 **Entrant** S.C. Moss

I have to confess that this was one of the few events where I was really tense. It poured with rain for much of the day, with cars slipping and sliding off the asphalt in all directions. Waiting around for more than two hours before I made my run did not help, either, and I was beaten in my class by both Eric Brandon and Colin Strang.

ABOVE *Refitting the Cooper's engine cover after some last-minute adjustments prior to winning my first race at Goodwood, a success achieved despite the grid order being determined by ballot.* (Guy Griffiths Collection)

LEFT *Displaying just a touch of opposite-lock in unpleasantly wet weather at Prescott. Third place in my class was the only reward for hanging around for ages in the sodden conditions.* (Guy Griffiths Collection)

18   1st

Goodwood, 500cc Race

Cooper-JAP 500 MkII

18 September 1948, Goodwood (GB)

Race distance 3 laps of 2.40-mile circuit **Race time** 6m 0.4s
Race speed 71.92mph **Fastest lap** 1m 58s, 73mph **Car no** 7
Entrant S.C. Moss

This was the most important race meeting in the post-war era at a circuit that would become one of my firm favourites. The 500cc race was a three-lap affair and, because grid positions were secured by ballot, I found myself starting well down the field. I quickly took the lead, though, and won by almost half a lap from Eric Brandon even though my father was signalling to me from the pits to slow down.

19   1st in class

Shelsley Walsh Hill Climb

Cooper-JAP 500 MkII

25 September 1948, Shelsley Walsh (GB)

Organising club Midland Automobile Club **Course length**
0.5 mile **Best time** 43.84s **Car no** 2 **Entrant** S.C. Moss

Earlier in the year I had been turned down for an entry at Shelsley Walsh due to my inexperience but the Midland Automobile Club clearly felt I had done enough to be accepted once its September meeting came around, although the class structure was not ideal because it meant I would have to compete in the 750cc category.

Despite this I managed to win the class and was flattered by the over-approving tone kindly adopted by *The Autocar*'s correspondent, who referred to the 'sheer genius' of my cornering technique.

20   Retired

British Grand Prix, 500cc Race

Cooper-JAP 500 MkII

2 October 1948, Silverstone (GB)

Organising club British Racing Drivers' Club **Circuit length** 3.67 miles **Reason for retirement** Engine drive sprocket **Car no** 5 **Entrant** S.C. Moss

21   1st

Dunholme Lodge, 500cc Race

Cooper-JAP 500 MkII

9 October 1948, Dunholme Lodge aerodrome, Lincolnshire (GB)

Race time 22m 36.4s **Race speed** 78.56mph **Car no** 2 **Entrant** S.C. Moss

This race supported the first British Grand Prix to be held at Silverstone. I qualified on the front row of the grid and, at the end of the first lap, led from Colin Strang, R.M. 'Curly' Dryden and John Cooper. After three laps, I was just under a second in front of Spike Rhiando but then, out on the back of the circuit, an engine drive sprocket worked loose. I had to run back to the pits to get the tools necessary to repair it, then run back to the car again. Spike Rhiando won.

I rounded off the season with another win, this time at an aerodrome circuit near Lincoln.

It was then time for my father and I to reflect on my achievements in 1948 and start planning seriously for the year ahead. I could hold my head up as I had not done too badly. By then, though, we knew that the JAP engine had to go as it only gave about 45bhp on alcohol, with a compression ratio of 14:1. I knew, deep down, that I would need to buy one of the double-knocker Nortons, which were in short supply – and expensive. So the Moss team held a Council of War.

LEFT *The programme cover from the first post-war British Grand Prix at Silverstone. The artist, incidentally, put green livery on his interpretation of an Alfa Romeo 158!* (Stirling Moss Collection)

RIGHT *Preparing for the start of the 500cc supporting race to the British Grand Prix at Silverstone. In those days the startline was on the exit of what is now the Abbey chicane.* (Guy Griffiths Collection)

24   1st

British Grand Prix, 500cc Race

Cooper-JAP 500 MkIII

14 May 1949, Silverstone (GB)

Organising club British Racing Drivers' Club
Race distance 17 laps of 3-mile circuit **Race time**
44m 26.2s **Race speed** 68.81mph **Fastest lap**
70.95mph **Car no** 23 **Entrant** S.C. Moss

My race preceded the British Grand Prix and, for some reason, it was decided that the 500s would have an Indianapolis-style rolling start behind an Austin A90. This would have been quite an interesting experiment had it not been for the fact that the 'pace car' went rather slowly, with the result that several competitors found their cars oiling up.

My engine had not been pulling to its maximum in practice, but I managed to lead from start to finish and set the fastest lap in the process. After I took the chequered flag the whole Moss family sat down to watch the Grand Prix, which was won by Baron 'Toulo' de Graffenried in a Maserati.

ABOVE *Wearing a slightly concerned expression – and a BRDC badge proudly in my lapel – prior to the British Grand Prix supporting race.* (Guy Griffiths Collection)

25   Retired

Douglas, Manx Cup

Cooper-JAP 1,000 MkIII

26 May 1949, Douglas (IoM)

Organising club British Racing Drivers' Club **Race distance** 18 laps of 3.88-mile circuit **Reason for retirement** Magneto drive after 15 laps **Fastest lap** 3m 26s, 67.78mph (record) **Car no** 7 **Entrant** S.C. Moss

B y this time, I had made up my mind that I wanted to compete abroad to measure myself against the best possible opposition, but, before I did so, I decided to try my hand on this challenging road circuit.

I qualified on pole position and led easily from the start, building up a big lead over Dudley Folland's new 2-litre Ferrari V12. After I had built up a cushion of more than half a minute, my father signalled that I should slow down. Then Folland's Ferrari retired with clutch trouble, so I slowed up even more. Then my magneto drive broke, and I came into the pits to see if anything could be done. I rejoined the race for a short period, but the car stopped for good out on the circuit.

26   1st in class

Blandford Hill Climb

Cooper-JAP 500 MkIII

28 May 1949, Blandford, Dorset (GB)

Organising club West Hants & Dorset Car Club **Course length** 0.5 mile **Best time** 35.62s **Car no** 101 **Entrant** S.C. Moss

T he trip to the Isle of Man had obviously been a big disappointment, but it served to convince me that the 1,000cc Cooper was really very good. Before I embarked on my first proper Continental trip to Lake Garda

in Italy, I managed to squeeze in three more hill climbs, the first of which was at Blandford, where I set the fastest time in my class, using the 500cc engine.

27   2nd in class

Shelsley Walsh Hill Climb

Cooper-JAP 1,000 MkIII

11 June 1949, Shelsley Walsh (GB)

Organising club Midland Automobile Club **Course length** 0.5 mile **Best time** 38.57s **Car no** 17 **Entrant** S.C. Moss

T his Shelsley Walsh meeting was considered by many to have attracted one of the best entries for years. Using the 1,000cc engine, I was satisfied to set the fastest time for an unsupercharged competitor, and I finished second in the 1,100cc class.

28   2nd in class

Bo'ness Hill Climb

Cooper-JAP 1,000 MkIII

25 June 1949, Linlithgow, Scotland (GB)

Organising club Scottish Sporting Car Club **Course length** 0.5 mile **Best time** 36.1s **Car no** 59 **Entrant** S.C. Moss

T he Bo'ness Hill Climb was near Linlithgow in Scotland, at the venue that had hosted the very first round of the British Hill Climb Championship in May 1947. I came second in the 1,100cc class and fourth overall.

RIGHT *Building up a commanding lead in the Manx Cup on the superb Douglas street circuit on the Isle of Man. Note the pannier fuel tanks fitted to the Cooper for this extra-long race and the slightly more comfortable seat that offered me more support than the normal one. Pity I failed to finish.* (LAT)

29   1st in class

9th Circuito del Garda, Heat 1

Cooper-JAP 1,000 MkIII

10 July 1949, Circuito del Garda, Lake Garda (I)

Organising club AC Brescia **Circuit length** 10.17 miles
Race distance 83 miles **Race time** 1h 12m 15.4s
Race speed 67.5mph **Car no** 46 **Entrant** S.C. Moss

I received £50 starting money for competing on this superb Italian road circuit. I made the trip with a couple of friends in a Bedford van we had bought, with the Cooper tucked inside. The journey took two days and, looking back on it, serves as a reminder of just how big Europe seemed in those distant days before the present autoroutes were constructed.

The atmosphere at this lakeside circuit was extremely relaxed. Anxious not to miss anything, I was out early sitting in my car on the starting grid when Luigi Villoresi strolled past. I asked him whether we were a bit late starting the race but he was pretty relaxed, suggesting that there was no hurry and it would be a good idea to have lunch first!

Once the race eventually started, I tucked in behind the Ferraris of Villoresi and Count Sterzi from the start, but I quickly became concerned about the rather erratic manner in which Sterzi was driving. Eventually, he overdid things and spun backwards over the tramlines into a telegraph pole, which snapped in two, before his Ferrari careered over the edge of a drop. Sterzi survived the incident, but he was badly injured and, I must say, it shook me up for a while.

I finished the race third overall, behind the Ferraris of Villoresi and Mario Tadini, and won my class.

30   1st in class

9th Circuito del Garda, Final

Cooper-JAP 1,000 MkIII

10 July 1949, Circuito del Garda, Lake Garda (I)

Organising club AC Brescia **Circuit length** 10.17 miles
Car no 46 **Entrant** S.C. Moss

LEFT & BELOW Cuttings from my album recalling memories of my first proper overseas race at Lake Garda. The relaxed mood of some of the competitors rather took me aback, I have to confess, but this was part of the Italian charm and general tempo of life. (Stirling Moss Collection)

Despite my strong performance in the first heat, we were worried about the final because the car was showing signs that the magnetos were overheating. We had to improvise pretty quickly because there was not much time before the final was due to start. We cut a hole in the under-tray, bending the edges down into the airflow in order to direct cool air on to the magnetos.

Our impromptu surgery seemed to do the trick. I managed to repeat the result achieved in the heat, finishing third overall behind Villoresi and Tadini, and winning my class. I received a great ovation from the spectators and £200 in prize money.

When the Italians first saw my Cooper they referred to it as a jukebox! I managed to show that it was a quick one.

31   Unclassified

Reims, Coupe des Petites Cylindrées

Cooper-JAP 1,000 MkIII

17 July 1949, Reims-Gueux (F)

Organising club Automobile Club de Reims **Race distance** 26 laps of 4.853-mile circuit **Car no** 2 **Entrant** S.C. Moss

After the Garda race, we drove straight back across Europe to be at Reims in time for the following weekend's race, which supported the French Grand Prix. There were three Coopers on the grid (mine, Bill Aston's, and the Vincent-powered version of George Abecassis) but none of us finished. My drive chain broke, so I had no choice but to push the car the best part of a mile back to the pits, where it was repaired. I rejoined but retired with magneto problems after another 13 laps.

l'action automobile

le Grand Prix de France

II REIMS *JUILLET 1949*

PROGRAMME OFFICIEL   NUMERO COURSES

BRITISH DRIVER WINS

The 18-year-old British driver, Stirling Moss, in a Cooper Jap, won the 1,000 c.c. class event in the "Tour Lake Garda" motor races, near Rome, yesterday.

Watched by a crowd of 100,000 people, Moss covered the 83 miles course at an average speed of about 67½ m.p.h.

24   1st

British Grand Prix, 500cc Race

Cooper-JAP 500 MkIII

14 May 1949, Silverstone (GB)

Organising club British Racing Drivers' Club
Race distance 17 laps of 3-mile circuit **Race time**
44m 26.2s **Race speed** 68.81mph **Fastest lap**
70.95mph **Car no** 23 **Entrant** S.C. Moss

M y race preceded the British Grand Prix and, for some reason, it was decided that the 500s would have an Indianapolis-style rolling start behind an Austin A90. This would have been quite an interesting experiment had it not been for the fact that the 'pace car' went rather slowly, with the result that several competitors found their cars oiling up.

My engine had not been pulling to its maximum in practice, but I managed to lead from start to finish and set the fastest lap in the process. After I took the chequered flag the whole Moss family sat down to watch the Grand Prix, which was won by Baron 'Toulo' de Graffenried in a Maserati.

ABOVE *Wearing a slightly concerned expression – and a BRDC badge proudly in my lapel – prior to the British Grand Prix supporting race.* (Guy Griffiths Collection)

25   Retired

Douglas, Manx Cup

Cooper-JAP 1,000 MkIII

26 May 1949, Douglas (IoM)

Organising club British Racing Drivers' Club **Race distance** 18 laps of 3.88-mile circuit **Reason for retirement** Magneto drive after 15 laps **Fastest lap** 3m 26s, 67.78mph (record) **Car no** 7 **Entrant** S.C. Moss

B y this time, I had made up my mind that I wanted to compete abroad to measure myself against the best possible opposition, but, before I did so, I decided to try my hand on this challenging road circuit.

I qualified on pole position and led easily from the start, building up a big lead over Dudley Folland's new 2-litre Ferrari V12. After I had built up a cushion of more than half a minute, my father signalled that I should slow down. Then Folland's Ferrari retired with clutch trouble, so I slowed up even more. Then my magneto drive broke, and I came into the pits to see if anything could be done. I rejoined the race for a short period, but the car stopped for good out on the circuit.

26   1st in class

Blandford Hill Climb

Cooper-JAP 500 MkIII

28 May 1949, Blandford, Dorset (GB)

Organising club West Hants & Dorset Car Club **Course length** 0.5 mile **Best time** 35.62s **Car no** 101 **Entrant** S.C. Moss

T he trip to the Isle of Man had obviously been a big disappointment, but it served to convince me that the 1,000cc Cooper was really very good. Before I embarked on my first proper Continental trip to Lake Garda

in Italy, I managed to squeeze in three more hill climbs, the first of which was at Blandford, where I set the fastest time in my class, using the 500cc engine.

27   2nd in class

Shelsley Walsh Hill Climb

Cooper-JAP 1,000 MkIII

11 June 1949, Shelsley Walsh (GB)

Organising club Midland Automobile Club **Course length** 0.5 mile **Best time** 38.57s **Car no** 17 **Entrant** S.C. Moss

T his Shelsley Walsh meeting was considered by many to have attracted one of the best entries for years. Using the 1,000cc engine, I was satisfied to set the fastest time for an unsupercharged competitor, and I finished second in the 1,100cc class.

28   2nd in class

Bo'ness Hill Climb

Cooper-JAP 1,000 MkIII

25 June 1949, Linlithgow, Scotland (GB)

Organising club Scottish Sporting Car Club **Course length** 0.5 mile **Best time** 36.1s **Car no** 59 **Entrant** S.C. Moss

T he Bo'ness Hill Climb was near Linlithgow in Scotland, at the venue that had hosted the very first round of the British Hill Climb Championship in May 1947. I came second in the 1,100cc class and fourth overall.

RIGHT *Building up a commanding lead in the Manx Cup on the superb Douglas street circuit on the Isle of Man. Note the pannier fuel tanks fitted to the Cooper for this extra-long race and the slightly more comfortable seat that offered me more support than the normal one. Pity I failed to finish.* (LAT)

29   1st in class

9th Circuito del Garda, Heat 1

Cooper-JAP 1,000 MkIII

10 July 1949, Circuito del Garda, Lake Garda (I)

Organising club AC Brescia **Circuit length** 10.17 miles
Race distance 83 miles **Race time** 1h 12m 15.4s
Race speed 67.5mph **Car no** 46 **Entrant** S.C. Moss

I received £50 starting money for competing on this superb Italian road circuit. I made the trip with a couple of friends in a Bedford van we had bought, with the Cooper tucked inside. The journey took two days and, looking back on it, serves as a reminder of just how big Europe seemed in those distant days before the present autoroutes were constructed.

The atmosphere at this lakeside circuit was extremely relaxed. Anxious not to miss anything, I was out early sitting in my car on the starting grid when Luigi Villoresi strolled past. I asked him whether we were a bit late starting the race but he was pretty relaxed,

suggesting that there was no hurry and it would be a good idea to have lunch first!

Once the race eventually started, I tucked in behind the Ferraris of Villoresi and Count Sterzi from the start, but I quickly became concerned about the rather erratic manner in which Sterzi was driving. Eventually, he overdid things and spun backwards over the tramlines into a telegraph pole, which snapped in two, before his Ferrari careered over the edge of a drop. Sterzi survived the incident, but he was badly injured and, I must say, it shook me up for a while.

I finished the race third overall, behind the Ferraris of Villoresi and Mario Tadini, and won my class.

30   1st in class

9th Circuito del Garda, Final

Cooper-JAP 1,000 MkIII

10 July 1949, Circuito del Garda, Lake Garda (I)

Organising club AC Brescia **Circuit length** 10.17 miles
Car no 46 **Entrant** S.C. Moss

Despite my strong performance in the first heat, we were worried about the final because the car was showing signs that the magnetos were overheating. We had to improvise pretty quickly because there was not much time before the final was due to start. We cut a hole in the under-tray, bending the edges down into the airflow in order to direct cool air on to the magnetos.

Our impromptu surgery seemed to do the trick. I managed to repeat the result achieved in the heat, finishing third overall behind Villoresi and Tadini, and winning my class. I received a great ovation from the spectators and £200 in prize money.

When the Italians first saw my Cooper they referred to it as a jukebox! I managed to show that it was a quick one.

31   Unclassified

Reims, Coupe des Petites Cylindrées

Cooper-JAP 1,000 MkIII

17 July 1949, Reims-Gueux (F)

Organising club Automobile Club de Reims **Race distance** 26 laps of 4.853-mile circuit **Car no** 2 **Entrant** S.C. Moss

After the Garda race, we drove straight back across Europe to be at Reims in time for the following weekend's race, which supported the French Grand Prix. There were three Coopers on the grid (mine, Bill Aston's, and the Vincent-powered version of George Abecassis) but none of us finished. My drive chain broke, so I had no choice but to push the car the best part of a mile back to the pits, where it was repaired. I rejoined but retired with magneto problems after another 13 laps.

LEFT & BELOW *Cuttings from my album recalling memories of my first proper overseas race at Lake Garda. The relaxed mood of some of the competitors rather took me aback, I have to confess, but this was part of the Italian charm and general tempo of life.* (Stirling Moss Collection)

> **BRITISH DRIVER WINS**
> The 18-year-old British driver, Stirling Moss, in a Cooper Jap, won the 1,000 c.c. class event in the "Tour Lake Garda" motor races, near Rome, yesterday.
> Watched by a crowd of 100,000 people, Moss covered the 83 miles course at an average speed of about 67½ m.p.h.

ABOVE *Piling on opposite-lock during the 500cc race at Zandvoort. The Dutch seaside circuit through the dunes was always very slippery due to the sand that invariably blew across it.* (LAT)

32   2nd in class

Bouley Bay Hill Climb

Cooper-JAP 1,000 MkIII

21 July 1949, Bouley Bay, Jersey (CI)

RAC British Hill Climb Championship, round 3

Organising club Jersey Motor Club & Light Car Club **Course length** 1,011yds **Best time** 56.2s **Car no** 4 **Entrant** S.C. Moss

33   1st

Dutch Grand Prix, 500cc Race

Cooper-JAP 500 MkIII

31 July 1949, Zandvoort, Haarlem (NL)

Organising club Royal Dutch Automobile Club
Race distance 10 laps of 2.6-miles circuit **Race time** 23m 21.2s
Race speed 66.92mph **Car no** 30 **Entrant** S.C. Moss

This was a particularly satisfying performance because I tied for the third fastest time of the day with Dennis Poore in his supercharged Alfa Romeo. I finished second in the 1,100cc class and third overall. It was a result that elevated me to third place in the RAC British Hill Climb Championship behind Joe Fry and Dennis Poore, a position that I retained until the end of the season.

This was my first visit to the famous windy Dutch seaside circuit of Zandvoort and I qualified on the front row, but there was a nasty moment at the start that gave me quite a shock. The mechanic working on John Habin's car alongside me on the grid was still on the track when the starting flag dropped. Somehow, concentrating on the flag, I didn't see him. He stepped back in front of my rear wheel and I hit him, flinging him into the air, after

which he was run over by 'Curly' Dryden.

I was convinced that the mechanic must have been killed or, at the very least, seriously injured and I slowed down, preparing to stop. As I approached the pits at the end of the lap, I was frantically waved on by the pit crew, so I concluded – rightly – that he was not too badly hurt. I caught up the field and won the race.

I should also mention that this meeting at Zandvoort had a profound effect on me for another reason. It was the first time I saw Giuseppe Farina in action behind the wheel of his Alfa Romeo and his driving position impressed me. Rather than being hunched up over the steering wheel like so many drivers of the time, he sat well back in the cockpit with his arms almost outstretched before him. This, I concluded, was a famous driver on whose style I would model my own.

34   2nd

Silverstone, *Daily Express* International Meeting

Cooper-JAP 500 MkIII
20 August 1949, Silverstone (GB)

Organising club British Racing Drivers' Club **Race distance** 10 laps of c3-mile circuit **Race time** 22m 22.6s **Race speed** 79.59mph **Car no** 18 **Entrant** S.C. Moss

35   Retired

Prix du Leman

Cooper-JAP 1,000 MkIII
27 August 1949, Lausanne (CH)

Category Formula 2 **Organising club** Lausanne Automobile Club **Reason for retirement** Engine trouble after 20 laps **Car no** 26 **Entrant** S.C. Moss

This was a particularly significant race because it was the first major event to be promoted by the British Racing Drivers' Club, whose badge I have worn on my lapel almost every day since I was elected a member in 1948.

For this race, we were using the so-called 'sloper' engine – the 1,000cc V-twin with one cylinder removed – but it just did not seem to be giving its expected power. Eric Brandon and 'Curly' Dryden led me from the start and, although I eventually got past 'Curly', there was just no way I could get past Eric, even though I tried to out-fumble him by dodging about in his slipstream, trying to confuse and unsettle him.

After Silverstone, we all piled into the Bedford van for the long haul to Switzerland, with my friend Gilbert Hill and Charlie, a mechanic provided by JAP. This was a Formula 2 event supporting the Lausanne Grand Prix and the trio of Simca-Gordinis driven by Raymond Sommer, Robert Manzon and Maurice Trintignant completely dominated the race.

I ran fifth, close behind Hans Stuck's AFM-BMW, but after 20 of the scheduled 60 laps the pace proved too much for the JAP engine, which blew up and I retired.

LEFT *Waiting to go out on to the grid at Silverstone for the 500cc supporting race at the International Trophy meeting. I tried everything to overtake Eric Brandon, but he wasn't to be flustered. It was quite a lesson.* (LAT)

ABOVE *Jacking up the rear of the Cooper at Goodwood as my mother keeps hold of the engine cover, while my father – in the BRDC-badged shirt – scrutinises the left front tyre.* (Guy Griffiths Collection)

36   3rd overall

Prescott Hill Climb

Cooper-JAP 1,000 MkIII

11 September 1949, Prescott (GB)

RAC British Hill Climb Championship

Organising club Bugatti Owners' Club **Course length** 1,127yds **Best time** 44.77s (class record) **Car no** 61 **Entrant** S.C. Moss

37   1st

Goodwood, Madgwick Cup

Cooper-JAP 1,000 MkIII

17 September 1949, Goodwood (GB)

Organising club British Automobile Racing Club **Race distance** 5 laps of 2.4-mile circuit **Race time** 8m 46.2s **Race speed** 82.1mph **Car no** 4 **Entrant** S.C. Moss

38   Retired

Goodwood Trophy

Cooper-JAP 1,000 MkIII

17 September 1949, Goodwood (GB)

Organising club British Automobile Racing Club **Race distance** 10 laps of 2.4-mile circuit **Reason for retirement** Uncertain **Car no** 4 **Entrant** Cooper works

At this outing at Prescott, I was pleased to demonstrate that I had not lost my touch at hill climbing. I beat Joe Fry's record in the *Freikaiserwagen* by more than a second. I was pleased to win my class, setting a new class record, and was third overall. Only Sydney Allard and Dennis Poore in his Alfa Romeo were faster than me and this was the final order in the British Hill Climb Championship, of which this was the final round.

This was the day on which I celebrated my 20th birthday. Eric Brandon got away from the grid first, but I was ahead by the end of the opening lap and stayed there right to the finish. Eric was second, ahead of Bill Whitehouse, in a Cooper one-two-three.

This event was run at the same meeting as the Madgwick Cup. I had to use John Cooper's works car, after my own developed gear selection problems, and unfortunately it lasted only two laps before it failed and I had to retire.

39   1st

Shelsley Walsh
Hill Climb

Cooper-JAP 1,000 MkIII

24 September 1949, Shelsley Walsh (GB)

Organising club Midland Automobile Club **Course length**
0.5 mile **Best time** 38.19s **Car no** 25 **Entrant** S.C. Moss

M y penultimate event of the year was
at Shelsley Walsh, where I had the
satisfaction of setting the fastest time of the day,
a full second quicker than Sydney Allard's time.

41   3rd

Brough Aerodrome,
Final

Cooper-JAP 500 MkIII

2 October 1949, Brough, North Yorkshire (GB)

Organising club Blackburn Aircraft Motor Club
Circuit length 1,144yds **Entrant** S.C. Moss

T he final at Brough Aerodrome took place
later that day. Things got no better but
I managed to take third place for the second
time that day.

42   Retired

Brough Aerodrome,
Handicap Race

Cooper-JAP 500 MkIII

2 October 1949, Brough, North Yorkshire (GB)

Organising club Blackburn Aircraft Motor Club **Circuit length**
1,144yds **Reason for retirement** Engine **Entrant** S.C. Moss

T his handicap race at Brough was at the
same race meeting. The engine finally
gave up the ghost and I had to retire from
third place.

40   3rd

Brough Aerodrome,
Heat 2

Cooper-JAP 500 MkIII

2 October 1949, Brough, North Yorkshire (GB)

Organising club Blackburn Aircraft Motor Club
Circuit length 1,144yds **Entrant** S.C. Moss

A t this meeting I was handicapped by a
very tired engine, which only got worse
as the day went on. I could not manage better
than third place in this heat.

RIGHT *Working the suspension of the*
Cooper-JAP 1,000 as hard as possible while
heading for fastest time at Shelsley Walsh.
(Guy Griffiths Collection)

1950

A PAID PROFESSIONAL

John Heath, working almost single-handedly, did more than almost anyone else to restore Britain's motor racing reputation in Europe.

British Racing Motors – BRM – may have had a higher profile, but the truth is that HWM achieved more in terms of hard results during this period than the much-vaunted, so-called 'national racing car' – the BRM.

After spending the 1949 season racing an Alta-powered special, Heath and his business partner, George Abecassis, took the decision to build a team of racing cars themselves. They built three cars over the winter and it was said at the time that, in total, they only cost £10,000 to build, whereas around £200,000 had been spent on the BRM project, which was going nowhere fast.

The HWM chassis was quite light. It used Citroën-type rack-and-pinion steering, front suspension units from a Standard 12, and independent rear suspension with transverse leaf springs. It was powered by the latest Alta engine, which developed around 120bhp with a compression ratio of 13.5:1. The two-seater bodywork was configured so that the car could compete in racing or sports car events.

John Heath and George Abecassis were going to race two of the cars, and Heath wanted me to drive the third.

I duly tried the HWM for the first time at Odiham aerodrome in Hampshire. Unfortunately, I ran over a landing light and smashed the sump, but John was really decent about it. He offered me a contract that guaranteed me a 25 per cent share of the start and prize monies, which I signed, and embarked on what turned out to be a hugely exciting season, full of diversity and fresh challenges.

I was very patriotic when I was young and, because of the war, I decided that I would only drive British cars. This was all right when there were competitive cars around but, in Formula 1, this was not realistically the case until 1957. Sticking to my convictions probably prevented me from ever winning the World Championship, but I was proud to be a British driver in a British car.

While John Heath and his team worked wonders preparing the HWM, circumstance and good fortune combined for me to meet the engineer Ray Martin, whose ingenuity and hard work ensured that my Cooper was quickly modified so that, by mid-season, we were able to replace the original JAP engine with a Norton. Ray and I subsequently went on to form a business alliance at the start of the 1951 season, after he designed the remarkable Kieft F3 car.

I also ordered a brand new Cooper-JAP MkIV so that I could continue racing in the closely fought 500cc category. That turned out to be a pretty good investment because it carried me to victory in the prestigious Monaco Grand Prix supporting race.

Other opportunities arose later in the year. In September I drove Tommy Wisdom's Jaguar XK120 at Dundrod in the RAC Tourist Trophy, the classic sports car race. The following month I had enormous pleasure driving one of the nicest 2-litre sports cars made, a Frazer-Nash BMW, which is misleadingly called a Le Mans Replica. Just before Christmas, Lance Macklin and I drove an Aston Martin DB2 in the *Daily Express* Rally of GB for fun – this was my first rally.

LEFT *Driving the HWM-Alta 'offset' at Silverstone during the 1950 International Trophy meeting. This season was a steep learning curve for me as it represented my first as a fully paid professional racing driver seeking to make his living exclusively from the sport.* (Tom March Collection)

43   6th

Goodwood, Chichester Cup

HWM-Alta 'offset'

10 April 1950, Goodwood, West Sussex (GB)

Category *Formule Libre* **Organising club** British Automobile Racing Club **Race distance** 5 laps of 2.4-mile circuit **Car no** 6 **Entrant** Works

This meeting was my first event with the HWM team, and I was very excited about it because the HWM-Alta 'offset' certainly had potential. I had also intended to compete in the 500 race driving my new Cooper but the car was not ready in time.

There were two HWM entries for Goodwood. Beforehand, there was also some question over whether I could compete because I had had my driving licence taken away for a month after what the police considered to be some excessively exuberant manoeuvres at the wheel of my Morris Minor. I had appealed to the Quarter Sessions at

Reading that I would, in effect, be out of work if they deprived me of my driving licence because, at the time, the RAC automatically suspended your competition licence if you lost your road licence. However, the RAC was not obliged to do this and I appealed, successfully, to its Competition Committee.

I finished sixth overall in the five-lap *Formule Libre* race, with George Abecassis seventh in the other HWM. It was a promising start but we were clearly unable to get on terms with the Formula 1 Maseratis of Reg Parnell, Prince Bira and Baron 'Toulo' de Graffenried.

LEFT *Chasing Duncan Hamilton's Maserati with the HWM-Alta during the Goodwood Easter Handicap in which I finished a close second.* (Guy Griffiths Collection)

It had started to rain heavily during the Richmond Trophy – the day's main race, in which I did not compete – and was still wet when I went out on the circuit again for the Third Easter Handicap event. I was on the 1m 40s mark with Duncan Hamilton's Maserati close behind, and within three laps I was holding second place close behind Duncan.

Despite the wet conditions – or perhaps because of them – I managed to hang on to the Maserati and took the chequered flag only a couple of seconds behind. We were both well ahead of the scratch men – Bira, Parnell and de Graffenried.

44   2nd

Goodwood, Easter Handicap

HWM-Alta 'offset'

10 April 1950, Goodwood, West Sussex (GB)

Organising club British Automobile Racing Club
Race distance 5 laps of 2.4-mile circuit **Car no** 6
Entrant Works

45   Retired

Brands Hatch, Heat 3

Cooper-JAP 500 MkIV

16 April 1950, Brands Hatch, Kent (GB)

Organising club British Racing & Sports Car Club
Circuit length 1 mile **Race distance** 20 miles **Reason for retirement** Holed piston after 4 laps **Entrant** S.C. Moss

While the HWMs were being prepared to embark on their season's first sortie abroad, I finally took delivery of my new Cooper-JAP MkIV. This was lighter than my previous cars and I had decided, being a man with a mission, to give it something of a personal touch by equipping it with special upholstery and anodised green bodywork.

Unfortunately, this did not do anything for the car's performance and it proved to be a big disappointment. The piston seized on the fourth lap of its first race and that was that.

46   Retired

Montlhéry, Paris Grand Prix

HWM-Alta 'offset'

30 April 1950, Montlhéry, Paris (F)

Race distance 103 miles **Reason for retirement** Con-rod after 40 laps **Entrant** Works

George Abecassis and I drove out to Montlhéry with John Heath in his Citroën. With an absence of any serious Italian opposition in the entry list, we were hopeful of achieving a good result.

In the race, things were looking promising and I got up to third behind two Talbot-Lagos and I felt quite comfortable holding that position. Unfortunately, at around half-distance my engine broke a connecting rod and that was the end of my race. When the results were being discussed after the race, it was suggested that somebody had noticed a crack in one of the connecting rods after my engine was checked following a pre-race test. But the crack did not appear to have moved, so the suspect rod was left in…

47   1st

British Grand Prix, 500cc Race, Heat 1

Cooper-JAP 500 MkIV

13 May 1950, Silverstone, Northamptonshire (GB)

Organising club British Racing Drivers' Club **Race distance** 30 miles **Race speed** 77.4mph **Car no** 30 **Entrant** S.C. Moss

This was an historic day for British motor racing because the 1950 British Grand Prix not only attracted Royal patronage from their Majesties King George VI and Queen Elizabeth, but the race was also the inaugural round of the first official Formula 1 World Championship.

In the 500cc support race, I managed to win the first heat after a close battle with the Iota of Wing Commander Frank Aikens and the other Coopers of Bill Whitehouse and Alan Brown.

48   2nd

British Grand Prix, 500cc Race, Final

Cooper-JAP 500 MkIV

13 May 1950, Silverstone (GB)

Organising club British Racing Drivers' Club **Race distance** 30 miles **Car no** 30 **Entrant** S.C. Moss

In the 500cc final, Peter Collins emerged as a strong competitor in his Cooper, but neither of us was able to get the upper hand over Wing Commander Aikens. In the closing stages, we were slipstreaming each other like mad, dodging and darting in all directions, but I just could not find a gap to squeeze past and had to settle for second place, 2.2 seconds behind, after the JAP engine's piston failed on the final corner.

49   6th

Prix de Mons, Heat 1

HWM-Alta 'offset'

14 May 1950, Mons (B)

Category Formula 2 **Race distance** 15 laps of 4.73-mile circuit **Car no** 23 **Entrant** Works

HWM fielded three cars at this event, driven by me, John Heath, and the popular band leader Johnny Claes. I finished sixth in the first heat, but the Ferraris of Luigi Villoresi and Rafe Vallone dominated the proceedings and had the legs of the rest of us.

RIGHT *This shot of the opening lap of the British Grand Prix 500cc final gives a good impression of just how frantic the competition was in this category. I am in number 30, taking a wide line on the outside of the pack during this first-lap scrum. Note that the driver of the car in front of me, Don Parker, is not wearing a helmet.* (Guy Griffiths Collection)

BELOW *A great day. Being presented to His Majesty King George VI at the 1950 British Grand Prix. I am standing between Duncan Hamilton and Peter Collins.* (LAT)

57   5th

Goodwood, Sports Car Race

Cooper-MG

17 June 1950, Goodwood, West Sussex (GB)

Category 1,500cc **Organising club** British Automobile Racing Club **Race distance** 7 laps of 2.4-mile circuit **Fastest lap** 74.5mph **Entrant** Works

This 1,500cc-class race was the only occasion on which I drove the little Cooper-MG sports car and I have to admit that I really do not remember a great deal about it at all. My archives show that I finished fifth, and I suspect it was a little under-powered, but it certainly made no great impression on my memory.

RIGHT *Coming up to take the chequered flag at Brands Hatch in the days when the circuit ran anti-clockwise. My Cooper has just climbed up Paddock Bend on to the start/ finish straight.* (Guy Griffiths Collection)

58   1st

Brands Hatch 500cc Races, Heat 1

Cooper-JAP 500 MkIV

25 June 1950, Brands Hatch, Kent (GB)

Organising club British Racing & Sports Car Club **Race distance** 15 laps of 1-mile circuit **Race speed** 65.94mph **Fastest lap** 65.94mph **Car no** 44 **Entrant** S.C. Moss

In the first race of this busy programme of events at Brands Hatch I really only had strong opposition from local driver George Wicken, who chased me very hard until the last corner of the race, when he spun off.

59   1st

Brands Hatch 500cc Races, Final

Cooper-JAP 500 MkIV

25 June 1950, Brands Hatch, Kent (GB)

Organising club British Racing & Sports Car Club **Race distance** 15 laps of 1-mile circuit **Race time** 14m 4s **Race speed** 63.98mph **Car no** 44 **Entrant** S.C. Moss

In the final I headed a Cooper one-two-three, with John Cooper following me home and Alan Brown in third place.

60   1st

Brands Hatch, 500cc Production Cars, Heat 1

Cooper-JAP 500 MkIV

25 June 1950, Brands Hatch, Kent (GB)

Organising club British Racing & Sports Car Club **Race distance** 15 laps of 1-mile circuit **Car no** 44 **Entrant** S.C. Moss

I cannot really recall much about this particular race because the events were coming thick and fast that afternoon…

61 — 1st

Brands Hatch, 500cc Production Cars, Final

Cooper-JAP 500 MkIV

25 June 1950, Brands Hatch, Kent (GB)

Organising club British Racing & Sports Car Club
Race distance 15 laps of 1-mile circuit **Race time** 14m 8s
Race speed 63.68mph **Car no** 44 **Entrant** S.C. Moss

I also have little memory of this race, but my little Cooper was positively singing around that tight little circuit and I was well in the swing of things, taking another victory.

62 — 1st

Brands Hatch, 'Ten Fastest Cars Race'

Cooper-JAP 500 MkIV

25 June 1950, Brands Hatch, Kent (GB)

Organising club British Racing & Sports Car Club
Race distance 20 laps of 1-mile circuit **Race time** 18m 44.8s **Race speed** 64mph **Car no** 44 **Entrant** S.C. Moss

This was the fifth event of the day and for the ten fastest cars in the meeting, but it seemed to take the organisers some little time to sort out who the ten fastest were! I won from the Cooper-JAP of J.W. Burgoyne.

LEFT *The flat horizons of the Champagne region dominate my first outing at Reims in the Cooper-JAP. Unfortunately I could only finish sixth, my car proving incapable of running with the leaders from the start.* (LAT)

63 — 6th

Reims, Coupe des 'Racers 500'

Cooper-JAP 500 MkIV

2 July 1950, Reims-Gueux (F)

Organising club Automobile Club de Reims **Race distance** 13 laps of 4.86-mile circuit **Entrant** S.C. Moss

This race proved to be a rather disappointing start to this weekend's racing in France. My diary, and my memory, are hazy on precisely why I was unable to run with the leading bunch, but I finished third with the Cooper in the main Formula 2 event.

64 — 3rd

Reims, Coupe des Petites Cylindrées

HWM-Alta 'offset'

2 July 1950, Reims-Gueux (F)

Organising club Automobile Club de Reims
Race distance 26 laps of 4.86-mile circuit
Car no 12 **Entrant** Works

This race was the curtain-raiser to the French Grand Prix, a *grande épreuve* and the fifth Formula 1 race to qualify for inclusion in the newly inaugurated World Championship. I was driving the third HWM to be built, which had previously been driven by Johnny Claes and Rudolf Fischer. It was a little under-geared for this extremely fast circuit, but I was satisfied to finish third behind Alberto Ascari's Ferrari and the Gordini of André Simon. John Heath and Lance Macklin finished fourth and fifth respectively, much to the satisfaction of the large contingent of British spectators who were attending the meeting.

65 · 3rd

Bari Grand Prix

HWM-Alta 'offset'

9 July 1950, Bari (I)

Category Formula 2 **Race distance** 58 laps of 3.44-mile circuit **Entrant** Works

It took a lot of hard effort to transport the cars from Reims right down to Italy's Adriatic coast in time for another race the following weekend. Our preparations were also disrupted in an unwelcome and unexpected fashion when the entire HWM team was very nearly destroyed by fire on the evening before the race. The mechanics had been working even later than usual, putting the final touches to the three cars, and were cleaning the upholstery with petrol when a short circuit apparently ignited the fumes.

What made it potentially much worse was that Alf Francis suddenly saw one of the mechanics, Rex Woodgate, standing in the middle of it all with only a small extinguisher in his hand. Alf grabbed another extinguisher from the wall and banged it hard on the ground, only to discover that it was empty. Thankfully the owner of the garage in which the cars were being prepared rushed up and handed Alf an extinguisher that worked.

The blaze was put out as quickly as it had started but Rex was quite badly burned, the seats were badly damaged, and the paintwork around the cockpit seriously blistered. That meant the remaining mechanics were in for yet another long night's work – but when the cars were pushed out on to the starting grid for the following day's race they were as good as new.

I was very satisfied with my drive, but I also discovered that Giuseppe Farina, who would go on to become the first official World Champion that same year, was a dirty driver. He and Fangio both lapped me in their Alfettas and, at one point, I felt that Farina chopped me unnecessarily going into a turn. It was really rough and not what I was expecting. The only amusing thing was that, in chopping me, he over-cooked it quite badly, putting himself so far off-line that I was able to re-pass him on the way out of the corner!

Of course, Farina quickly came past me again, but as Fangio went by I could see he was roaring with laughter. Farina was out of order, in my view, but he was always a very tough competitor.

66 · 1st

Naples Grand Prix, Heat 1

HWM-Alta 'offset'

22 July 1950, Posillipo, Naples (I)

Category Formula 2 **Race distance** 50 laps of 2.54-mile circuit **Car no** 20 **Entrant** Works

The intention was to remain in Italy after the Bari race because we could take a fortnight's break in Capri before the next race in Naples. However, we had a change of plan, and Lance Macklin and I borrowed John Heath's Citroën and opted for the 700-mile drive to Monte Carlo, where Lance's mother had a house. The object of the exercise was the pursuit of crumpet, but this quest turned out to be rather less successful than expected and we were soon retracing our steps back south towards Capri. We thrashed the Citroën until its front tyres were almost bald, so we swapped the less worn rears on to the front wheels before handing the car back to John. Thank goodness he didn't look at the rears.

Then it was off to the Posillipo road circuit on the edge of Naples and the next race of our hectic summer schedule. I won my heat quite easily despite the presence of Franco Cortese in a 2-litre Ferrari and Alfa Romeo veteran Luigi Fagioli in an OSCA. Then I prepared for the final, which did not go to plan.

LEFT *My drive in the HWM-Alta in the 1950 Naples Grand Prix ended on a bruised and painful note after an unfortunate accident as I was lapping a much slower car.* (Rodolfo Mailander, Ludvigsen Library)

67   Retired

Naples Grand Prix, Final

HWM-Alta 'offset'

22 July 1950, Posillipo, Naples (I)

Category Formula 2 **Race distance** 50 laps of 2.54-mile circuit
Reason for retirement Accident **Car no** 20 **Entrant** Works

Five minutes before the start of the final, there was a problem with my car. Alf Francis noticed water dripping from the engine. I asked Alf whether he thought the water in the radiator would be enough to last for the full race distance. He replied that he hoped so, but the manner of his reply left me convinced that I would have to drive absolutely flat-out to give myself a margin for a possible pit stop if necessary.

Franco Cortese led from the start and I was stuck farther back, behind a particularly slow competitor who baulked me badly and repeatedly. I tried the inside line but he moved across on me. Then I went for the outside line and he did exactly the same. Eventually, I got far enough alongside him to prevent him from cutting across me, although even then he tried hard to do so. Soon I was up into second place and chasing Cortese hard, with Lance Macklin following in third. I kept getting signals from

John Heath and Alf reminding me to watch for overheating, but in response all I did was gesticulate towards the front of the car. I continued to build up the biggest possible lead in case I had to come in and top up the radiator.

Suddenly I was stopped in my tracks, quite literally. I came up to lap the Italian amateur Bernardo Taraschi in his 500cc supercharged Guia just as we went into a really high-speed curve. Normally I might well have waited until the following straight to lap him, but in these particular circumstances every second counted.

I went around the outside of Taraschi but, as he tried to tuck his car tightly towards the inside of the corner to give me room, his tail broke away and he slid into me. One of his hubcaps hit my left-front wheel and burst the tyre.

Immediately, my HWM was pitched into a spin at about 85mph, and then it hit a tree. My face slammed into the rear-view mirror on the side of the cockpit, knocking out my front teeth, and my left knee was broken as it smashed into the dashboard. But although I was stunned by the impact, I quickly pulled myself together, lifted myself out of the cockpit, and staggered away a short distance from the car before collapsing into the company of a group of spectating monks. My mind had flashed to the memory of Dick Seaman, who was fatally burned in the 1939 Belgian Grand Prix because he had not been quick enough to get out of the cockpit of his burning Mercedes. If the HWM was going to catch fire, then I wanted to be as far away from it as possible.

68   1st

Brands Hatch, 500 Open Challenge Trophy, Heat 2

Cooper-JAP 500 MkIV

7 August 1950, Brands Hatch, Kent (GB)

Organising club British Racing & Sports Car Club
Race distance 35 miles **Entrant** S.C. Moss

Only 14 days after the crash in Italy, my left leg was out of plaster and I was back at Brands Hatch getting into the swing of things again. The day started on a positive note when I won my heat easily.

69   2nd

Brands Hatch, 500 Open Challenge Trophy, Final

Cooper-JAP 500 MkIV

7 August 1950, Brands Hatch, Kent (GB)

Organising club British Racing & Sports Car Club
Race distance 35 miles **Entrant** S.C. Moss

Later that day, my car developed gearbox trouble during the race and I was unable to fend off George Wicken, also in a Cooper, who went past me to win.

LEFT *Ready for the start at Brands Hatch on 7 August. I had quite a successful day, winning two of the 500cc races in which I competed.* (Guy Griffiths Collection)

70 — 1st

Brands Hatch, *Daily Telegraph* Trophy, Heat

Cooper-JAP 500 MkIV

7 August 1950, Brands Hatch, Kent (GB)

Organising club British Racing & Sports Car Club
Race distance 35 miles **Race speed** 64mph **Entrant** S.C. Moss

After the problems with my own car earlier in the day, John Cooper lent me his spare car for this heat and I went on to win.

71 — Retired

Brands Hatch, *Daily Telegraph* Trophy, Final

Cooper-JAP 500 MkIV

7 August 1950, Brands Hatch, Kent (GB)

Organising club British Racing & Sports Car Club **Race distance** 35 miles **Reason for retirement** Carburettor **Entrant** S.C. Moss

Just to round off a disappointing day, I was forced to retire from the final race with carburettor problems in John Cooper's car.

72 — Retired

Prix de Berne

HWM-Alta 'offset'

12 August 1950, Bremgarten (CH)

Category Formula 2 **Race distance** 95 miles **Reason for retirement** Gearbox **Fastest lap** 67.67mph **Entrant** Works

After missing two of the scheduled races I was due to compete in with the HWM, I was back behind the wheel again at Bremgarten for the Prix de Berne. It was some consolation that I led the race and set the fastest lap, but eventually the gearbox broke and I had to retire again.

73 — 6th

Ostend, Coupe de Monde, Heat 1

Cooper-JAP MkIV

14 August 1950, Ostend (B)

Entrant S.C. Moss

I qualified on pole position and finished sixth, but I have only fleeting memories of this race.

74 — Retired

Ostend, Coupe de Monde, Final

Cooper-JAP MkIV

14 August 1950, Ostend (B)

Entrant S.C. Moss

I retired in the final, but I have been unable to discover precisely why.

75 — 1st

Silverstone, 500cc Race

Cooper-Norton 500 MkV

26 August 1950, Silverstone (GB)

Organising club British Racing Drivers' Club **Race distance** 10 laps of 2.88-mile circuit **Race time** 21m 42s **Race speed** 79.87mph **Entrant** S.C. Moss

By the middle of 1950, it was becoming clear that the JAP 500 engines were down on power compared with the twin-overhead-camshaft 'double-knocker' TT-type Norton engines, which were increasingly being used by the 500cc Formula 3 front-runners.

My father and I had been trying for some months to get our hands on one of these engines, but very few were being made available for car racing. Finally, five days before Silverstone, we managed to get hold of one.

This was not the end of our problems, though, because the engine mountings for the JAP engine were totally different from those required for the Norton, and it looked as though we might not be able to get the work completed in time.

However, a few months earlier I had been introduced to a fellow called Ray Martin, who ran a small garage near Victoria in London. Ray was very much what you would describe as an intuitive engineer. He had previously worked for Alvis and the de Havilland aircraft company, but clearly liked doing things his own way. We met through a mutual friend, another John Cooper who was the sports editor of *The Autocar* magazine, and it was on his recommendation that I commissioned Ray to do the work on my 500.

Working around the clock, Ray completed the job in time. To finish the project, he welded up an oil tank for the car made from an old oil drum, which is why I drove with an oil tank labelled 'Castrol' when in fact I was running on Shell.

The car went very well at Silverstone. I qualified on pole position, but just as I came up to take my place on the grid the clutch seized and I was unable to keep the engine running. My father and Ray had to pull me to the back of the grid, where I received a push-start after the field had departed.

Raymond Sommer led off the line, but by the end of the first lap 'Curly' Dryden was in the lead. On the second lap, having made my way up the field, I took the lead and pulled away. I won by 7 seconds from Sommer, Alf Bottoms and Dryden.

76 — 9th

Silverstone, BRDC *Daily Express* International Trophy, Heat 2

HWM-Alta 'offset'

26 August 1950, Silverstone (GB)

Organising club British Racing Drivers' Club **Race distance** 35 laps of 2.88-mile circuit **Car no** 18 **Entrant** Works

77 — 6th

Silverstone, BRDC *Daily Express* International Trophy, Final

HWM-Alta 'offset'

26 August 1950, Silverstone (GB)

Race distance 35 laps of 2.88-mile circuit **Race speed** 86.17mph **Car no** 18 **Entrant** Works

78 — 4th

Circuit de Mettet, Heat 1

HWM-Alta 'offset'

10 September 1950, Mettet (B)

Category Formula 2 **Circuit length** 4.59 miles **Race distance** 98 miles **Entrant** Works

This was to be the HWM team's first appearance at Silverstone and there was a great sense of enthusiasm and expectation from the huge crowd, which included the Duke of Edinburgh.

The first heat was won by Farina in the Alfetta at just over 90mph and the start of the second was memorable for all the wrong reasons because the BRM V16, making its race début and driven by Raymond Sommer, broke its transmission on the starting line. Not a good omen for the future, we all thought.

I was running mid-field, just ahead of Louis Chiron in his supercharged 1.5-litre Maserati, when there was a sudden downpour that flooded not only the circuit but also the cockpit of my HWM.

Visibility was impossible, so I pulled into the pits to ask for a helmet visor, but there wasn't one to be found. The race was won by Fangio, whose average speed was much reduced, and the ERAs of Brian Shawe-Taylor and Bob Gerard were second and third. After my delay, I could manage only a distant ninth place.

Before the start of the final – my third race on this same rainy day – my father managed to borrow a visor for me, although it didn't look very flattering and somebody said I looked as though I was wearing a bay window.

My team-mate for this race in the second HWM was the motorcyclist Fergus Anderson, who was standing in for John Heath, and he ran ahead of me in the opening stages. It was not long before I got up to seventh and I managed one lap at just over 90mph, which was satisfying to me, at least. As expected, the battle for the lead developed into a two-horse race between the Alfas, with Fangio and Farina coming through Abbey Curve on the last lap virtually side by side, Fangio easing off at the last moment to ensure his team-mate won.

I went into the last lap still holding seventh place. Peter Whitehead's Ferrari 125 was running third with Cuth Harrison's ERA right behind. Then came Bob Gerard and Brian Shawe-Taylor, but on the last lap Gerard slid off at Stowe corner as he tried to avoid Pierre Levegh's dawdling Talbot and I passed him to finish sixth.

Just days before I was due to have a big opportunity driving in the Tourist Trophy at Dundrod in Northern Ireland, we squeezed in yet another race meeting. This one was on the Mettet circuit in Belgium, where some stiff opposition included the 2-litre Ferraris of Alberto Ascari and Dorino Serafini and a number of new Gordinis, one of which was being driven by Johnny Claes. The event took place across two heats for an aggregate result.

In the first heat, in the dry, I finished fourth and Lance Macklin came fifth, the race being won by Robert Manzon in a Gordini.

79 — 1st

Circuit de Mettet, Heat 2

HWM-Alta 'offset'

10 September 1950, Mettet (B)

Category Formula 2 **Circuit length** 4.59 miles **Race distance** 98 miles **Entrant** Works **Aggregate result** 2nd

It was clearly going to be difficult to beat the Ferraris in the dry, but it rained heavily before the start of the second heat and I won quite easily ahead of Lance Macklin in the other HWM and the Gordinis of Robert Manzon and André Simon. Manzon won on aggregate, I was second, and Lance was third.

LEFT *The BRDC International Trophy meeting marked my first outing at Silverstone with the HWM team and I grabbed sixth place in the final on the last lap from Bob Gerard's ERA.* (Guy Griffiths Collection)

80   1st

RAC Tourist Trophy

Jaguar XK120

16 September 1950, Dundrod, Belfast, Northern Ireland (GB)

Organising club Royal Automobile Club **Race distance** 225.5 miles in 3 hours **Race speed** 75.15mph **Car no** 7 **Entrant** Tommy Wisdom

I had asked all the sports car manufacturers to let me drive one of their cars in the RAC Tourist Trophy at Dundrod. However, none had agreed because they were afraid that I was driving too fast for my age and experience and thought that I might have a shunt and kill myself, which would be bad publicity.

I had been impressed with the Jaguar XK120 ever since I had watched it race for the first time at Silverstone in 1949. I knew that Tommy Wisdom, the motoring correspondent of the *Daily Herald*, had just acquired one but I also knew that he had been invited to drive for the factory Jowett team in the Tourist Trophy at Dundrod.

I chatted to him in the Steering Wheel Club, the social haunt of the motor racing fraternity in Brick Street in London's West End. My parents had known him for many years because, back in the early 1930s, when my mother was competing in trials with a Marendaz sports car, they loaned the car to Tommy to drive in a race in France.

I think Tommy had been impressed by my performance in the HWM at Silverstone and he eventually reached the conclusion that lending me his car would be a good idea, although he insisted that I obtain my father's approval

RIGHT *Splashing through the rain to victory in the RAC Tourist Trophy at the wheel of Tommy Wisdom's Jaguar XK120. The narrowness of the Dundrod circuit is dramatically emphasised in this shot taken as I lap an MG TD.* (LAT)

because I would still be under 21 – by just one day! – when the race took place.

I think the Jaguar top brass were a little apprehensive about allowing a youngster like me into what was, to all intents and purposes, a works car, even though Tommy had bought it himself from the factory. As most of these £1,000 machines were earmarked for export to the USA to earn crucial dollars during that economically stringent post-war period, Tommy was one of the lucky few in Britain to get hold of one, owing to his position in the national press.

After racing the HWM at Mettet, I flew directly to Belfast for the TT, which was being held on the Dundrod circuit, about 12 miles west of the city. This was a seriously demanding road circuit with humps, bumps, bridges and high grass banks, and fields in all directions. The weather was absolutely terrible and the circuit was lashed by heavy rain and gusting winds. On the first practice day I just went round and round in the rain, getting to know the car and the track. On the second day, in the dry, I lapped in 5 minutes 28 seconds, an average of 81.39mph, which was 105 per cent of my ideal speed to make the most of the race's handicapping system. By now I was feeling pretty confident, although it was clear that it was going to be a very long three-hour event if the rain returned on race day.

Sure enough, just before I climbed into the XK120 at the start, torrential rain began to fall in the teeth of a howling gale. Leslie Johnson was first away, in another XK120, but I had pulled up on to his tail by the time we were halfway round the opening lap. On the second lap I took the lead and I stayed there all the way to the finish.

Although I did not really enjoy such adverse conditions, driving the XK120 in the wet certainly suited my style. Going through the corners I was thinking, "Gosh, this car feels really, really good". Once I began passing some of the other competitors I really felt a tremendous lift.

My first win at Dundrod was a very satisfying personal achievement and, of course, a crucial milestone in my career. I like to think it was also a testimony to Tommy Wisdom's judgement in offering me the drive. Certainly it caught the attention of both Jaguar boss Bill – later Sir William – Lyons and his racing team manager, 'Lofty' England, because that evening they offered me a contract to lead the official Jaguar works team the following year.

81 — 1st

Brands Hatch, Open Challenge, Heat 2

Cooper-Norton 500 MkV

17 September 1950, Brands Hatch, Kent (GB)

Organising club British Racing & Sports Car Club
Race speed 60.1mph **Car no** 7 **Entrant** S.C. Moss

I had to stay in Belfast for the TT prize presentation on the evening after the race and that meant catching an early flight back to London the following day because I was to compete at Brands Hatch with my Cooper-Norton. I managed to win the first heat comfortably and after the race the crowd sang "21 today" to celebrate my coming of age.

82 — Retired

Brands Hatch, Open Challenge, Final

Cooper-Norton 500 MkV

17 September 1950, Brands Hatch, Kent (GB)

Organising club British Racing & Sports Car Club
Reason for retirement Gearbox **Car no** 7 **Entrant** S.C. Moss

Unfortunately I accidentally changed from top gear straight into bottom during this race, with the result that the gearbox broke and I had to retire. I enjoyed a 'monster' 21st birthday party that evening, though.

83 — 2nd

Circuit de Périgueux, Heat 1

HWM-Alta 'offset'

24 September 1950, Périgueux (F)

Category Formula 2 **Circuit length** 1.087 miles
Race distance 85 miles **Entrant** Works

This was a really challenging street circuit right in the middle of Périgueux, precisely the sort of track that really appealed to me. The opposition was a bit like that which we had encountered at Mettet a few weeks earlier. Alberto Ascari and Dorino Serafini were in 2-litre Ferraris and there were the three Gordinis for Robert Manzon, André Simon and Maurice Trintignant. I finished second in my heat after a good drive.

84   3rd

Circuit de Perigueux, Final

HWM-Alta 'offset'

24 September 1950, Périgueux (F)

Category Formula 2 **Circuit length** 1.087 miles
Race distance 85 miles **Entrant** Works

85   7th

Goodwood, Formula 2 Race

HWM-Alta 'offset'

30 September 1950, Goodwood (GB)

Organising club British Automobile Racing Club **Race distance** 10 laps of 2.4-mile circuit **Car no** 16 **Entrant** Works

86   2nd

Goodwood, 500cc Race

Cooper-Norton 500 MkV

30 September 1950, Goodwood (GB)

Organising club British Automobile Racing Club **Race distance** 5 laps of 2.4-mile circuit **Race speed** 72.39mph **Entrant** S.C. Moss

This was another race in which the Ferraris finished out of contention but the HWM could not quite match the speed of the Gordinis. Those driven by Manzon and Simon finished first and second, and I came home third.

Although this race meeting at Goodwood was little more than a club event, this particular race caused a great deal of excitement because Reg Parnell was entered in the BRM V16. Thanks perhaps in part to rain, he won this minor league event. I finished seventh in the HWM.

I had a poor starting position on the fifth row of the grid. I managed to climb through the field but, by the time I reached second place, there was not enough of the race left for me to catch 'Curly' Dryden, who won.

LEFT *The day after my Tourist Trophy win I was back at Brands Hatch celebrating my 21st birthday with victory in my 500cc heat, but I had to retire in the final.* (Guy Griffiths Collection)

BELOW *Lining up the HWM-Alta in the rain prior to the start of the Goodwood Formula 2 race at the end of September. I slithered home in seventh place.* (Guy Griffiths Collection)

87   1st

Castle Combe, 2-Litre Race

HWM-Alta 'offset'

7 October 1950, Castle Combe, Chippenham, Wiltshire (GB)

Race distance 20 laps of 1.84-mile circuit
Race speed 78.54mph **Entrant** Works

This 20-lapper proved to be a close battle between my HWM and Ken Wharton's supercharged 1.5-litre ERA. I made up on the corners what I lost to the ERA's extra power on the straight to beat Ken in a close finish.

88   1st

Castle Combe, 500cc Heat 2

Cooper-Norton 500 MkV

7 October 1950, Castle Combe, Chippenham, Wiltshire (GB)

Race speed 72.04mph **Entrant** S.C. Moss

This race was a pretty straightforward win, although the fine detail of the event escapes me after all this time.

89   Retired

Castle Combe, 500cc Final

Cooper-Norton 500 MkV

7 October 1950, Castle Combe, Chippenham, Wiltshire (GB)

Reason for retirement Engine **Entrant** S.C. Moss

I was out of luck in the final of this 500cc event and retired with a piston failure.

90   1st

Castle Combe, Sports Car Race

Frazer Nash Le Mans Replica

7 October 1950, Castle Combe, Chippenham, Wiltshire (GB)

Race speed 74.77mph **Car no** 16 **Entrant** Works

The Frazer Nash was a car whose appearance tended to deceive. At first glance you did not expect it was going to be anything special but, once you got used to its rather tricky high-geared steering, it was very pleasant to drive. I won by a few lengths from a similar car driven by Tony Crook.

91   1st

Castle Combe, Team Handicap Sports Car Race

Frazer Nash Le Mans Replica

7 October 1950, Castle Combe, Chippenham, Wiltshire (GB)

Car no 16 **Entrant** Works

Rounding off the first meeting at which I drove this car, I won the team handicap race with the Nash to complete a day of varied achievement.

RIGHT *I won two races at the October Castle Combe meeting at the wheel of the works Frazer Nash Le Mans Replica. This was a neat little car that I enjoyed driving very much. (Guy Griffiths Collection)*

92 Retired

10th Circuito del Garda

HWM-Alta 'offset'

15 October 1950, Circuito del Garda (I)

Organising club AC Brescia **Race distance** 68 miles **Reason for retirement** Broken stub axle **Car no** 20 **Entrant** Works

93

Montlhéry record attempts

Jaguar XK120

24 October 1950, Montlhéry, Paris (F)

Duration 24 hours **Distance** 2,579 miles **Speed** 107.46mph
Co-driver Leslie Johnson **Entrant** Works

95

Montlhéry record attempts

Kieft-Norton 350 & 500

21 & 23 November 1950, Montlhéry (F)

Class J (Kieft 350) 50km, 78.44mph; 50 miles, 78.75mph; 100km, 79.08mph; 1 hour, 79.37mph; 100 miles, 79.62mph; 200km, 77.11mph **Class I (Kieft 500)** 50km, 90.06mph; 50 miles, 90.63mph; 100km, 90.87mph; 1 hour, 91.34mph; 100 miles, 91.4mph; 200km, 88.5mph; 200 miles, 86.99mph
Co-drivers Ken Gregory and Jack Neill **Entrant** Works

This was the last race of the season and I suppose some people might say I was fortunate that it was not the last of my entire career. We were back at the Lake Garda circuit, the scene of my first foray into European motor racing the previous year, and I was running flat-out on one of the fastest parts of the circuit when the right-front stub axle broke and the wheel came off. It was just the same as I had experienced at the Caracalla Baths circuit in Rome earlier in the year.

I walked back to the pits and explained what had happened. John Heath told me that I had better go back, find the car, and retrieve the wheel. At the time, I thought he might just be relieved that I had got away unscathed from another stub axle failure, but it wasn't that at all! The Borrani wheels we were using cost about £50 each, which made them extremely expensive items – especially considering that HWM was receiving about £200 a car in starting money at these European events.

So I went back to where I had lost the wheel and discovered that it had bounced to a halt in a nearby garden. I asked the bloke whether I could have our wheel back and he replied, "Yes, as soon as you've repaired the wall it has just knocked down."

I looked around and there was a pile of rocks scattered about the place, but one could hardly call it a proper wall. So I put the stones back in place and he gave me the wheel back.

This was the first of two endurance runs in which I participated at Montlhéry, near Paris, and the purpose of this one was to try to average 100mph for 24 hours in one of the new Jaguar XK120 roadsters. Leslie Johnson was well-acquainted with William Lyons, the managing director of Jaguar, and persuaded him and his engineering chief, Bill Heynes, to back this successful record bid. Leslie shared the driving with me.

94 Unclassified

Daily Express Rally

Aston Martin DB2

17 November 1950 (GB)

Co-driver Lance Macklin **Entrant** Works

This outing with Lance Macklin in an Aston Martin DB2 was not really a terribly serious exercise, more in the nature of a 'crumpet tour', you might say. Either way, it was all pretty unsuccessful. Although we cleared the road sections, I messed up the final driving test and we were not classified.

Even though Ken Gregory had started to work in the role of my manager, he was still competing from time to time and had plenty of experience driving 500s, so when Cyril Kieft approached me to take part in some record attempts at Montlhéry, I had no hesitation in recruiting Ken and Jack Neill to share the driving duties. The conditions were anything but favourable: near-gales blew across the circuit and the runs were undertaken in very cool weather conditions.

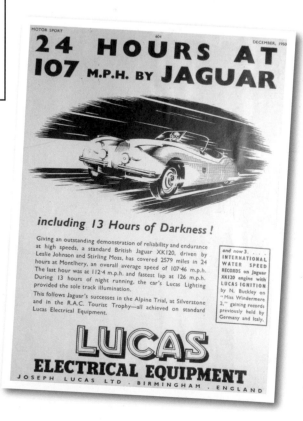

LEFT *At Garda my HWM suffered another stub axle breakage. I was glad I didn't hit one of the concrete posts lining the circuit.* (Rodolfo Mailander, Ludvigsen Library)

RIGHT *Jaguar's advertising promoting our Montlhéry record run included this full-page celebration in several motoring magazines.* (Stirling Moss Collection)

1951

LEARNING MORE WITH HWM

The 1951 season brought another busy and varied F2 programme driving for HWM. My motivation to achieve international success at the wheel of a British car was still as intense as ever.

John Heath's plucky team now built three more conventional-looking single-seaters, although they retained the Alta engines and Armstrong Siddeley pre-selector gearboxes, which were very heavy. John and George Abecassis still drove from time to time, and Lance Macklin joined me full-time in the team.

It was a fantastic time. We were not paid much but our quality of life was exceptional for two young Englishmen. We drove from town to town all over Europe, racing nearly every weekend, had a party at each race, and met all the local ladies!

Jaguar decided to enter one of their XK120s in the Mille Miglia. I took Frank Rainbow along as my passenger. He was an excellent mechanic from Jaguar's racing department. Unfortunately, I lost control on some oil – there were no flag marshals to warn us of the spillage – and we crashed out, fortunately without injury. I also had my first outing at Le Mans, driving the superb Jaguar C-type

During this period, the possibility of being able to drive the temperamental, controversial 1.5-litre supercharged BRM V16 was still nagging at me. This was Britain's sole, fully fledged Grand Prix car to be built to the same regulations as the contemporary Ferrari 125s and Alfa Romeo 158s. My first BRM test came in July, and then in the autumn there were long, frustrating and in the end fruitless sessions at Monza. Raymond Mays, who ran the team, wanted me to sign to drive for BRM for 1952, but in the end I only did one race for them that season.

In 1950 three friends of mine had decided to build a really different 500cc Formula 3 car. John Cooper, Sports Editor of *The Autocar*, was the real brains behind this project, Dean Delamont, Competition Manager of the RAC, came in on the deal because he knew everybody within motor racing, and Ray Martin was the mechanical genius. Initially, they called the car the Martin-Norton as it had a 'double-knocker' Norton fitted, and they asked me to drive it.

The Martin-Norton soon became known as the Kieft. This was because Cyril Kieft, a Welsh enthusiast, formed a company to produce cars similar to, but not the same as, my Martin.

The original car had a revolutionary lightweight but very rigid space-frame chassis and was probably the very first space-frame, rear-engined racing car ever built. It had rubber suspension, front and rear, but the rear wheels had an enormous amount of camber, allowed by the fact that the suspension was a swing axle system. The engine was mounted in a sort of 'box' formed by the space-frame chassis. Further forward came the driver, which was me. The seat position was so far forward that I could actually touch the front tyres. This made it possible for me to move into the correct position on the starting grid without any outside assistance!

It was a fantastic car – and quite a bit superior to any of the other Formula 3 cars of the day.

LEFT *The 1951 HWM was a good-looking car that significantly enhanced my international racing experience. Here I am during the Grand Prix OstSchweiz on the Erlen road circuit where a front wishbone failed while I was dicing for the lead with Rudi Fischer's Ferrari.* (Rodolfo Mailander, Ludvigsen Library)

96

Chiltern night trial

Morris Minor

10 February 1951, GB

Entrant A. Woods

I had always enjoyed myself driving my own Morris Minor, which pre-dated the Mini as one of the great designs produced by Sir Alec Issigonis. It handled very well and in 1950, after I broke my leg at Naples, I had my own Minor fitted with a hand-operated clutch that enabled me to drive with my leg in plaster.

My sole competitive outing in one of these cheerful little cars was the 1951 Chiltern night trial, when I shared a friend's Minor convertible. We were heavily penalised for a map-reading error, but hugely enjoyed ourselves even so.

97   1st

Goodwood, Lavant Cup

HWM

26 March 1951, Goodwood, West Sussex (GB)

Organising club British Automobile Racing Club
Race distance 5 laps of 2.4-mile circuit **Race speed** c81mph **Car no** 1 **Entrant** Works

There were only two of the new HWMs on the grid for the opening race of the year because George Abecassis had injured himself testing in the wet at Goodwood a week earlier, but he gamely persuaded his doctors to allow him out of bed to witness the new car's début.

Goodwood had been resurfaced for the start of the season and, despite the fact that I was quick in practice, the bookies tipped Eric Brandon's 1,100cc Cooper as the pre-race favourite. I took it steadily with the new car and ran third from the start, behind Bill Aston's Cooper. Then I settled down into the swing of things, picked up the pace, and managed to catch and pass Brandon on the last lap to win by four-fifths of a second. It was a satisfying note on which to open the new season.

98   5th

Goodwood, Richmond Trophy

HWM

26 March 1951, Goodwood, West Sussex (GB)

Organising club British Automobile Racing Club
Race distance 20 laps of 2.4-mile circuit **Car no** 1 **Entrant** Works

The main race of the day was for Formula 1 machinery and the Formula 2 HWMs were outclassed in terms of sheer speed. Prince Bira won convincingly in the 4.5-litre OSCA after Reg Parnell spun wildly in his Maserati and lost a lot of ground, bouncing for about 100 yards across the grass before regaining the track. My fifth place was as much as I could manage in an F2 car against fully fledged F1 opposition.

99   3rd

Marseilles Grand Prix

HWM

8 April 1951, Marseilles (F)

Race distance 99 laps of 1.66-mile circuit
Race time 2h 5m 39.8s **Car no** 16 **Entrant** Works

Arriving at the Bristol Hotel in Marseilles, we found that it was too expensive at 1,400 Francs for a bed only, so we crossed the road and switched to more modest accommodation costing 650 Francs, which seemed much better value.

Before practice began, we changed the cars' axle ratios and inflated the tyres to around 30–35lb, but the real challenge was the state of the circuit. It was one of the most bumpy I had ever driven on, dusty and extremely tiring. Robert Manzon qualified fastest in the Gordini, while I was fifth fastest.

The race was run in the dry, but with a stiff wind blowing in from the Mediterranean. Alberto Ascari led strongly in the Ferrari from the start, only to lock up and slide into the straw bales, damaging his steering. André Simon then took the lead in his 1.5-litre non-supercharged Gordini, but he had to pit for a wheel change, handing the win to Luigi Villoresi, the first person I had ever seen win a race, in another 4.5-litre unsupercharged Ferrari. Maurice Trintignant was second for Gordini and I came home third. All in all, a good day.

100   5th

San Remo Grand Prix

HWM

22 April 1951, Ospedaletti (I)

Race distance 90 laps of 2.07-mile circuit
Car no 16 **Entrant** Works

A fter a quick visit to Coventry to try out the Jaguar XK120, which was being prepared for the Mille Miglia, I flew out to San Remo for my next race in the HWM. On my first day there I remember hiring a Vespa scooter for two days, which cost me only 4,000 Lire – very good value.

During first practice my car was reluctant to run at much over 5,000rpm so we changed the axle ratios and removed the cylinder head for a quick check-up, but nothing seemed to be wrong.

I qualified fifth, 10 seconds slower than Ascari's pole position time of 1m 52s, but – to keep this in perspective – I was competing in a Formula 1 race with a 2-litre unsupercharged Formula 2 car. In the race I got up to seventh before finally ending up fifth, helped in part by Villoresi crashing his Ferrari into Reg Parnell's Maserati, which had stopped on the circuit. This was not too bad, considering that I did not have a good race. I spun twice and had a couple of trying moments when I stupidly applied the accelerator rather than the brakes and when I selected second gear instead of fourth.

OPPOSITE *Race debut of the new HWM at Goodwood in March 1951. I am wearing a woolly jumper knitted by my mother and carrying what one might today call Kieft 'branding'!* (Guy Griffiths Collection)

BELOW *With the HWM on my way to fifth place on the challenging Ospedaletti circuit, venue for the San Remo Grand Prix.* (LAT)

Luxembourg 500cc Grand Prix, Heat

Kieft-Norton 500

3 May 1951, Findel (LU)

Race distance 12 laps of 2.4-mile circuit
Reason for retirement Uncertain **Entrant** S.C. Moss

After the Mille Miglia I flew straight to Brussels on my way to the Luxembourg Grand Prix for Formula 3 cars. The new Kieft was not ready at this point, but Eric Brandon brought over my old one in his van.

Practice day was simply shocking. Alf Bottoms was killed driving his JBS, in my opinion after the brakes failed. He tried to aim up an escape road, but it was crowded with people. He successfully avoided them but hit a parked car. It was a real tragedy because he was a good, clean sportsman.

I retired from my heat after five laps and never made it to the final. I was so embarrassed by this poor showing that I handed back most of the starting money to the organisers, keeping only enough to cover some expenses. In those days I was still very naïve!

101 **Retired**

Mille Miglia

Jaguar XK120

28/29 April 1951, Brescia (I)

Race distance 1 lap of 992 miles **Reason for retirement** Crash
Co-driver Frank Rainbow **Car no** 432 **Entrant** Works

ABOVE *On my way to sixth place in my heat at the BRDC International Trophy meeting. The final was held in torrential rain and hail so heavy that the race had to be abandoned after only six laps.* (Tom March Collection)

I put a lot of preparation into my first Mille Miglia and spent four days based in Brescia familiarising myself with sections of the route. Unfortunately, as things transpired, the effort was to be completely wasted.

My passenger Frank Rainbow and I were up at 3am on the day of the race. The weather was cold and wet. We left the starting ramp at 4.32am, three minutes after Leslie Johnson in the other works-entered XK120. The car went well from the start and we were soon running at about 115mph in the darkness, but after 15 miles our race came to an abrupt end.

A small Fiat saloon had broken down and dropped a huge oil slick on to the soaking asphalt. Suddenly I saw a chap at the side of the road trying to wave me down, so I applied the brakes. Nothing happened. I turned the steering wheel. Nothing happened.

On that cocktail of oil and water there was simply no grip, so I skidded into the Fiat and bent one of the Jaguar's front wings back on a wheel. While backing away from the Fiat, the gearbox also jammed in reverse and, although we got to a local garage, repairs took a couple of hours. In addition, the bonnet would not close so we had to retire there and then. Damn it!

103 **6th**

Silverstone, BRDC International Trophy, Heat 1

HWM

5 May 1951, Silverstone (GB)

Organising club British Racing Drivers' Club **Race distance** 15 laps of 2.9-mile circuit **Car no** 19 **Entrant** Works

Practice for this event was run in pouring rain, my HWM sliding around all over the place and the engine misfiring badly. In my heat, however, I had a steady drive to sixth place.

104 14th

Silverstone, BRDC International Trophy, Final

HWM

5 May 1951, Silverstone (GB)

Organising club British Racing Drivers' Club **Race distance** 30 laps of 2.9-mile circuit; race stopped after six laps **Car no** 19 **Entrant** Works

BELOW *Conditions at Silverstone dried out in time for me to score my first win of the season in the production sports car race with a factory Jaguar XK120.* (Tom March Collection)

We thought it had rained during practice but that was nothing compared with the downpour that began just before the start of the International Trophy final. Rolls of thunder drowned the noise of the cars' exhausts and everybody was drenched within moments. The race started but then conditions got worse as huge hailstones came crashing down.

By the end of the second lap, Reg Parnell had stormed through to take the lead in Tony Vandervell's 4.5-litre ThinWall Special Ferrari. The conditions were so bad that the race was flagged to a halt after only six laps. I was climbing through the field, only to collide with a marker tub that had been knocked on to the track at Stowe corner by Ken Richardson's ERA. It got wedged in the HWM's front suspension and I had to come into the pits to get someone to kick it free. That delay dropped me right down to the back of the field and when the race was finally stopped I was in 14th place.

105 1st

Silverstone, Production Sports Car Race

Jaguar XK120

5 May 1951, Silverstone (GB)

Organising club British Racing Drivers' Club **Race distance** 30 laps of 2.9-mile circuit **Race time** 1h 1m 32s **Race speed** 84.5mph **Car no** 26 **Entrant** Works

This was my first win of the season. I took the lead at the start and had quite an easy drive, the weather having improved after the soaking I got in the previous race. The XK120 was going really well and getting through Woodcote corner in one long drift, with tyres howling, at just under 100mph in a standard production sports car was extremely satisfying.

which was the closest airfield to Goodwood that was operational that particular day.

Ken Gregory had practised the car for me on Saturday but I was back in time to take it over for the race. Ken told me he thought the Kieft was "fantastic" but everything went wrong during the immediate pre-race preparations. After warming up the engine, nobody had bothered to replace the 'soft' sparking plug with a 'hard' racing plug.

When the field raced away I realised that I could not keep up. My problems were exaggerated by the fact that the throttle cable had stretched and I was losing speed all the time. I just managed to scrape home ninth, guaranteeing me a place in the final by the skin of my teeth.

109 1st

Goodwood, International Trophy, Final

Kieft-Norton 500

14 May 1951, Goodwood, West Sussex (GB)

Organising club British Automobile Racing Club
Race distance 15 laps of 2.4-mile circuit
Race time 26m 15.4s **Race speed** 82.28mph
Fastest lap 84.55mph (record)
Car no 57 **Entrant** S.C. Moss

Happily, in the final I made up for all that disappointment when I was fully able to demonstrate the pent-up potential of the new Kieft. I just ran away from the opposition, at one point passing Eric Brandon on the outside of Madgwick corner and, as I did so, pointing down to the Kieft and mouthing across at him, "You'll have to buy one of these!" The first prize of £200 brightened my day, as well.

BELOW *Concentrating hard on Bremgarten's treacherously wet 'pavé' track surface during the opening stages of the Swiss Grand Prix. Later the HWM's screen was smashed and the full force of the slipstream felt as though it would tear off my helmet!* (LAT)

110 Retired

Genoa, Formula 3 Race

Kieft-Norton 500

20 May 1951, Genoa (I)

Reason for retirement Suspension failure after 22 laps
Car no 40 **Entrant** S.C. Moss

I very nearly found myself unable to compete in this race because the Kieft's timing was up the spout and we just could not get it to

fire up. As a result, I could not take part in qualifying and consequently the organisers refused to let me race, but eventually we persuaded them to let me start from the back of the grid.

After a couple of laps, I had fought my way through to second place behind Felice Bonetto's Volpini, and then went past him into the lead. I stayed in front until three laps from the finish, when the swing axle suspension cable broke and I spun at about 80mph. I was unharmed, but unfortunately out of the race.

111 Retired

Genoa, Columbian Centenary Grand Prix

HWM

20 May 1951, Genoa (I)

Reason for retirement Differential seized after 26 laps
Entrant Works

Once again the HWM demonstrated good speed in this very demanding street race, but yet again it let me down.

The circuit ran along the seafront and back, with floral gardens separating the two roads. It was twisty and bumpy, and on the bends we were leaping off the ground and landing near the kerb. The place suited me because I did not care in those days.

At the start, my team-mate Lance Macklin went into the lead with me behind him, but I passed him a little further round the opening lap. I held the lead quite comfortably but this time the differential failed, putting paid to our hopes of a decent result. I think I could have won this race.

I walked back to the pits and arrived there just in time to see Alberto Ascari's Ferrari, which had been leading, catch fire and go up in smoke. Lance came third. What a day!

112 8th

Swiss Grand Prix

HWM

27 May 1951, Bremgarten (CH)

F1 World Championship, round 1

Race distance 42 laps of 4.524-mile circuit
Car no 14 **Entrant** Works

There was no time to waste after the Genoa race because John Heath had been invited to field two of the HWMs in the opening round of that year's World Championship, at Bremgarten, Berne.

The weekend started on a troubled note. On the Friday, the boys changed my magneto but the car still misfired after a few laps. They decided they would have to lift the cylinder head and take a close look at the number-three cylinder, which was oiling up, but the car was doing 7mpg, which we thought would at least ensure that I could run through the race without having to stop to refuel.

The main battle for outright victory was, of course, between the 1.5-litre supercharged Alfa Romeos and the 4.5-litre Ferraris, but when race day dawned wet and dismal I thought we might be in with a chance of a strong showing.

Unfortunately, it all went wrong for me. As the rain and spray intensified, something was thrown up at the front of my car and smashed the HWM's windscreen. Suddenly my face was taking the full force of the slipstream and the torrential rain while the wind got under my visor and threatened to rip off my helmet. It was the worst experience I had ever known. But I just had to soldier on for the remaining 30 laps, which, in those conditions on that 4.5-mile circuit, seemed likely to take around an hour and a half.

For much of that time I was in effect driving one-handed as I tried to hang on to my helmet. I was heading for seventh place as I came up towards the finishing line, but my car ran out of fuel and Louis Chiron just pipped me at the last moment as I coasted in with a dead engine.

113   1st

Aix-les-Bains, Circuit du Lac, Heat 2

HWM

3 June 1951, Aix-les-Bains (F)

Category Formula 2 **Race distance** 40 laps of 1.09-mile circuit
Race time 54m 38.4s **Race speed** 48.04mph **Car no** 16
Entrant Works

I raced at Aix-les-Bains the weekend after Bremgarten and there was no time for relaxation in the short gap between the two races. I accompanied John Heath on a brief two-day trip to Germany to discuss magnetos with Bosch in an effort to sort out the misfiring problems the HWMs had been experiencing.

Soon after the start of my heat, Franco Cortese's Ferrari spun in front of me and I had to take evasive action and stalled, but Maurice Trintignant and a few others were involved in a multiple crash which allowed Robert Manzon to pull away in the lead with his Gordini. I managed to catch him up once I had restarted and I overtook him after 13 laps to win easily.

114   2nd

Aix-les-Bains, Circuit du Lac, Final

HWM

3 June 1951, Aix-les-Bains (F)

Category Formula 2 **Race distance** 57 laps of 1.09-mile circuit
Race time 1h 15m 26.2s **Car no** 16 **Entrant** Works

I had complained about the HWM's handling after the heat earlier in the day, and just before the start of the final Alf Francis noticed,

while walking round the front of my car, that a track rod and steering arm were bent. On closer examination, it turned out that the front wheels had toe-out of about 2.5 inches.

John Heath immediately told Alf to get his own car ready for me, so I jumped into the cockpit and they began to push me out to the starting grid. Only then did it become clear that John's car had suffered a major engine problem during his heat, so I made a quick switch back to the car with the bent steering arm.

Under the circumstances, I must say the car ran very well and I was able to keep ahead of Franco Cortese in the Ferrari and André Simon in the Gordini, although I could not keep up with Rudi Fischer's particularly fast Ferrari, which finished just over 10 seconds ahead of me. After the race we heard rumours that Fischer was still using an oversized engine that had been in the car for the Swiss Grand Prix the previous weekend. We would not have done anything about it even it were true – it had been a good result for me.

115   4th

Rome Grand Prix

HWM

10 June 1951, Caracalla Baths, Rome (I)

Category Formula 2 **Race distance** 126.26 miles
Car no 20 **Entrant** Works

After Aix-les-Bains, John Heath decided to split the team up, with Lance Macklin and most of the mechanics going on to Angoulême for the Circuit des Remparts meeting while John and I drove down to Rome as we had been offered very good starting money of £350 in recognition of my performance the previous year.

The weekend started on a bad note. I had covered only a few hundred yards at the start of first practice when the timing chain broke, bending all the valves, so on the Saturday the mechanics worked late into the night replacing the camshaft bearers and adjusting the valve clearances.

The race did not start until 5pm. I was second by the end of the second lap, but the throttle jammed open and I had to make a pit stop. Then the plugs oiled up, so I made another stop. Then the magneto gave trouble and, finally, the gearbox played up. I finished fourth, but I know I could have won had it not been for those delays.

116   1st

British Empire Trophy

Frazer Nash Le Mans Replica

14 June 1951, Douglas (IoM)

Race distance 35 laps of 3.88-mile circuit
Race time 1h 57m 38s **Race speed** 67.27mph
Fastest lap 3m 23s, 68.78mph (record) **Car no** 22
Entrant Gilby Engineering

The day after the race in Rome, I flew back to England, arriving at Heathrow at 6pm. I was met by my father, and we went home to Tring. That evening he and I set out at 11pm to drive in the family Land Rover up to Liverpool, where we arrived at 2.45am. After a couple of hours' sleep we were up again to catch the boat to the Isle of Man, where I was due to race Syd Greene's Gilby Engineering Frazer Nash.

This was a handicap event and I must admit that I did not think I had much of a chance, particularly because the two Lester-MGs, one of which was driven by Pat Griffith, received three laps' credit over my Frazer Nash. That meant, in effect, that I was giving them a 12-mile start. In the race itself Griffith led comfortably, but I got up to second place and took the win after the Lester-MG suffered engine failure with two laps to go.

RIGHT *Holding second place amidst the jostling pack on the first lap of the British Empire Trophy. I worked my Frazer Nash through to second place and then inherited the lead when Pat Griffith's Lester-MG retired late in the race.* **(Guy Griffiths Collection)**

117 Retired

Le Mans 24 Hours

Jaguar C-type

24/25 June 1951, Sarthe (F)

Race distance 24 hours of 8.38-mile circuit (2,243.88 miles, 267 laps) **Reason for retirement** Broken oil pipe after 92 laps (18h 33m, 105.85mph)
Fastest lap 4m 46.8s, 105.2mph (record)
Co-driver Jack Fairman **Car no** 22 **Entrant** Works

This was my first experience of Le Mans and also the first of several races in my career when I shared the driving with Jack Fairman. 'Jolly' Jack was a good, solid driver, a dependable bloke who never beat up the cars. He was not the fastest in the business, but his was a safe pair of hands and he could generally be relied upon to keep out of trouble.

The other two C-types were shared by Peter Walker and Peter Whitehead, and Leslie Johnson and Clemente Biondetti. At the pre-race conference in the Jaguar pit, it was decided that Whitehead, Johnson and I should drive the opening stints of three and a half hours each. 'Lofty' England, the Jaguar team manager, told me that my job as the team's pacemaker was to encourage the leading Talbot driver José

Froilán González to over-tax his engine and the works Ferraris to wear out their brakes.

I lined up 22nd for the famous Le Mans-style start, sprinted across the road as quickly as I could and leaped into the C-type, which had been left fully prepared already in bottom gear. I passed 14 cars getting away from the start and another seven down the long Mulsanne straight. That put me into the lead, but González came back at me and re-passed going into the tight right-hand Mulsanne corner. I went ahead again as we came up the long straight towards the start-line. It took only five laps or so of baiting the Talbot for González to cook his brakes – not his engine – and drop away.

When I came in to hand over the C-type to Fairman, I was a full lap ahead of Juan Manuel Fangio, who had taken over the Talbot from González.

After we had been leading the race for eight hours, my heart sank as I watched the needle on the oil-pressure gauge sink to zero. The engine blew up immediately, so I had to struggle back to the pits on foot. It was pouring with rain and I kept being forced to leap into the flooded ditches along the edge of the circuit because of cars passing close by. The walk was about three miles and by the time I arrived back at the pits, soaked to the skin, it was about 2am on Sunday morning and I am told that I looked "rather mournful". That was rather an understatement.

118 Retired

AVUS Rennen

HWM

1 July 1951, AVUS, Berlin (D)

Category Formula 2 **Race distance** 60 laps of 3.17-mile circuit
Reason for retirement Broken crankshaft after 3 laps
Car no 109 **Entrant** Works

This was my first experience of the AVUS circuit, a section of dual-carriageway autobahn between Berlin and Potsdam joined by a 45-degree banked turn at one end and a tight hairpin at the other. The most obvious and immediate problem was that the HWM team did not have sufficiently high gear or axle ratios to achieve the potential speeds offered by the circuit.

Under the circumstances I was not really looking forward to practice. I also had other

BELOW *The Jaguar C-type was always one of my favourite cars, but at Le Mans a loss of oil pressure while leading after eight hours cost Jack Fairman and me a possible victory.* (Ludvigsen Library)

matters on my mind as I had received word that a telegram had arrived at home in Tring from Enzo Ferrari himself, inviting me to drive one of his new 4.5-litre Tipo 375s in the Grand Prix d'Europe at Reims on the same day as the race at the AVUS. I telephoned my manager, Ken Gregory, to discuss the matter but I felt I could not let John Heath down, even though I am sure he would have released me had I asked.

As it turned out, the AVUS race proved to be very disappointing. My engine was misfiring from the start and broke a connecting rod after only a couple of laps. Perhaps I should have accepted the invitation to drive the Ferrari after all…

119 — Retired

Rouen Grand Prix

HWM

8 July 1951, Les Essarts (F)

Category Formula 2 **Race distance** 60 laps of 3.17-mile circuit **Reason for retirement** Gearbox after 27 laps **Car no** 2 **Entrant** Works

I took the train from Paris to Rouen at the start of what proved to be a rather disagreeable weekend involving a succession of niggling disputes with the race officials.

With the Gordini squad ranged against various Ferraris, it seemed as though the French team was being given a helping hand by officialdom. The rules stated that 'no cars may be push-started'. But the HWMs were not fitted with electric starters, so I do not know what they expected me to do during the refuelling stops. Keep the engine running, perhaps? No, they told me that was not permitted, either.

In the event, the gearbox failed after 27 laps so I coasted into the pits and climbed out of the cockpit, only to be told that I must move my car immediately. I responded with some French invective that, I think, took the wind out of the bloke's sails. I later wrote to apologise to the organisers – but it was certainly worth it at the time.

Incidentally, Yves Giraud-Cabantous was driving the other HWM in this event.

120 — 1st

British Grand Prix, 500cc Race

Kieft-Norton 500

14 July 1951, Silverstone, Northamptonshire (GB)

Race distance 20 laps of 2.889-mile circuit **Race time** 42m 12.2s **Race speed** 82.13mph **Fastest lap** 2m 2s, 85.23mph **Car no** 7 **Entrant** S.C. Moss

The Kieft ran superbly well at this important race, the principal supporting event to the British Grand Prix, which saw José Froilán González score Ferrari's first World Championship Formula 1 victory. I broke the two-minute barrier with a pole time of 1m 59.6s for the 500cc race, even though we had to change the engine, the latest version from Norton, back to an older one because it had seized on my first practice lap.

I took the lead from the start and never looked back. As I told Ray Martin afterwards, I could drive the entire circuit pretty well flat out, without lifting my foot from the throttle, apart from a momentary lift at Becketts. I joked that we could almost have left the brakes off altogether.

121 — 4th

Circuit de Mettet

HWM

15 July 1951, Mettet (B)

Category Formula 2 **Race distance** 40 laps of 5.25-mile circuit **Race time** 2h 19m 0s **Entrant** Works

I was not able to stay at Silverstone to watch the British Grand Prix because I was due in Mettet the following morning to race the HWM and had to catch a flight to Brussels.

Obviously I had to start from the back of the grid because I had not taken part in practice, but, despite the troublesome number-three cylinder oiling up because one of the piston rings had gone, I eventually worked my way up to second place behind Robert Manzon's Simca-Gordini. Unfortunately I had to make three stops to change the plugs, which were oiling up, and that dropped me back to fourth place at the finish behind a Gordini one-two-three.

BELOW *On the way to victory in the British Grand Prix 500cc supporting race in the Kieft-Norton, carefully avoiding getting too close to those heavy oil drums that marked the corners.* (Stirling Moss Collection)

122 — 1st

Dutch Grand Prix, 500cc Race

Kieft-Norton 500

22 July 1951, Zandvoort, Haarlem (NL)

Race distance 17 laps of 2.64-mile circuit **Race time** 36m 27.7s
Race speed 72.89mph **Car no** 26 **Entrant** S.C. Moss

Before I departed for Holland, I accepted an invitation to drive the BRM V16 for the first time at the Folkingham airfield, near the team's headquarters at Bourne, Lincolnshire. I went up there by train and was collected at Grantham. After the test, I was returned to London in Raymond Mays's Ford Consul and I headed off to Holland.

Almost up to the start of the race, there was some doubt over whether I would be allowed to compete because the organisers feared, on the strength of my drive at Silverstone, that I would have a runaway victory in the Kieft. Although this was contrary to my nature, it was agreed that I would be accepted on condition that I make a race of it to keep the crowds entertained. I battled with the JBS cars of Les Leston and John Habin, the three of us passing and re-passing, and then with two laps remaining I pulled away to win the race by 9 seconds.

123 — 3rd

Dutch Grand Prix

HWM

22 July 1951, Zandvoort, Haarlem (NL)

Race distance 90 laps of 2.64-mile circuit
Car no 28 **Entrant** Works

With neither the Alfa Romeo nor the Ferrari teams competing in this non-championship Formula 1 race, I thought we might have a good chance of a strong result. But Giuseppe Farina was there, driving a two-stage supercharged San Remo Maserati, and there were five 4.5-litre Talbot-Lagos driven by Louis Rosier, Louis Chiron, 'Phi-Phi' Etancelin, Johnny Claes and Duncan Hamilton.

Farina led from the start and I settled into sixth place right behind Rudi Fischer's Ferrari. After 19 laps Farina had to stop to top up with oil, which was obviously the start of a problem that caused his retirement because he made a second pit stop around the half-distance mark before stopping for good out on the circuit. By this stage, I had climbed to third place behind Rosier and Etancelin, but when the latter came in to the pits to change a punctured tyre with 15 laps to go, I moved up into second place.

Suddenly, with two laps to go, the HWM engine began to misfire. I rushed into the pits, the bonnet was ripped off, and a loose magneto wire was diagnosed and hastily fixed. Then I realised that Etancelin was due, so I jumped back into the cockpit and shouted to the mechanics to push-start me back into the race. In the rush there was no time to re-fix the bonnet, so I rejoined without it. I thought there was a chance I might hang on ahead of the Talbot, but Etancelin passed me on the last lap and I finished third.

124 — Retired

German Grand Prix, 500cc Race

Kieft-Norton 500

29 July 1951, Nürburgring (D)

Race distance 6 laps of 14.1-mile circuit **Reason for retirement** Broken steering arm after 3 laps **Entrant** S.C. Moss

This race supporting the German Grand Prix attracted an amazing entry of 49 competitors. In practice I was easily fastest with a lap of 11m 31.8s – an average speed of 73.71mph. Eric Brandon's Cooper-Norton took a brief lead from the start but I went past him by the time we exited the downhill wooded Hatzenbach section and the road circuit opened out towards Flugplatz and Schwedenkreuz. Halfway around the second lap, I was over half a minute in front of Brandon, but then the Kieft broke a steering arm and that was that. Brandon was left to win ahead of Alan Brown and Bill Whitehouse, also in Coopers.

125 — 4th

Freiburg Hill Climb, Formula 2 Class

HWM

5 August 1951, Freiburg (D)

Best time 8m 24.08s **Best speed** 53.3mph **Car no** 131
Entrant Works

As the HWM team was in the middle of its continental tour, it seemed a good idea to take in the spectacular Freiburg hill climb because it fell between major fixtures at Zandvoort and Erlen. I was pretty satisfied to finish fourth in the Formula 2 class at this venue, which was totally new to me, although my hill-climbing experience certainly helped.

126 — 1st

Freiburg Hill Climb, 500cc Class

Kieft-Norton 500

5 August 1951, Freiburg (D)

Best time 8m 18.99s **Best speed** 53.8mph
Entrant S.C. Moss

The Kieft-Norton came straight to Freiburg from my disappointing retirement at the Nürburgring and all the effort was rewarded with a trouble-free run to a class victory.

RIGHT *Back to my roots. In the gap between Zandvoort and Erlen I drove the HWM in the Freiburg hill climb – a new venue for me.* (Rodolfo Mailander, Ludvigsen Library)

127   Retired

Grand Prix OstSchweiz

HWM

12 August 1951, Erlen (CH)

Race distance 60 laps of 1.74-mile circuit **Reason for retirement** Broken suspension 1 lap from end **Car no** 4 **Entrant** Works

After the Freiburg hill climbs, I drove across to Switzerland in my Morris Minor to meet the rest of the HWM team at Erlen.

I set the fastest practice time, although there was a bit of a dispute with the Veritas driver Toni Ulmen, who told me, rather pompously, that overtaking other competitors on the right was against international regulations.

Everybody seemed to agree with me, so I gathered a deputation of drivers and went to the organisers to make the point that we should be permitted to overtake on either side if a rival would not pull over. The officials were slightly taken aback but, after a short discussion, amended the rules on the spot.

I set the second-fastest time, sharing the front row with Rudi Fischer's Ferrari. At the start he took the lead, but I overtook him on the first lap. He repassed me, then I overtook him again and built up a 9-second lead. Just as it seemed as though I would win, the left-front suspension wishbone snapped at about 100mph. The wheel folded inwards and I was very lucky to pull up without being involved in a big accident.

Before returning home after the Erlen race, I accepted an invitation to meet Enzo Ferrari at Maranello, which meant quite a detour in my Morris Minor. Ferrari told me that he wanted me to drive his latest car at Bari, assuming of course that it would be ready in time, or otherwise in the Italian Grand Prix at Monza a fortnight later. We also talked about the possibility of my driving for him in the seven-race winter series in South America.

128 Did not start

Bari Grand Prix

Ferrari 166

2 September 1951, Bari (I)

Reason did not start Practice accident **Race distance** 65 laps of 3.46-mile circuit **Entrant** David Murray

My father and I flew to Rome and then had a terrible overnight journey to Bari by train. Early in the morning of the practice day, I went into the Ferrari garage expecting to be welcomed and shown to the new car. In fact, they looked slightly surprised at my presence and told me that Piero Taruffi was going to drive the car instead. I was taken aback and exceedingly angry about it – so angry, in fact, that it coloured the rest of my motor racing career and I vowed that I would never race for a man with such poor ethics.

In a very generous gesture, David Murray sportingly offered to lend me his own Formula 2 Ferrari 166. It was hardly a potential winner but I accepted on the spot. Unfortunately, I suffered brake failure and crashed heavily on the first day of practice, then the engine broke on the second and I was unable to start.

129 1st

Curragh, Wakefield Trophy

HWM

8 September 1951, Curragh (ROI)

Race time 1h 52m 59.8s **Race speed** 81.21mph **Fastest lap** 3m 31.8s, 83.96mph (record) **Car no** 3 **Entrant** Works

Although this was not a major international event, it was certainly a very challenging one because the so-called 'long' Curragh circuit in County Kildare was a tricky and bumpy road circuit that demanded great concentration and discipline. My car's back axle seized during practice so I took over my team-mate Duncan Hamilton's HWM and lapped second fastest, in 3m 34s. I managed to win the race pretty decisively, heading an HWM one-two-three with Duncan and Oscar Moore following me home.

BELOW LEFT *Dressed for bad weather prior to the start of the Tourist Trophy at Dundrod, where I drove a works Jaguar C-type.* (Stirling Moss Collection)

BELOW *Taking the chequered flag after leading the TT from start to finish at Dundrod.* (LAT)

OPPOSITE *Relaxing with a rare cigarette after scoring my second TT victory.* (LAT)

The Wakefield Trophy race also incorporated a handicap-based competition for the O'Boyle Trophy, and I won this as well.

130 1st

RAC Tourist Trophy

Jaguar C-type

15 September 1951, Dundrod, Belfast, Northern Ireland (GB)

Organising club Royal Automobile Club
Race distance 43 laps of 7-mile circuit **Race time** 3h 42m 6.4s
Race speed 83.55mph **Car no** 7 **Entrant** Works

After the race at the Curragh, I had enjoyed a leisurely drive up to Belfast in preparation for my second RAC Tourist Trophy, this time driving one of the works

Jaguar C-types. The TT took place on the Saturday and the Italian Grand Prix on the Sunday, so I was tempted to enter. It would have involved some clever juggling of flights.

Theoretically it would have been possible to run in practice at Dundrod on Thursday, fly to Monza for practice on Friday, fly back to Dundrod for the race on Saturday, and then back again to Monza for the Grand Prix on Sunday. Reading this, you might think that I was getting a little bit too carried away with things, and eventually I decided that such a schedule would be asking too much.

I led the TT from start to finish, so I had made the right decision.

This was to be the HWM team's final outing in Europe. I caught a flight to Paris on 18 September before driving down to the villa owned by Lance Macklin's mother near Monte Carlo. On the morning of the 21st we were delayed in leaving for Modena because Lance had got involved in a dispute and clouted some fellow the previous evening. We eventually arrived in Modena at 8.45pm.

Practice was a bit frustrating because Lance's car seemed to have better pick-up out of the corners. I tried different tyres, but that was no good. I could qualify only on the fourth row of the grid. In the race I was quickly up to fourth place behind the Ferraris of Alberto Ascari and Luigi Villoresi, and André Simon in the Gordini. Then the magneto began to play up again – the old HWM problem. I made a pit stop to change the plugs, then another one to change the magneto, but eventually I had to retire when the number-three plug blew out of the head.

131 Retired

Modena Grand Prix

HWM

23 September 1951, Modena (I)

Race distance 66 laps of 2.35-mile circuit Reason for retirement Magneto/sparking plug Car no 18 Entrant Works

LEFT *Struggling with the HWM on the Modena aerodrome circuit, where I eventually retired when a sparking plug blew out of the head.* (Rodolfo Mailander, Ludvigsen Library)

BELOW *All smiles at Modena. With HWM boss John Heath and team-mate Lance Macklin.* (Rodolfo Mailander, Ludvigsen Library)

132 1st

Goodwood, Madgwick Cup

HWM

29 September 1951, Goodwood (GB)

Organising club British Automobile Racing Club
Race distance 5 laps of 2.4-mile circuit **Race time** 8m 25s
Race speed 84.83mph **Fastest lap** 1m 39s, 86.54mph
Car no 6 **Entrant** Works

This was the final Goodwood meeting of the year and I opened the day with an easy drive to victory, heading Lance and George Abecassis home for an HWM one-two-three.

BELOW *Leading the September Goodwood sports car race all the way in the works Jaguar C-type, pursued here by a trio of XK120s.* (LAT)

133 1st

Goodwood, Sports Car Race

Jaguar C-type

29 September 1951, Goodwood (GB)

Organising club British Automobile Racing Club
Race distance 5 laps of 2.4-mile circuit **Race time** 8m 32s
Race speed 83.67 mph **Fastest lap** 1m 41s, 84.83mph
Car no 60 **Entrant** Works

Later in the day I started from pole position and led the sports car race comfortably all the way. Contemporary reports suggested that the C-type was fitted with a low 7:1 compression ratio so that it could run on the low-grade 'pool' petrol that was available to most motorists in this immediate post-war period. I have no recollection whether or not this was the case. Either way, the Jaguar ran perfectly.

134 1st

Goodwood, 29th September Handicap, 1

Jaguar C-type

29 September 1951, Goodwood (GB)

Race distance 5 laps of 2.4-mile circuit **Race time** 9m 20.2s
Race speed 84.16 mph **Fastest lap** 1m 39.6s, 86.02mph
Car no 60 **Entrant** Works

This was a straightforward and very brief handicap race that gave me a good second win of the day.

OPPOSITE *At the Winfield aerodrome circuit in Scotland, where I took the HWM to victory in the Formula 2 class in an event staged concurrently with a Formule Libre race.* (LAT)

1952

ERA IN ERROR

Although the 1951 season had finished on a disappointing note with two frustrating weeks of testing the BRM at Monza during November, over the winter a definite target came into view as it was being suggested that BRM might compete in the Turin Grand Prix on 6 April. By this stage, Alfa Romeo had indicated that they would not be competing in Formula 1 races during 1952, so only Ferrari was left with a fully fledged Formula 1 car to offer as direct competition to BRM. Race organisers across Europe were waiting to see what would happen before deciding whether to commit to running races under the existing Formula 1 regulations or switch to the interim Formula 2 rules that had been introduced as a stop-gap for rounds of the World Championship, pending the arrival of new 2.5-litre regulations for 1954.

I returned to Monza for more tests with BRM in March 1952 and it looked as though the car might be ready to race at Turin. But then, suddenly, the BRM Trust took the staggering decision to order the cars back to Britain only a few days before the Turin event. We very soon learned that Juan Manual Fangio and José Froilán González were arriving from Argentina to test the BRM at Folkingham. The BRM management were clearly star-struck by the interest shown by these two experienced drivers…

I would eventually have my one and only drive in the BRM V16 in June at Dundrod for the Ulster Trophy Race, which turned out to be a complete and utter fiasco. It was in this race that I passed the great Fangio – but only because he had spun and was going backwards!

Then I made what turned out to be a crucial wrong decision. I decided to leave HWM to drive the brand-new Bristol-engined G-type ERA, which was being developed by my friend Leslie Johnson at his base in Dunstable, Bedfordshire. The chassis, the brainchild of a high-calibre university graduate, was revolutionary, made from very substantial Electron tubing of five or six inches in diameter. Unfortunately, it did not work too well. I understood that the idea was to develop the car through the 1952 and 1953 seasons before making a Formula 1 version in time for the start of the revised Formula 1 regulations in 1954.

The remainder of my 1952 season was as frantically busy as usual. This was the first year that I drove for Rootes in rallies in a Sunbeam-Talbot and I won a *Coupe des Alpes* – the award for a penalty-free run – on the Alpine Rally at my first attempt.

I took every opportunity I could to drive the Kieft-Norton, which I bought from the company for £400 and fitted with a new Norton engine, costing another £250.

I also continued as a member of the Jaguar sports car team, although my C-type failed to finish both at Le Mans and in the Mille Miglia. However, I did manage to score several other victories in the car, most notably in the sports car race at Reims, which was the first race ever won by a car with disc brakes. Here was a great example of how development through racing can make a gigantic contribution to passenger cars, in the same way as I believe today's KERS (Kinetic Energy Recovery System) will be standard on all production vehicles within the next ten years.

All in all, though, it was a pretty disappointing year.

LEFT *At the wheel of the G-type ERA at Silverstone. I thought it would be the right thing to do, leaving HWM to drive this new challenger. In fact it proved to be a crucial wrong turning for my career and in many ways resulted in a wasted season.* (Guy Griffiths Collection)

Monte Carlo Rally

Sunbeam-Talbot 90

22/29 January 1952, Monte Carlo (MON)

Event distance c2,000 miles **Co-drivers** Desmond Scannell and John Cooper **Car no** 341 **Entrant** Works

I competed in this event with Desmond Scannell, Secretary of the BRDC, and John Cooper of *The Autocar* as my co-drivers. They picked me up with the car in Paris, because I had been skiing in Switzerland. At this time the Monte Carlo Rally followed a route around a large part of Europe and competitors started from a number of different places. We chose to start the event from Monte Carlo itself, rather than Glasgow, which meant that we could, in effect, practise the tough, final part of the journey on the outward leg before tackling it again on the final run-in to Monte Carlo.

All went well enough until we reached the leg between Luxembourg and Liège, which was covered in sheet ice and deeply rutted frozen snow. I think my two passengers were rather shaken by the speed I was driving, flat out with the car weaving and juddering spectacularly.

But the crucial section of the route was from St Flour to Le Puy, high in the mountains. The car leaped from one mound of packed ice to the next. I discovered that on ice the only way to keep straight was to press on as fast as the car was able to go, and, if it began to snake, you did not correct it with the steering otherwise you would over-correct and fly off the road.

The outcome of the rally was finally settled on a regularity trial on the snow-covered Col de Braus. I slid gently nose-first into a snow bank but we managed to haul the Sunbeam-Talbot out and get it back on the road. Because we were such an amateur team none of us had any idea how long we were stationary. Now Desmond and John had to calculate how much time we had lost and how much we needed to make up to arrive at the next scheduled time check within our allotted time.

First we decided to make up two minutes. Then we decided to lose them. Finally we opted to split the difference. In the end we were 28 seconds too fast, 4 seconds faster than Sydney Allard's Allard, which beat us to overall victory by this tightest of margins.

Kitching Trophy Trial

Harford 3 special

17 February 1952, Derbyshire (GB)

Car no 60 **Co-driver** John Cooper **Entrant** Cuth Harrison

This was my first serious experience of cross-country 'mud-plugging', which came about when Cuth Harrison – who also raced an ERA – invited me to drive one of his specials, the so-called Harford 3, alongside Reg Parnell in a Harford 2 and John Bolster in a Dellow. The car was so oddly shaped that I should think the weight distribution was 90 per cent to the rear wheels and 10 per cent to the front. I took John Cooper of *The Autocar* along as my passenger and, although we were both bouncing up and down like mad as we tackled the first hill, we did not manage to synchronise our bounces. But we just managed to beat Parnell and Bolster, which was our main aim.

LEFT *With John 'Autocar' Cooper and Desmond Scannell, and the Sunbeam-Talbot 90 that I drove to second place in the Monte Carlo Rally.* (LAT)

RIGHT *Mud, mud, glorious mud! Fighting for grip at the wheel of Cuth Harrison's Harford 3 special in the Kitching Trophy Trial. Passenger John Cooper looks rather less than convinced.* (LAT)

143 — 2nd in class

Lyons-Charbonnières Rally

Jaguar XK120

24/26 March 1952, Lyons-Charbonnières (F)

Event distance 2,200km **Co-driver** Gregor Grant **Car no** 143 **Entrant** S.C. Moss

Before the main 1952 racing season began I took my own Jaguar XK120 coupé on the gruelling Lyon-Charbonnières Rally with Gregor Grant, the founder and editor of *Autosport* magazine, as my co-driver. Run from the Cote d'Azur through a large section of southern France, the 2,200km route combined some arduous road sections with challenging speed and hill climb sections.

My most vivid memory of this event was on the section from Grenoble to Chambéry in the French Alps, by which time the rally had developed pretty much into an out-and-out road race. The section comprised a series of sharp turns, steep climbs, tunnels and narrow roads coated with a generous helping of ice and melted snow. It was quite an experience and slightly out of the ordinary for me, I have to admit. We did pretty well, finishing second in our class and 15th overall.

144 — 1st

Castle Combe 500 Races, Heat 3

Kieft-Norton 500

12 April 1952, Castle Combe, Chippenham, Wiltshire (GB)

Race distance 6 laps of 1.84-mile circuit **Race time** 8m 53.6s **Race speed** 74.48mph **Fastest lap** 1m 27s, 76.15mph **Car no** 7 **Entrant** S.C. Moss

This was a little club meeting held on the Saturday of Easter weekend and I treated it as a useful warm-up for the traditional Easter Monday Goodwood meeting a couple of days later. In my heat I had an easy win ahead of another Kieft driven by André Loens and Don Grey's Cooper-JAP.

145 — 1st

Castle Combe 500 Races, Final

Kieft-Norton 500

12 April 1952, Castle Combe, Chippenham, Wiltshire (GB)

Race distance 10 laps of 1.84-mile circuit **Race time** 14m 56s **Race speed** 74.39mph **Fastest lap** 1m 25s, 77.9mph (record) **Car no** 7 **Entrant** S.C. Moss

This was another straightforward victory on the same day, interrupted only by a little bit of strategic gamesmanship to ensure that Loens and Jack Westcott finished second and third behind me, completing a Kieft one-two-three.

146 — Unclassified

Castle Combe 500 Races, Relay Event

Frazer Nash Le Mans Replica

12 April 1952, Castle Combe, Chippenham, Wiltshire (GB)

Race distance 10 laps of 1.84-mile circuit **Co-driver** Roy Salvadori **Entrant** Gilby Engineering

This was my second drive in the Frazer Nash owned by Syd Greene and I shared it with Roy Salvadori. We were not classified at the finish.

147 — 1st

Goodwood, Earl of March Trophy

Kieft-Norton 500

14 April 1952, Goodwood, West Sussex (GB)

Organising club British Automobile Racing Club **Race distance** 6 laps of 2.4-mile circuit **Race time** 11m 4s **Race speed** 78.07mph **Fastest lap** 1m 48.6s, 79.56mph (record) **Car no** 7 **Entrant** S.C. Moss

This was another easy win with the Kieft. I was not challenged from start to finish, taking the chequered flag comfortably ahead of Alan Brown's Ecurie Richmond Cooper, with John Coombs coming home third in a similar car entered by Ecurie Britannique.

148 — 4th

Goodwood, Easter Handicap

Jaguar C-type

14 April 1952, Goodwood, West Sussex (GB)

Organising club British Automobile Racing Club **Race distance** 6 laps of 2.4-mile circuit **Race time** 12m 40.6s **Fastest lap** 1m 44.6s, 82.6mph **Car no** 8 **Entrant** Works

This event, the first Easter Handicap, was a much-publicised duel between myself and motorcycle ace Geoff Duke, who was having his first car race outing in the Aston Martin DB3. I thought the handicapping was pretty harsh, with the result that I could finish only fourth, about 10 seconds behind Geoff. I seem to recall that Geoff suggested to me that the next time we competed against each other we should both be on Norton motorcycles.

RIGHT *Waiting for the start of the handicap race at Goodwood, where my Jaguar C-type was pitted against motorcycle star Geoff Duke's Aston Martin DB3. (Guy Griffiths Collection)*

149 Retired

Mille Miglia

Jaguar C-type

4 May 1952, Brescia (I)

Event distance 1 lap of 992-mile circuit **Reason for retirement** Steering **Co-driver** Norman Dewis **Car no** 619 **Entrant** Works

This was my second Mille Miglia and this time I was competing in what became one of my favourite cars – the Jaguar C-type. A couple of years later the streamlined D-type became an ideal machine for the smooth surface and high speeds of Le Mans, but for sheer driving pleasure I always preferred the C-type as a more versatile 'driver's car'.

The opposition included 4.1-litre Ferraris for Piero Taruffi and Giannino Marzotto. Although our C-types were now fitted with Dunlop disc brakes, most of the attention was centred on the new, lightweight Mercedes-Benz 300SL coupés.

I was sharing the car with Norman Dewis from Jaguar and the race started in pouring rain again. I found myself wishing that Jaguar could have prepared for it in the way Mercedes did. That whole team, with mechanics and spare cars, was out in Italy months before the race. The drivers had all done two or three trips around the circuit and had decided where to set up their refuelling and servicing stations.

My clearest memory of the opening stages of that 1952 event is of a section near Ravenna, where I was doing around 150mph. It was pouring with rain and a nasty cross-wind made it very difficult to keep the car on the road.

Norman Dewis had his head down and, as a matter of fact, I was frightening myself stiff. I thought I was pressing on as hard as anybody could, when suddenly a gullwing Mercedes went flying past. I managed to overtake it again later, but I can tell you it really shook me.

My biggest problem in this race was a split fuel tank, which meant the team had to try to improvise a revised refuelling schedule. Later it was clear just how much the C-type was wilting under the stress of the Mille Miglia. It took a terrible pounding. The shock absorbers were beginning to pack up, but, after the punishing section over the mountains to Bologna, I was lying third. Then, with about 145 miles to go, the Jaguar gave up the ghost. Everything seemed to happen to it but the chief problem was the steering, which came adrift because of the punishment the car had taken.

152   1st

Silverstone, Production Sports Car Race

Jaguar C-type

10 May 1952, Silverstone (GB)

Organising club British Racing Drivers' Club
Race distance 17 laps of 3-mile circuit **Race time** 35m 32s
Race speed 84.02mph **Fastest lap** 2m 1s, 87mph **Car no** 40
Entrant Works

Three C-types lined up for this race, driven by Tony Rolt, Peter Walker and me. Walker led off the line, but I took the lead midway round the second lap. I won by 14 seconds from Reg Parnell in an Aston Martin DB3.

ABOVE *Lapping a couple of MGs on my way to victory in the Silverstone production car race with the works Jaguar C-type.* (Tom March Collection)

153   1st

Silverstone, Race of Champions

Jaguar XK120

10 May 1952, Silverstone (GB)

Organising club British Racing Drivers' Club
Race distance 5 laps of 3-mile circuit **Race time** 11m 15s
Race speed 78.05mph **Fastest lap** 2m 12s, 79.83mph **Car no** 5
Entrant Works

No sooner I had I hopped out of the C-type than it was time to take part in this so-called 'Race of Champions' celebrity race over five laps – my fourth race of the day.

There were six new Jaguar XK120s in the field and we drivers drew ballots for our grid positions. The other competitors included Paul Pietsch (Switzerland), Johnny Claes (Belgium), Prince Bira (Siam), 'Toulo' de Graffenried (Switzerland) and Tony Gaze (Australia). After dodging round the slow-starting Bira off the line, I managed to pull out almost 2 seconds a lap over de Graffenried to win quite easily.

154   Retired

Brussels Grand Prix, Heat 2

Kieft-Norton 500

11 May 1952, Bois de la Cambre, Brussels (B)

Category Formula 3 **Reason for retirement** Crash
Car no 8 **Entrant** S.C. Moss

Immediately after the BRDC's Saturday fixture at Silverstone I flew to Brussels for what was to prove an ill-fated F3 event in the Bois de la Cambre. I made a bad start in the second heat, but was climbing through the field when local driver Lex Beels suddenly spun, triggering a multiple accident involving several other cars.

I swerved to avoid the pile-up, but clipped a trackside straw bale and somersaulted the Kieft. I looked out and saw a mass of other cars arriving on the scene facing in all directions, so I ducked back into the cockpit again. I was shaken, but unhurt. The Kieft was a total write-off.

155 Retired

Swiss Grand Prix

HWM

18 May 1952, Bremgarten, Berne (CH)

F1 World Championship, round 1

Category Formula 2 **Race distance** 62 laps of 4.524-mile circuit **Reason for retirement** Withdrawn by team **Car no** 46 **Entrant** Works

This was my first Formula 2 outing of the year – but not in the long-awaited ERA. For this race I was invited to drive a fourth HWM alongside Lance Macklin, George Abecassis and Peter Collins, the young 500cc driver who had replaced me in the team's permanent line-up.

My trip down from Brussels to Berne was every bit as eventful as the two races at either end of my journey. At the start of 1952 I had taken delivery of a green-and-cream-painted Jaguar XK120 fixed-head coupé with the intention of towing a caravan around Europe to stay in at all the races.

Ken Gregory and I duly set out from Brussels having spent many weeks finalising the caravan's specification. Unfortunately, as we approached Namur the towing bolt sheared and, to my horror, I suddenly realised that the XK120 was being overtaken by our caravan! It knocked down some signposts and a kilometre stone before coming to rest on its side, really badly wrecked. In the space of a few days I had lost not just my Kieft but also my new caravan.

At Berne I was ninth on the starting grid, but even as we went out on to the grid I was feeling a little worried because John Heath and I could not agree on which sparking plugs would be most appropriate for the race. After two laps I was up to third place, behind the Ferraris of Giuseppe Farina and Piero Taruffi. Unfortunately the plugs 'cooked', as I had anticipated, with the result that I had to pit at the end of the third lap for a complete change to harder plugs, resuming in 17th place.

Suddenly, everything went wrong for the HWM team. On the 12th lap Abecassis was negotiating a very fast corner when the rear axle broke and a wheel came off. The car crashed into a bank and George was thrown out on to the road. He suffered serious bruises and was lucky not to be killed. Then the same thing happened to Collins, but he managed to fight his HWM to a standstill at the edge of the track. Lance Macklin and I were quite relieved when John Heath decided to call us in and withdraw our cars from the race.

BELOW *A very satisfying second place came in the Eifelrennen behind Rudi Fischer's Ferrari.* (Stirling Moss Collection)

156 — 1st

Luxembourg Grand Prix, Heat 2

Kieft-Norton 500

22 May 1952, Findel (LU)

Category Formula 3 **Race time** 23m 47s **Race speed** 73mph **Fastest lap** 1m 50s, 76.95mph **Car no** 7 **Entrant** D. Annable

---

158 — Retired

Eifelrennen 500cc Race

Kieft-Norton 500

25 May 1952, Nürburgring (D)

Race distance 5 laps of 14.17-mile circuit **Reason for retirement** Wheel came off **Car no** 168 **Entrant** D. Annable

---

160 — Retired

British Empire Trophy

Frazer Nash Le Mans Replica

29 May 1952, Douglas (IoM)

Race distance 52 laps of 3.85-mile circuit **Reason for retirement** Ignition **Car no** 20 **Entrant** Gilby Engineering

---

As my own Kieft had been wrecked in Belgium a fortnight earlier, my friend Derek Annable very kindly loaned me his similar car for the next few Formula 3 races. My first race with it was in Luxembourg, but I soon discovered that, being what you might call a 'production' car, it was not quite the same as the one-off 'hand-built' version that Ray Martin had prepared for me.

Even so, I managed to win my heat at Luxembourg by 4 seconds from Ken Carter's Cooper-Norton.

157 — 6th

Luxembourg Grand Prix, Final

Kieft-Norton 500

22 May 1952, Findel (LU)

Category Formula 3 **Car no** 7 **Entrant** D. Annable

This race was on the same day as the heat. I led from the start, but eventually a plug lead worked loose and I had to make a pit stop. It dropped me to ninth place, but I climbed back to sixth by the time the chequered flag had dropped.

I began to wonder if things could really get much worse. From pole position, I took the lead from another Kieft, driven by André Loens, going into the first corner and was well ahead by the end of the opening lap. Then, just as I swung into the South Curve, a wheel came off and that was that.

159 — 2nd

Eifelrennen Formula 2 Race

HWM

25 May 1952, Nürburgring (D)

Race distance 7 laps of 14.17-mile circuit **Race time** 1h 17m 39.5s **Race speed** c76mph **Car no** 139 **Entrant** Works

---

Again I was in an HWM. Beating Rudi Fischer's powerful 2-litre Ferrari was going to be a tall order, even at the Nürburgring, but I led him for the first two laps before things again began to go wrong for me. The fire extinguisher in the HWM's cockpit suddenly went off, dousing me in foam. But the car kept going and I finished only 18 seconds behind Fischer. I was terrifically pleased – it was wonderful to finish anywhere at all!

I returned to the Isle of Man hoping that I might be able to repeat my 1951 victory driving Syd Greene's Frazer Nash, but things were to work out very differently. Although I got on the front row alongside Duncan Hamilton's C-type Jaguar and Geoff Duke's Aston Martin DB3, the race was not a success for me. First, I had to stop to have a new fan belt fitted, then I lost another 11 minutes in the pit lane having the car's fuel pump changed. Soon afterwards the car stopped for good.

161 — Retired

Prix de Monte Carlo

Frazer Nash Le Mans Replica

2 June 1952, Monte Carlo (MON)

Race distance 65 laps of 1.95-mile circuit **Reason for retirement** Wheel-fixing damage after 49 laps **Fastest lap** 1m 50s, 76.95mph **Car no** 26 **Entrant** Works

---

I took pole position on the starting grid but Franco Bordoni's amazingly fast little 1.3-litre OSCA catapulted straight into the lead and was 6 seconds ahead of my Frazer Nash after only a single lap. Robert Manzon was also racing quickly through the field, having started at the back of the grid in the spare Gordini.

Eventually Manzon nipped ahead of me but I quickly repassed him. Suddenly I became aware of a slight rear-end imbalance to my car. I immediately came into the pits, where

the mechanics found that the wheel-securing bolt holes on the left rear had stretched and elongated, with the result that the whole wheel was wobbling about violently. I went back into the race for a while but there was no point just hobbling about at reduced speed, so there was no other option but to retire.

162 Disqualified

Monaco Grand Prix

Jaguar C-type

2 June 1952, Monte Carlo (MON)

Race distance 100 laps of 1.95-mile circuit
Reason for disqualification Receiving outside assistance
Car no 78 **Entrant** Works

The Monaco Grand Prix was held for sports cars in 1952 and I thought both my driving style and the works Jaguar C-type would be ideally suited to the challenge. I missed out on pole position by 0.3 seconds to Pierre Levegh's streamlined Talbot, which he was testing in preparation for Le Mans, but I took the lead at the start of the race and began to pull away.

After about 17 laps it was beginning to look as though Robert Manzon's Gordini was starting to catch me, but the race was thrown into chaos by a multiple pile-up at the Ste Devote right-hander just beyond the pits, triggered by Reg Parnell's Aston Martin blowing its engine and dropping oil all over the road. Antonio Stagnoli spun his Ferrari, hit the Aston and briefly trapped poor Reg against a straw bale, leaving him with a very badly bruised leg. Then Manzon, who had just slipped past me to take the lead, slid into the stationary Aston and I did the same, badly

LEFT The backdrop at Monte Carlo has changed little over the years since I led the 1952 Grand Prix for sports cars in the works Jaguar C-type. Disappointingly, I was disqualified after my car had been pushed by two spectators, following a shunt caused by oil on the track. (Rodolfo Mailander, Ludvigsen Library)

bending both of the C-type's front wings. I came into the pits for repairs and then rejoined the race to catch up as best I could.

For the next 20 laps I drove absolutely as fast as I could, climbing back to fifth place. But then the race officials, after conferring for almost an hour, decided to show me the black flag for allegedly 'receiving outside assistance, other than in the pits'. This referred to the Ste Devote incident and the willing efforts of a couple of enthusiastic British spectators who proffered their help to get me going again and thus clear the track. The decision by the race officials was technically correct, but by no means popular.

163 Retired

Ulster Trophy

BRM V16

7 June 1952, Dundrod, Belfast, Northern Ireland (GB)

Race distance 34 laps of 7.5-mile circuit **Reason for retirement** Clutch and overheating after 4 laps **Car no** 8 **Entrant** Works

Looking back, it seems extraordinary that I did not get round to racing the BRM V16 until the summer of 1952, considering that I had taken part in the tests at Monza some nine months before.

Having missed the Turin Grand Prix in April, the BRMs were scheduled to compete next at Albi on 1 June. It then emerged that the BRM Trust had promised Northern Ireland's Prime Minister, Viscount Brookeborough, that three BRMs would be on the grid for the Ulster Trophy at Dundrod on 7 June. Given the cars' unreliability, this looked like a tall order.

My first impression was that the car handled better, but on the narrow Dundrod circuit its tendency to wander and feel unstable seemed extremely pronounced compared with its handling on the broad asphalt at Monza. In practice, I thought the BRM certainly did not feel safe, particularly in view of the fact that a wet race was predicted. In the event, only two BRMs were fielded, the first for Fangio and the second for me, but the whole meeting degenerated into a fiasco as far as I was concerned.

Unknown to me, my car was switched with Fangio's overnight. I had agreed that such a step might be taken if necessary because Fangio was the number-one driver, but it would have been nice if they had mentioned it to me before the race…

When the starter held up the 30-second board, I put the clutch out and selected first gear. I always did that earlier than strictly necessary to make sure I was in gear when the flag dropped. There were about 10 seconds to go when the clutch began to take up and the car began to creep. There was not much I could do because I had the clutch hard down. I had to heel-and-toe with my right foot on the brake as well as the accelerator to hold the car still. Just as the flag was about to fall the clutch burned out and the engine stalled.

I looked across and saw that Fangio had stalled his engine on the line too, seconds before the flag fell. So while the field rushed off in a cloud of spray, we were just left sitting there on the back of the grid. The mechanics rushed out and push-started us.

Once we got going I found my clutch was slipping badly so Fangio quickly lost me. Then, as I came round the left-hand corner before the hairpin, I encountered Fangio facing me, going backwards quickly. So there were two BRMs, nose to nose, going down the hill towards the hairpin. I think Fangio was going faster backwards than I was forwards!

On the second lap the gear knob came off in my hand. I think I slung it to somebody as a souvenir. Both Fangio and I were having big trouble getting round the hairpin and therefore we had to slip our clutches – and, of course, it did not help that mine had virtually burned out on the line. Anyway, that was the least of my problems because I came into the pits at the end of the second lap with chronic overheating. I crawled round a bit more and was almost relieved to call it a day after four laps.

I later wrote to Raymond Mays telling him that I did not want to drive the BRM again in its present state. The truth was that, at this stage in its history, the BRM organisation just was not up to the job. Those guys thought they were on a par with Alfa Romeo or Mercedes, but the sad truth was that they really had not got a clue.

164 Retired

Le Mans 24 Hours

Jaguar C-type

14/15 June 1952, Sarthe (F)

Race distance 24 hours of 8.38-mile circuit (2320.07 miles, 277 laps) **Reason for retirement** Overheating
Co-driver Peter Walker **Car no** 17 **Entrant** Works

Looking back to that moment in the Mille Miglia when one of the new Mercedes-Benz 300SL coupés simply rocketed past my Jaguar near Ravenna, I see that that was when I inadvertently sowed the seeds of Jaguar's 1952 Le Mans disaster. I had sent a telegram to William Lyons saying 'we must have more speed for Le Mans'. As a result of this comment, the Jaguar racing department had gone after improved top speed by completely redesigning the C-type bodywork with a long sweeping tail and a smaller radiator lower down in the nose.

Soon after the start of practice, it became clear that there was something radically wrong with the cars. The brakes were not too good, but we had declined the opportunity to run Dunlop disc brakes on this occasion. The cars were difficult to hold down the long straights and, more worrying, suffered persistent overheating, which would cause them to come into the pits after only a handful of laps with their radiators boiling.

It was clear that the revised radiator set-up was not working properly. Rough louvres were cut in the side of the bodywork in a bid to solve the problems. On closer examination, it looked as though hot water from the cylinder head was passing straight to the header tank and back, completely bypassing the radiator. At the last moment, William Lyons personally gave instructions that two of the cars should be modified to accept the original radiators for the race.

But it was too little, too late. I was paired with Peter Walker while the other two C-types were driven by Tony Rolt and Duncan Hamilton, and Ian Stewart and Peter Whitehead. Stewart was out with overheating after 15 laps, I lasted about another nine laps before boiling my way into the pit lane, and Hamilton retired shortly afterwards.

I was a disappointed man in many ways.

RIGHT *My sole race with the BRM V16 was the Ulster Trophy at Dundrod and it turned out to be a complete and utter fiasco for both Fangio and myself.* (Klemantaski Collection)

LEFT *In the works Jaguar C-type in the opening stages at Le Mans. The aerodynamically modified nose was a disaster and all three cars retired early with dire overheating.* (LAT)

165 Retired

Belgian Grand Prix

ERA G-type

22 June 1952, Spa-Francorchamps, Liège (B)

F1 World Championship, round 3

Race distance 86 laps of 8.479-mile circuit **Reason for retirement** Accident on opening lap **Car no** 17 **Entrant** Works

166 1st

Reims Sports Car Grand Prix

Jaguar C-type

29 June 1952, Reims (F)

Race distance 50 laps of 4.58-mile circuit **Race time** 2h 16m 39s **Race speed** 98.26mph **Car no** 50 **Entrant** T. Wisdom

It is no exaggeration to say that this was a crucial race for Leslie Johnson and me. Leslie was keen to get his programme with the G-type ERA back on track, in the literal sense, after a run of disappointments. And I just wanted to get back to finishing races. Apart from this, I was 17 points behind Mike Hawthorn in the contest for the British Racing Drivers' Club's Gold Star award and, with Mike having his first Continental Grand Prix outing with the Cooper-Bristol at Spa, I really felt I needed a strong performance in this event.

After the first practice session, it was clear that the ERA's Bristol engine was not producing sufficient power. It was decided that a replacement should be flown out from England and the mechanics worked overnight to install it in the car. Because of my poor practice times, I had to start from the back of the grid, but by the time I got round to the Malmédy section of the circuit on the opening lap I had passed 17 cars and was up to fifth place.

Suddenly, my race turned into a disaster. A connecting rod in the Bristol engine punched a hole through the side and then burst into flames. The car snapped luridly sideways, shot off the road, and came to rest after mowing down a kilometre marker stone. In the pouring rain, all that was left for me to do was to struggle back to the pits, soaked to the skin yet again.

After the rain at Spa I now found myself in sweltering conditions at Reims, where I drove Tommy Wisdom's light-green Jaguar C-type in the sports car race supporting the Formula 2 event. I managed to get round in 2m 37s during practice but Robert Manzon in the 2.3-litre Gordini lapped 6 seconds quicker. That little car was really fast and the Jaguar could not hold it.

As anticipated, Manzon led in the opening stages, although I made such a strong start that I was ahead for the first few corners. After five laps he was 20 seconds ahead of me, but the Gordini eventually broke a stub axle and lost a wheel at Garenne, crashing into a telegraph pole.

Luckily, Manzon escaped with a scraped arm. I was left with a big lead and came home an easy winner ahead of Guy Mairesse in his Talbot and the Ecurie Ecosse Jaguar XK120 driven by Jamie 'Sir James' Scott-Douglas. It was the C-type's first victory equipped with Dunlop disc brakes and the first ever disc-braked race win in motor racing history.

RIGHT *The start of the Belgian Grand Prix. I passed 17 cars on the opening lap only for the ERA G-type's Bristol engine to punch a hole through the side of the cylinder block, as a result of which I shot off the road.* (LAT)

Marne Grand Prix

HWM

29 June 1952, Reims (F)

Category Formula 2 **Race distance** 3 hours
of a 4.58-mile circuit **Entrant** Works

With no ERA available, I was asked to drive for HWM again at Reims. Conditions, if anything, were hotter than they had been for the sports car race earlier in the day.

I made a poor start but pulled through to battle with Mike Hawthorn's Cooper-Bristol for fifth place. Then everything began to go wrong again. I had to make a long pit stop for plugs, oil and water. Once out on the circuit again, I found myself gradually becoming soaked with leaking oil. There was nothing for it but to keep stopping to replenish the oil in the tank and getting fresh cloths for to wipe my goggles clean. I finished the race in such a distant 10th place that I was unclassified.

168	Coupe

Alpine Rally

Sunbeam-Talbot 90

11–16 July 1952

Event distance 2,045 miles **Co-driver** John Cutts
Car no 316 **Entrant** Works

During the 1950s the Alpine Rally was one of the most gruelling and challenging of tests to be held for production motor cars anywhere in Europe. Of the 90 cars that left Marseilles on 11 July, only 23 reached the finish in Cannes on 16 July after completing a 2,045-mile route that included more than 40 of the most hazardous mountain passes in the Alps and the Dolomites.

It was a tough challenge, but we survived it without incurring any penalties, although at one point we lost 26 minutes when the car

shed its exhaust system, which had to be replaced. Making up that lost time meant my driving pretty much at ten-tenths, which resulted in John Cutts, my co-driver, hanging on for dear life. Mike Hawthorn was also in the team, which included Sunbeam's most experienced rally driver, George Murray-Frame. Not only did we each win a coveted *Coupe des Alpes* award, but we also scooped the team prize.

169   1st

British Grand Prix, 500cc Race

Kieft-Norton 500

19 July 1952, Silverstone (GB)

Race distance 15 laps of 2.93-mile circuit **Race time** 31m 46s
Race speed 82.50mph **Fastest lap** 2m 4s, 84.98mph (record)
Car no 7 **Entrant** D. Annable

I had a close race-long battle with Don Parker's Cooper. On the last lap I knew it would be an all-or-nothing affair. We rushed down to Stowe with only Club corner and Woodcote left. I could only hope that Don would make a mistake and let me through because he seemed to have the speed to hold me off. Going into Stowe, flat out in top gear, I saw Don change down into third. Coming out of the corner he rammed the lever back into top so hard that I thought something must break. It did – the chain! So I went through to a clear victory.

OPPOSITE *The Sunbeam-Talbot 90 I drove to win a coveted* Coupe des Alpes *award on the Alpine Rally. This photo dramatically illustrates just how wild and woolly some of the mountain passes were back in the 1950s.* (LAT)

ABOVE *My expression looks slightly dejected in this shot of the ERA G-type in the British Grand Prix – the car suffered a terminal misfire.* (Tom March Collection)

170   Retired

British Grand Prix

ERA G-type

19 July 1952, Silverstone,
Northamptonshire (GB)
F1 World Championship, round 5

Race distance 85 laps of 2.93-mile circuit
Reason for retirement Cylinder head after 36 laps
Car no 12 **Entrant** Works

The ERA handled quite well but simply did not have the power to perform strongly on a fast circuit such as Silverstone. It was also misfiring badly and I had to make a succession of pit stops to try to sort it out. I decided to drive safely and strategically in an effort to finish but eventually, after a long conference with Leslie Johnson, the decision was taken to retire the car.

177   1st

Boreham, 100-mile Sports Car Race

3.4 Jaguar C-type

2 August 1952, Boreham, Essex (GB)

Race distance 34 laps of 3-mile circuit **Race time** 1h 9m 28.4s
Race speed 88.09mph **Fastest lap** 90mph **Car no** 40
Entrant T. Wisdom

In this race I was driving Tommy Wisdom's Jaguar C-type and up against the similar cars of Duncan Hamilton and Ian Stewart. The opposition included the new Aston Martin DB3s of Reg Parnell and George Abecassis. I made the best of the Le Mans-style start and got away first, leading the race quite comfortably to the finish. Duncan Hamilton finished in second place.

178   3rd in class

Boreham, *Daily Mail* International Trophy

ERA G-type

2 August 1952, Boreham, Essex (GB)

Race distance 67 laps of 3-mile circuit **Race speed** 80.61mph
Car no 1 **Entrant** Works

There was much interest in the main race of the day, generated by the presence of the BRM V16s driven by José Froilán González and Ken Wharton. The race started in torrential rain, which helped me to get up as high as sixth place in the opening stages, but the ERA was no match for the Cooper-Bristols of Mike Hawthorn and Alan Brown, who both eventually passed me to take first and second places in the Formula 2 section of the race.

179   2nd

Brands Hatch, August Sprint Races, Heat 4

Kieft-Norton 500

4 August 1952, Brands Hatch, Kent (GB)

Organising club Half-Litre Club **Race distance**
10 laps of 1-mile circuit **Car no** 7 **Entrant** D. Annable

This was a minor race outing, organised by the Half-Litre Club, in which my main aim was to score points for the prestigious BRDC Gold Star contest, for which I was locked in a close fight with Mike Hawthorn.

180   2nd

Brands Hatch, August Sprint Races, Final

Kieft-Norton 500

4 August 1952, Brands Hatch, Kent (GB)

Organising club Half-Litre Club **Race distance** 10 laps of 1-mile
circuit **Fastest lap** 71.43mph (record) **Car no** 7 **Entrant** D. Annable

This was another brief contest on a busy day at the little Kent circuit, where races were still being run in an anti-clockwise direction – the opposite of today.

181   1st

Brands Hatch, *Daily Telegraph* International Trophy, Heat 3

Kieft-Norton 500

4 August 1952, Brands Hatch, Kent (GB)

Organising club Half-Litre Club **Race distance** 30 laps of 1-mile
circuit **Race speed** 67.9mph **Car no** 7 **Entrant** D. Annable

Again driving the Kieft-Norton, I managed to win this heat of the *Daily Telegraph* International Trophy, held over 30 laps.

182   Retired

Brands Hatch, *Daily Telegraph* International Trophy, Final

Kieft-Norton 500

4 August 1952, Brands Hatch, Kent (GB)

Organising club Half-Litre Club **Race distance** 30 laps of 1-mile
circuit **Reason for retirement** Broken con-rod **Car no** 7
Entrant D. Annable

There was a disappointing end to the day at Brands Hatch because I failed to finish in the final of the *Daily Telegraph* International Trophy, my fourth race of the day, Don Parker winning the laurels.

183

Montlhéry, seven-day record attempt

Jaguar XK120

5–12 August 1952, Montlhéry, Paris (F)

Distance completed 16,851.73 miles **Average speed** 100.31mph
Co-drivers Leslie Johnson, Jack Fairman and Bert Hadley

After we had successfully averaged over 107mph for 24 hours with a Jaguar XK120 in 1950, Leslie Johnson persuaded Jaguar to support another record attempt, this time with an XK120 fixed-head coupé.

We really raised our sights for this attempt, with the aim of averaging more than 100mph for a week. As before, driving duties were divided into three-hour stints. The car was fitted with a two-way radio, which helped prevent us from becoming terminally bored, although, in fairness, we had a pretty strong incentive to maintain concentration because we were running within four feet of the lip of the banking at around 120mph.

British Jaguar betters two world records

MONTLHERY, Thursday.

A BRITISH 3½-litre Jaguar had tonight bettered, without being credited as having beaten, two world records by the time the second day's run in an expected seven-day record attempt ended on the track here.

The car, driven in three hourly spells by Leslie Johnson, Stirling Moss, Herbert Hadley and Jack Fairman, is trying to break Class C records (three to five litres) for

BELOW *Celebrating the successful conclusion of our seven-day record attempt with the Jaguar XK120 fixed-head coupé at Montlhéry.* (Stirling Moss Collection)

184   5th

Goodwood 9 Hours

Jaguar C-type

16 August 1952, Goodwood, West Sussex (GB)

Race distance 9 hours of 2.4-mile circuit, 267 laps
Co-driver Peter Walker **Car no** 1 **Entrant** Works

BELOW *Rear axle problems and a consequent long delay in the pits wiped out the early lead Peter Walker and myself had built up in the Goodwood 9 Hours, dropping our Jaguar C-type back to fifth at the finish.* (LAT)

This race offered a new format for spectators and fans, starting at 3pm and running through to its scheduled finish in darkness at midnight. There were three works C-types in the field and I was sharing one with Peter Walker. The race started in heavy rain, which offered a brief advantage to Reg Parnell's nimble Aston Martin DB3, but as the track dried out it was possible to assert the Jaguar's superior performance and I was up to second place behind Tony Rolt before it was time to hand over to Walker.

Race regulations required that drivers had to be changed after about 65 laps. Eric Thompson brought the Aston into the pits ready to hand over to Parnell but a drop of spilled fuel, possibly ignited by a red-hot brake component, caused the car to burst into flames. Marshals and team personnel quickly grabbed fire extinguishers and doused the blaze, although a couple of mechanics and John Wyer, the Aston Martin team manager, were quite badly burned.

With about two hours to go Walker and I were running first, ahead of Tony Rolt and Duncan Hamilton, when they broke a driveshaft and lost a wheel. Not long afterwards, Walker brought our car into the pits very slowly, reporting that something felt badly wrong with the rear suspension.

Our first reaction was that our race was over, but 'Lofty' England, our team manager, instructed the two mechanics allocated to the car that they should get on and replace the broken rear-axle locating arm. It was a job they successfully and impressively completed in just over half an hour. By then we were 16 laps behind the leading Aston Martin and I drove steadily on to an eventual fifth place.

185   1st

Dutch Grand Prix, 500cc Race

Cooper-Norton MkVI

17 August 1952, Zandvoort, Haarlem (NL)

Race time 35m 21.5s **Race speed** 75.16mph **Car no** 2
Entrant Works

As I was racing at Goodwood, Ken Gregory practised the Cooper at Zandvoort in my place. I flew over to Holland on race morning with my father and it was a bit of a rush to get to the circuit in time. I did not have a good grid position so I had to fight my way through the pack but eventually won quite easily by a couple of seconds from George Wicken.

186   Retired

Dutch Grand Prix

ERA G-type

17 August 1952, Zandvoort, Haarlem (NL)

F1 World Championship, round 7

Race distance 90 laps of 2.7-mile circuit
Reason for retirement Engine after 73 laps
Car no 36 **Entrant** Works

As in the Formula 3 race, the fact that I had been competing at Goodwood meant that I had to start the Grand Prix from the back of the grid. To conserve the engine, I was driving it to firmly prescribed rev limits, but I still passed 10 cars on the opening lap and settled down to run in eighth place. Unfortunately, with only 16 of the 90 laps left to go, the engine failed.

187   1st

Turnberry Sports Car Race, Heat 2

Jaguar C-type

23 August 1952, Turnberry, Scotland (GB)

Race distance 10 laps of 1.7-mile circuit **Race time** 11m 10.8s
Race speed 75.56mph **Car no** 106 **Entrant** T. Wisdom

I was invited to drive Tommy Wisdom's Jaguar C-type in this late-season meeting at the wind-blown Scottish coastal circuit. I beat Duncan Hamilton's similar car quite easily, with Bill Dobson's Jaguar XK120 coming home third.

188   1st

Turnberry Sports Car Race, Final

Jaguar C-type

23 August 1952, Turnberry, Scotland (GB)

Race distance 10 laps of 1.7-mile circuit **Race time** 11m 10.8s
Race speed 75.56mph **Car no** 106 **Entrant** T. Wisdom

This was another quite straightforward win for me – much like the heat.

189   1st

Turnberry 500cc Race

Cooper-Norton 500 MkVI

23 August 1952, Turnberry, Scotland (GB)

Race distance 10 laps of 1.7-mile circuit **Race time** 14m 12s
Race speed 71.03mph **Entrant** S.C. Moss

Completing a successful day, I switched to my new Cooper to win easily ahead of André Loens in his Kieft-Norton.

190   3rd

Grenzlandring Formula 3 Race

Cooper-Norton 500 MkVI

31 August, 1952, Grenzlandring (D)

Race distance 12 laps of 5.8-mile circuit **Race time** 41m 20.5s **Entrant** S.C. Moss

This was an extremely fast circuit in the Lower Rhine area of Germany. It was dauntingly fast – so much so that John Cooper had been using it to experiment with a car fitted with a streamlined body. It worked extremely well, with the result that John won the race easily.

I spent most of the race sitting in Eric Brandon's slipstream, backing right off the throttle and literally being sucked along by his car. When the time came for me to make my planned move on him, he blocked me quite expertly. "What, let you sit on my tail all the way and then beat me?" he said afterwards. "Not likely!"

191   Retired

Italian Grand Prix

Connaught A-type

7 September 1952, Monza (I)

F1 World Championship, round 8

Race distance 80 laps of 3.92-mile circuit
Reason for retirement Broken push-rod rocker after 61 laps **Car no** 32 **Entrant** Works

I really hoped that the ERA G-type would be ready for this race but, after I debated the matter with Leslie Johnson, we decided to

give the race a miss and I made a last-minute arrangement with Rodney Clarke to drive one of the works Connaught A-types.

Unfortunately the cars had to be driven on the road from Milan to Monza in a last-moment scramble to get them there in time. Dennis Poore, Ken McAlpine and I drove the trio of A-types – after dark – in line astern behind an Italian motorcycle policeman. It was the most fantastic dice.

I was particularly anxious to lap quicker than Mike Hawthorn's Cooper-Bristol and, thanks to a tow in the slipstream of Alberto Ascari's Ferrari on one of the long straights, I recorded a practice time 1.4 seconds faster than Mike's best. However, the race was disappointing because I failed to finish due to a broken push-rod rocker.

192　Retired

Goodwood, Madgwick Cup

ERA G-type

27 September 1952, Goodwood (GB)

Race distance 7 laps of 2.4-mile circuit
Reason for retirement Collision on first lap
Car no 17 **Entrant** Works

This Formula 2 race was over almost as quickly as it started. Accelerating away from the grid, I was hit by Dennis Poore's Connaught, which in turn seemed to be trying to avoid another incident. The front of the ERA was damaged and I retired.

193　1st

Goodwood, 500cc Race

Cooper-Norton 500 MkVI

27 September 1952, Goodwood (GB)

Race distance 5 laps of 2.4-mile circuit
Race time 9m 5.2s **Race speed** 79.24mph
Car no 47 **Entrant** S.C. Moss

This was an enjoyable race and I managed to keep Les Leston at bay in his Leston Special on the last lap to win by a couple of lengths.

194   2nd

Goodwood, Sports Car Race

Jaguar C-type

27 September 1952, Goodwood (GB)

Race distance 5 laps of 2.4-mile circuit **Race time** 8m 37.2s
Fastest lap 1m 41.2s, 85.37mph (record) **Car no** 70
Entrant T. Wisdom

This was a race around which there was an unfortunate misunderstanding. The Jaguar team had originally offered Mike Hawthorn a C-type for this race, but he was hospitalised after a crash at Modena while demonstrating his Cooper-Bristol to Roy Salvadori. Instead, this C-type was taken over by Tony Rolt, who just pipped me to the win.

I was a little upset about this at the time because, technically, under the terms of my contract as the number one Jaguar driver, I should always have been given the best car when the official team was entered in an event. The car driven by Rolt was actually a works car fitted with the latest type of cylinder head, which was not available on Tommy Wisdom's car, which I was driving. Jaguar later apologised, explaining that the team had not been aware that I would be driving at Goodwood.

195   5th

Goodwood Trophy

ERA G-type

27 September 1952, Goodwood (GB)

Race distance 5 laps of 2.4-mile circuit **Entrant** Works

This *Formule Libre* race proved to be a demonstration run by the two BRM V16s driven by José Froilán González and Reg Parnell. The ERA was not very fast and, bearing in mind that it had been repaired following the collision in the first race of the day, I did not take any chances as the steering arm was possibly weakened.

196   1st

Castle Combe 500cc, Heat 1

Cooper-Norton 500 MkV1

4 October 1952, Castle Combe, Chippenham, Wiltshire (GB)

Race distance 7 laps of 1.84-mile circuit **Race time** 9m 53.2s
Race speed 78.18mph **Car no** 7 **Entrant** S.C. Moss

A good start to a busy day produced a cracking win over André Loens in his Kieft by just over 3 seconds.

197   1st

Castle Combe 500cc, Final

Cooper-Norton MkVI

4 October 1952, Castle Combe, Chippenham, Wiltshire (GB)

Race distance 10 laps of 1.84-mile circuit **Race time** 13m 51.2s
Race speed 79.7mph **Fastest lap** 1m 22.2s, 80.58mph (record)
Car no 7 **Entrant** S.C. Moss

I won the Formula 3 final easily without much pressure from the opposition.

198   Retired

Castle Combe, Joe Fry Memorial Trophy

ERA G-type

4 October 1952, Castle Combe, Chippenham, Wiltshire (GB)

Race distance 20 laps of 1.84-mile circuit **Reason for retirement** Broken steering arm **Car no** 61 **Entrant** Works

I went straight into the lead at the start of this Formula 2 race but events were to prove that I had been right to take things cautiously a week earlier in the final race at Goodwood, following the collision earlier that day. The ERA's steering arm, clearly weakened as I had suspected, collapsed while I was leading and Roy Salvadori went through to win in a 2-litre Ferrari.

BELOW *On my way to winning the 500cc final at Castle Combe in the Cooper-Norton MkVI.* (Stirling Moss Collection)

Charterhall, Sports Car Race

Jaguar C-type

11 October 1952, Charterhall, Scotland (GB)

Race distance 20 laps of 2-mile circuit **Race time** 31m 12.8s
Car no 27 **Entrant** T. Wisdom

Charterhall, 500cc Race

Cooper-Norton 500 MkVI

11 October 1952, Charterhall, Scotland (GB)

Race distance 25 laps of 2-mile circuit **Race time** 40m 44s
Fastest lap 1m 33.8s, 76.9mph **Car no** 26 **Entrant** Works

Newcastle *Journal* Trophy

ERA G-type

11 October 1952, Charterhall, Scotland (GB)

Race distance 40 laps of 2-mile circuit
Car no 25 **Entrant** Works

Unfortunately, I found that Tommy Wisdom's by now rather tired C-type was again a little bit too slow and there was simply nothing I could do about young Ian Stewart in a similar car entered by Ecurie Ecosse. He never put a wheel wrong throughout the race, and I was right on his tail the whole way.

BELOW *Tommy Wisdom's Jaguar C-type was getting a little tired by the end of the season and at Charterhall I had to give best to Ian Stewart, who won the race for Ecurie Ecosse.* (LAT)

I had an unexpectedly close call in this event because, after I had been chasing John Coombs for most of the way in second place, his Cooper shed a wheel and just missed hitting me. I had to swerve pretty violently and that allowed Eric Brandon in Jock McBain's Cooper through into a lead that he held to the finish.

Coombs's wayward wheel went careering off among the marshals, narrowly missed hitting Jamie 'Sir James' Scott-Douglas's gleaming Aston Martin DB2 in the paddock, bounced off an MG, and came to rest harmlessly in a field. Coombs was totally unhurt and very calm about the whole incident.

I might not have had much luck in my sole Connaught outing of the year at Monza, but in this Formula 2 race my ERA simply could not keep up with the trio of A-types, which filled the top three positions, driven by Dennis Poore, Ken McAlpine and Mike Oliver. I had to settle for fourth in my last circuit race of the year.

202   13th

Daily Express Rally

Jaguar XK120

12–15 November 1952, GB

Event score 5.17 marks **Co-driver** John Cooper **Car no** 216
Entrant Works

I always made time for rallying when I could because I enjoyed both the social and competitive aspects of the major British events, so I had no hesitation in taking my Jaguar XK120 fixed-head coupé on the MCC *Daily Express* Rally late in the year, recruiting John Cooper of *The Autocar* as my navigator. We had an enjoyable time and finished 13th overall in a challenging mix of speed trials, road sections and driving tests.

RIGHT *Driving my own Jaguar XK120 fixed-head coupé in misty conditions to an eventual 13th place on the* Daily Express Rally. (Guy Griffiths Collection)

LEFT *I took this Humber Super Snipe on a publicity tour through 15 European countries and drove most of the way in very wintry conditions, accompanied by navigator John Cutts and mechanic David Humphrey. We started in Norway on 2 December and finished in Portugal just under four days later, having travelled through Sweden, Denmark, Germany, Holland, Belgium, Luxembourg, France, Switzerland, Liechtenstein, Austria, Yugoslavia, Italy and Spain – a total distance of 3,827 miles.* (LAT)

1953

STILL SEARCHING

After the profoundly disappointing 1952 season with the G-type ERA, I was hoping for a much better year if I was going to realise my ambition of racing full-time in Formula 1.

With that aim in mind, I made what was to turn out to be another career wrong-turn. I became involved with Ray Martin's Cooper-Alta which, my critics may say, was reflective of what some people thought was my slightly obsessive desire to race a British car at all costs.

It is also worth remembering that 1953 was the year that Mike Hawthorn signed to drive for Ferrari and, although this did not bother me as such, I was conscious that the press were fanning the flames of our supposed rivalry, and Mike's victory in a Ferrari over Juan Manuel Fangio's Maserati in the French Grand Prix at Reims had certainly raised his profile.

Given the excellent job that Ray Martin had done in designing the 500cc Formula 3 Kieft, it seemed a perfectly reasonable idea that he should design a Formula 2 chassis and John Cooper (of *The Autocar*), who was in on the ground floor of the Kieft programme, and I gave him our thoughts on its design.

While this new project was germinating, John Cooper approached Alf Francis – with my blessing – and suggested that he went to work for Ray Martin, This would mean Alf leaving Peter Whitehead, for whom he had worked after leaving HWM, and Alf agreed. This was the start of a professional partnership that would thrive until the early 1960s.

The Cooper-Alta was not a success. Long before the end of the year it became clear that the car was going nowhere and that it was time for me to try to get a seat with a factory Formula 1 team – otherwise my career was going to stall. By June, I had become so frustrated with the Cooper-Alta that I accepted another drive with Connaught in the Dutch Grand Prix, but that outing unfortunately ended in disappointment as well. We also rebuilt the Cooper-Alta around a Mk2 chassis frame, acquired from the 'other' Cooper company, run by Charles and John Cooper, and that was much more promising.

I enjoyed another reasonably successful year driving a C-type as a member of the Jaguar factory sports car team, finishing second at Le Mans, sharing with Peter Walker, and winning the Reims 12-hour race with Peter Whitehead. I managed to get a second *Coupe des Alpes* on the Alpine Rally in a Sunbeam-Talbot Alpine, and quite a few decent Formula 3 results also came my way.

Overall, however, 1953 was a holding season. Things were going to have to get a whole lot better if I was to realise my dreams.

LEFT *At Goodwood for the start of yet another new season, now at the wheel of the new Ray Martin-designed Cooper-Alta, unpainted in the rush to ready it for its debut. It was the beginning of another frustrating year for me.* (Guy Griffiths Collection)

203 — 6th

Monte Carlo Rally

Sunbeam-Talbot 90

20–27 January 1953, Monte Carlo (MON)

Car no 318 **Entrant** Works

In contrast to the previous year's Monte, on which we had finished second, the 1953 event was run in unusually mild conditions, which seemed unfamiliar in the extreme. The Rootes team won the team prize, but the absence of really slippery conditions shifted the emphasis from driving skill to sheer power, at least in some measure, so the best I could achieve, with navigators John Cooper and Desmond Scannell, was sixth place.

204

Jabbeke speed run

Sunbeam-Talbot Alpine

17 March 1953, Jabbeke (B)

Speed 120.459mph **Entrant** Works

Two high-speed runs, one on the Jabbeke-Aeltre stretch of dual carriageway in Belgium and the other at Montlhéry the following day, were essentially 'warm-ups' for the Alpine Rally, which fell between the French and British Grands Prix on the international calendar. Sheila van Damm and I drove the car at Jabbeke, and Sheila just managed to break the 120mph mark.

205

Montlhéry speed run

Sunbeam-Talbot Alpine

18 March 1953, Montlhéry, Paris (F)

Speed 116mph **Entrant** Works

In the second day of high-speed runs, at the banked Montlhéry circuit, I lapped at 116mph while Leslie Johnson achieved 112 miles in one hour. As at Jabbeke, we were driving the new Sunbeam-Talbot Alpine, a new two-seater convertible named in honour of Rootes' success in the 1952 Alpine Rally.

RIGHT *Through the winter sunshine towards the Côte d'Azur during the Monte Carlo Rally in which I finished sixth together with my crew of Desmond Scannell and John Cooper.* (LAT)

BELOW *Standing alongside the Sunbeam-Talbot Alpine during the Jabbeke speed run with Sheila van Damm behind the wheel.* (Stirling Moss Collection)

Goodwood, Lavant Cup

Cooper-Alta Special

6 April 1953, Goodwood, West Sussex (GB)

Race distance 7 laps of 2.4-mile circuit **Car no** 6
Entrant S.C. Moss

M y relationship with the Cooper-Alta Special began on a troubled note and never really got much better. When the idea was first mooted, I said that I would like to use a Maserati six-cylinder engine, but there was no way Maserati would sell us anything less than a complete car. That in itself was a propitious signal given the way events would unfold.

In the meantime, I accepted Alf Francis's suggestion that we use an Alta engine, but the original plan envisaged us using a standard Cooper Mk2 chassis frame. That came to nought because John '*Autocar*' Cooper wanted to use coil-spring and double-wishbone front suspension rather than the other Cooper's transverse leaf spring arrangement.

We therefore decided to build our own chassis frame, which, in the event, was insufficiently rigid. At Goodwood our team had endless problems, including trying to balance the front disc brake effect against the inboard rear drums' performance. Added to that, oil was leaking from the final drive all over the rear brakes and the car's handling was seriously unpredictable. You can see the problems we faced.

The car ran poorly to seventh place in the first event and then I decided we should withdraw it from the other two races in which it had been entered.

Goodwood, Earl of March Trophy

Cooper-Norton 500 MkVII

6 April 1953, Goodwood, West Sussex (GB)

Race distance 5 laps of 2.4-mile circuit **Race time** 8m 58s
Car no 7 **Entrant** S.C. Moss

A lan Brown led this race all the way, setting a new lap record in the process. I became involved in a close battle with Reg Bicknell and overtook him for second place. But he repassed me and I just failed to get back ahead of him by 0.4 seconds in a last-lap lunge from Woodcote up to the chicane. It was a good dice but a frustrating one!

LEFT *Meeting – for the first time – the great Juan Manuel Fangio at Goodwood during the Easter meeting that traditionally marked the start of the British racing season.* (Guy Griffiths Collection)

ABOVE *Pressing on hard during the Mille Miglia with the works Jaguar C-type. This proved to be another disappointing outing and the final occasion when Italy's famous road race was contested by the Coventry marque.* (LAT)

208 Retired

Mille Miglia

Jaguar C-type

26 April 1953, Brescia (I)

World Sports Car Championship, round 2

Race distance 1 lap of 992 miles
Reason for retirement Broken rear-axle tube
Co-driver Mort Morris-Goodall **Car no** 542 **Entrant** Works

After disappointing outings in the Mille Miglia the previous two years, Jaguar

made a big effort with the C-type and I covered an amazing 6,000 miles of reconnaissance work during the fortnight before the race itself. In retrospect, that seems remarkable but it equated to six laps of the route. My passenger on this occasion was Mort Morris-Goodall, who had taken over the Jaguar team management job – at least nominally – from 'Lofty' England.

Unfortunately all this detailed preparation went to waste because a rear-axle tube twisted in the differential housing and we retired before the first control at Ravenna. It was a big disappointment for us all and was to be the last Mille Miglia Jaguar ever attempted.

209   2nd

Silverstone, BRDC International Trophy, Heat 1

Cooper-Alta Special

9 May 1953, Silverstone (GB)

Organising club British Racing Drivers' Club
Race distance 15 laps of 2.93-mile circuit **Race time** 29m 4s
Fastest lap 1m 54s, 92.43mph (shared with de Graffenried)
Car no 7 **Entrant** S.C. Moss

210   9th

Silverstone, BRDC International Trophy, Final

Cooper-Alta Special

9 May 1953, Silverstone (GB)

Organising club British Racing Drivers' Club
Race distance 35 laps of 2.93-mile circuit **Car no** 7
Entrant S.C. Moss

I qualified poorly, but by the end of the opening lap I was up to second place and managed to keep within a second of 'Toulo' de Graffenried's Maserati A6GCM all the way to the finish.

LEFT & ABOVE *My Cooper-Alta looked good, but it wasn't!* (Guy Griffiths Collection)

Mike Hawthorn's Cooper-Bristol, the winner of the second heat, took pole for the final with Ken Wharton's similar car, de Graffenried's Maserati and me completing the front row of the grid. After de Graffenried was penalised one minute for a jumped start – and consequently withdrew from race – I got up to sixth before being forced to drop out with mechanical trouble just before the finish, leaving me classified ninth.

Silverstone, Saloon Car Race

Jaguar MkVII

9 May 1953, Silverstone (GB)

Organising club British Racing Drivers' Club **Race distance** 17 laps of 2.93-mile circuit **Race time** 40m 7s **Race speed** 74.42mph **Fastest lap** 76.36mph **Car no** 40 **Entrant** Works

Silverstone, Sports Car Race

Jaguar C-type

9 May 1953, Silverstone (GB)

Organising club British Racing Drivers' Club **Race distance** 17 laps of 2.93-mile circuit **Race time** 34m 51s **Race speed** 85.67mph **Car no** 35 **Entrant** Works

I led all the way, which was extremely satisfying after what occurred during practice at Silverstone. I had rolled a works C-type Jaguar, my entry for the last race of the meeting, and was feeling pretty battered and bruised.

I had a brand-new Jaguar C-type for this important domestic meeting but rather foolishly convinced myself in practice that it would be possible to take the very fast left-hand Abbey Curve flat out, without lifting off the throttle. Unfortunately, on one lap I made a mistake as I had to alter my line because a slower car was right in my path and kept my foot hard on the throttle rather than backing off. The car oversteered, I dropped a wheel over the track edge and on to the grass, it dug in, and I rolled at about 110mph. I was lucky to escape unhurt.

The car was repaired for the race, but was off the pace. I finished seventh.

BELOW *Sharing a selection of silverware with my contemporary and rival Mike Hawthorn after the Silverstone International Trophy meeting.* (Guy Griffiths Collection)

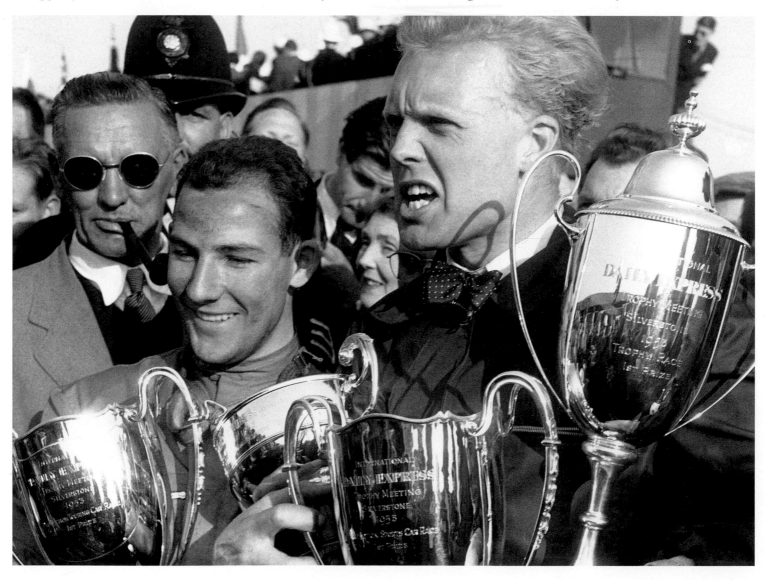

213   2nd

Ulster Trophy, Heat 1

Connaught A-type

16 May 1953, Dundrod, Belfast (GB)

Race distance 10 laps of 7.41-mile circuit **Race time** 52m 41s
Race speed 84.46mph **Fastest lap** 4m 46s, 90.91mph **Car no** 32
Entrant Works

This event was made up of two heats and a final and there was inevitably a lot more press coverage about the rivalry that existed between me and Mike Hawthorn, who was driving a factory Ferrari at this event.

We started in different heats and my day got off to a poor start when I lost 30 seconds with gearbox problems and resumed in sixth place. In the end I managed to get back to second place behind Duncan Hamilton's HWM, despite at one point bouncing into one of the trackside banks.

214   Did not start

Ulster Trophy, Final

Connaught A-type

16 May 1953, Dundrod, Belfast (GB)

Race distance 14 laps of 7.41-mile circuit **Reason did not start** Not allowed to change car **Car no** 32 **Entrant** Works

It was clear after my heat that my Connaught was still suffering quite serious gearbox problems, so they put me into Roy Salvadori's sister car for the final, only for the stewards to decree that it was not permissible to change cars and therefore I would not be allowed to start. I was quite irritated by that, even though I am pretty sure that the Connaught would have had little chance up against Mike's Ferrari, which easily won the final.

ABOVE In the bustling paddock at Crystal Palace during a busy weekend that saw me win the 500cc final. (Guy Griffiths Collection)

215   4th

Crystal Palace, Coronation Trophy, Heat 1

Cooper-Alta Special

25 May 1953, Crystal Palace, London (GB)

Race distance 10 laps of 1.39-mile circuit **Race time** 12m 15s
Car no 7 **Entrant** S.C. Moss

This was an extremely significant fixture on the British motor racing calendar because it was the first occasion since August 1939 that a race meeting had taken place at the tight little Crystal Palace circuit in south London. Tony Rolt's Connaught had the legs of the field and I had to settle for fourth place in the Cooper-Alta.

216   1st

Crystal Palace, 500cc Race

Cooper-Norton 500 MkVII

25 May 1953, Crystal Palace, London (GB)

Race distance 10 laps of 1.39-mile circuit **Race time** 12m 12.6s
Race speed 68.26mph **Fastest lap** 1m 10.8s, 70.68mph
Car no 27 **Entrant** S.C. Moss

I started from the second row and ran second behind Les Leston from the start before taking the lead on the third lap. By the fifth lap I was 3 seconds ahead and thereafter drove to a relatively comfortable win.

217   5th

Crystal Palace, Coronation Trophy, Final

Cooper-Alta Special

25 May 1953, Crystal Palace, London (GB)

Race distance 10 laps of 1.39-mile circuit **Race time** 12m 0.4s **Car no** 7 **Entrant** S.C. Moss

Having won the heat earlier in the day, Tony Rolt also ran away with the final. I had to be satisfied with fifth place behind Ken Wharton, Peter Whitehead and Lance Macklin.

218   1st

Eifelrennen 500cc Race

Cooper-Norton 500 MkVII

31 May 1953, Nürburgring (D)

Race speed 66.55mph **Entrant** S.C. Moss

In practice I set a new class record of 11m 23.1s. Race day turned out to be wet but I kept the same gearing because I had concluded that the Cooper-Norton was slightly under-geared in practice. I won the race quite convincingly and posted a new lap record in the process. It was very satisfying.

RIGHT *Continuing my quest to find a British car that would carry me to sustained success, my second outing in a Connaught came at the Dutch Grand Prix at Zandvoort.* (LAT)

219   6th

Eifelrennen

Cooper-Alta

31 May 1953, Nürburgring (D)

Race distance 7 laps of 13.69-mile circuit **Race time** 1h 29m 3.9s **Car no** 8 **Entrant** Works

Quite a mixed bag made up the entry for this prestigious Formula 2 race at the Nürburgring and my Cooper-Alta was ranged against a trio of HWMs, a variety of private Maseratis and some locally built Veritas specials. As at Silverstone, de Graffenried won for Maserati and I had a quiet race to sixth place.

220   9th

Dutch Grand Prix

Connaught A-type

7 June 1953, Zandvoort, Haarlem (NL)

F1 World Championship, round 3

Race distance 90 laps of 2.61-mile circuit **Race time** 83 laps **Car no** 34 **Entrant** Works

In first practice, I had a Goodwood ratio and was over-geared. I also tried the car with a full 55-gallon fuel load aboard and it seemed to handle better, but I found the track was very slippery due to the new surface that had been laid.

On race day, strangely, the car seemed to handle badly with a full load of fuel but it gradually improved as the fuel was consumed. But we were definitely much slower than the Maseratis or Ferraris. I was running in seventh place – the best-placed British car at that stage – when a stone broke a blanking pipe on a fuel pump and I lost over five minutes in the pits having it replaced. That dropped me down to ninth, a lap behind one of the HWMs. Alberto Ascari and Giuseppe Farina made it a Ferrari one-two.

221   2nd

Le Mans
24 Hours

Jaguar C-type

13/14 June 1953, Sarthe (F)

World Sports Car Championship, round 3

Race distance 24 hours of 8.38-mile circuit (2,540.2 miles, 304 laps) **Race speed** 104.63mph **Co-driver** Peter Walker **Car no** 17 **Entrant** Works

The Dunlop disc brakes on our Jaguar C-types meant that we were in another league from most of the opposition when it came to slowing for the tricky corners that abound at the Sarthe circuit. The team had developed three new special lightweight C-types for this important event, fitted with Weber carburettors rather than SUs and with transmission-driven servo assistance for the disc brakes.

Despite the fact that Mercedes-Benz was not competing on this occasion, the entry list was one of the strongest that I can ever recall for Le Mans. I shared my car with Peter Walker and I led in the early stages until, after only about 20 laps, the engine began running roughly, not pulling properly. I came into the pits, where they changed the plugs, but that did not seem to make much difference. The problem was only solved after I came in a second time and they changed what turned out to be a blocked fuel filter.

From then on the C-type never missed a beat. But we had lost too much time to get back on terms with Tony Rolt and Duncan Hamilton, who won the race at a record speed. Walker and I finished second, four laps – some 29 miles – behind them. It was a shame, because I am sure we would have won had we enjoyed a trouble-free run.

ABOVE *My prospects of winning Le Mans were again frustrated when the C-type I was sharing with Peter Walker was delayed with a blocked fuel filter while we were leading.* (LAT)

222   2nd

British Empire Trophy, Heat 3

Jaguar C-type

18 June 1953, Douglas (IoM)

Race distance 8 laps of 3.88-mile circuit Race time 25m 33s Car no 52 Entrant Works

This was a return to the scene of my previous outings in the Frazer Nash Le Mans Replica and I managed to finish second in the third heat, although by now the nimble new Aston Martins definitely had an edge on the C-type's performance, even allowing for our lightening programme.

I was using the car I had previously driven in the Mille Miglia but it seemed all over the place during the first day's practice. I could not initially manage a better lap than 3m 21s, which was 4 seconds away from what Reg Parnell recorded in the Aston. On the second day I got going and did a 3m 10s lap, which would have been a 3m 8s had I not been baulked by a slower car. But then Reg came back with a 3m 5s lap.

Predictably, in my heat there was no way I could catch Reg and I finished second, ahead of Hans Rüsch's 4.1-litre Ferrari. Ian Stewart clung on to me for seven of the race's eight laps but then his clutch failed.

223   4th

British Empire Trophy, Final

Jaguar C-type

18 June 1953, Douglas (IoM)

Race distance 16 laps of 3.88-mile circuit Race time 54m 41s
Race speed 72.05mph Car no 52 Entrant Works

In the handicap final I gave the 1.5-litre competitors three minutes' advantage and the 2-litre runners one minute over the 16 laps. At the start, I shot off into the lead, only to be passed fair and square by Reg Parnell in the Aston Martin. He took a good 150 yards off me up the back hill alone.

He carried on to win, with Ken Wharton second in a Frazer Nash ahead of Hans Rüsch, who by now had got used to his Ferrari and had passed me late in the race. Ninian Sanderson and Jimmy Stewart – whose younger brother Jackie would make his mark in Formula 1 more than 10 years later – both drove well, finishing just after me.

224   Unclassified

Rouen Grand Prix

Cooper-Alta Special

28 June 1953, Les Essarts (F)

Race distance 60 laps of 3.16-mile circuit Car no 16
Entrant S.C. Moss

In practice the handling was so bad that I could hardly hold the car in a straight line. Alf Francis worked on it and took off some castor, which improved things. We then noticed the position of the front of the Ferrari radius arms and copied it. This added a touch of positive camber, which made things better but not yet totally right.

My best time was 2m 20s, which would have put me on the front row, but, amazingly, the official timers missed it so I had to make do with a starting position on the fifth row. In practice I also had a go in John Lyons' Connaught, which was very nice but had too much understeer in my view.

In the race I started well from my lowly grid position. I was sixth at the hairpin on the opening lap and got ahead of the eventual winner, Harry Schell in the Gordini. But then I gradually dropped back with an apparent fuel-feed problem and later came in to refuel because a fuel pipe had come adrift. I had also lost first gear, which did not help. I was not classified at the finish, though I was in 10th place.

225   1st

Reims 12 Hours

Jaguar C-type

4/5 July 1953, Reims (F)

Race distance 12 hours of 5.19-mile circuit (1,282.10 miles, 243 laps) **Race speed** 105.44mph **Co-driver** Peter Whitehead **Car no** 4 **Entrant** Works

Jaguar had fitted 3.3:1 axle ratios to the C-types for this event, which meant we were pulling between 5,700 and 5,800rpm on the straights. That was all right but I felt we could have done with slightly more speed.

This race was held to a new format, starting at midnight on the Saturday and running through to midday on the Sunday, just before the start of the Grand Prix.

Peter Whitehead started the race in our car and was first away into the darkness, but was running fourth by the time I took over at 3am. Of the cars ahead of me, John Fitch flipped his Cunningham, but was unhurt, and the best-placed Ferrari was disqualified, so I was soon up into the lead. Peter took over again from 6am to 9am and then I resumed at the wheel for the run to the finish. In the closing stages I was getting very hot and the cockpit was filled with fumes due to a broken exhaust. In the end we won by four laps.

ABOVE *Standing to attention for the national anthem at Reims after winning with the Jaguar C-type – the first international victory for a disc-braked car.* (LAT)

French Grand Prix

Cooper-Alta Special

5 July 1953, Reims (F)

F1 World Championship, round 5

Race distance 60 laps of 5.19-mile circuit
Reason for retirement Clutch **Car no** 36 **Entrant** S.C. Moss

I n the first practice, the Cooper-Alta was so bad that I could do only one lap really quickly. The car was all over the road and the brakes were very poor indeed. Despite some adjustments, it was still awful in the second practice and, after George Abecassis and Peter Whitehead tried it, we decided to alter the steering arms. In the end I did a 2m 55s lap, which made the Cooper the fastest British car on the grid apart from Prince

Bira's Connaught, which everyone reckoned was mistimed.

In the race, which started soon after the 12-hour sports car race, which I had won, the car was much improved by those new steering arms. I had clutch-slip from the start but was still faster than the Cooper-Bristols driven by Ken Wharton and Bob Gerard. I made a pit stop for fuel after 27 laps and then the clutch burst down the straight, at 6,000rpm, and cut my leg to the bone.

That was the end of the original Cooper-Alta – and very nearly the last straw for me. I would miss the British Grand Prix because we decided to abandon the Ray Martin-developed chassis.

BELOW *Heading for a second successive* Coupe des Alpes *with the Sunbeam-Talbot Alpine on an unseasonably mild Alpine Rally.* (LAT)

Alpine Rally

Sunbeam-Talbot Alpine

10–16 July 1953, Marseilles to Cannes (F)

Event distance 2,078 miles **Co-driver** John Cutts
Car no 507 **Entrant** Works

T his event was slightly less demanding than I had expected, again partly because of the mild weather. By the time we completed the six mountain stages in the Sunbeam-Talbot Alpine and arrived in Cannes, we were among no fewer than 25 competitors to remain unpenalised, so John and I received our second straight *Coupe des Alpes*, awarded for a penalty-free run. We vowed that we would return in 1954 to try to achieve a hat trick.

228   1st

British Grand Prix, 500cc Race

Cooper-Norton 500 MkVII

18 July 1953, Silverstone (GB)

Race distance 15 laps of 2.93-mile circuit **Race time** 31m 5s **Race speed** 84.74mph **Fastest lap** 2m 2s, 83.37mph (equal with Stuart Lewis-Evans) **Car no** 7 **Entrant** S.C. Moss

I missed the first day's practice at Silverstone because I was returning from the Alpine Rally but, after the decision to get rid of the troublesome original Cooper-Alta, I was taking part only in the 500cc race, not the Grand Prix.

Conditions were very windy in practice, but the little Cooper-Norton was still pulling 6,000rpm down the Hangar Straight and up the hill to Woodcote. I managed a 2m 3s lap to take pole position ahead of Don Parker, with most of the others much slower. I made a bad start due to difficult ratios but took the lead from Eric Brandon when he lifted momentarily from the throttle coming through Woodcote for the first time. After three laps my clutch went, so I finished – still in the lead – with the car stuck in fourth gear. As I also managed to equal the lap record, I was quite pleased.

229   2nd

Lisbon, Jubilee Grand Prix

Jaguar C-type

26 July 1953, Monsanto, Lisbon (P)

Entrant Works

First practice served to emphasise how very bumpy the circuit was. The weather was hot and the brakes seemed particularly ineffective under these conditions. I spent a lot of time juggling with tyre sizes and pressures in an effort to get a better ride over the bumps and things improved after my mechanics softened the damper settings.

On the first lap of the race I was third, then Piero Taruffi's Ferrari blew up and I moved up to second place behind Felice Bonetto's Lancia. I stayed in that position to the end of the race, one lap behind the winner.

230   6th

German Grand Prix

Cooper-Alta MkII

2 August 1953, Nürburgring (D)

F1 World Championship, round 7

Race distance 18 laps of 14.173-mile circuit **Race time** 17 laps in 3h 6m 50.9s **Car no** 19 **Entrant** S.C. Moss

In the run-up to the German Grand Prix we fitted the Alta engine – now considerably improved thanks to attentive detail tuning from Alf Francis – into a straightforward Cooper MkII chassis frame, which we bought from John and Charles Cooper's company. It took 11 days of round-the-clock effort to build up the new car and it was a day late arriving at the Nürburgring, so I could only squeeze in a single practice session.

Even though I had some problems with low oil pressure and with the gearbox, I managed a lap of 10m 48.3s from a standing start, easily pulling 6,200rpm on the straight. The other Coopers were slower than the 11-minute mark, although Roy Salvadori achieved 10m 57.5s in the Connaught to line up alongside me on the fourth row of the grid.

LEFT *Not pin sharp, but an impressive head-on shot of my Cooper-Norton in a powerslide on the way to winning the British Grand Prix 500cc supporting race.* (Stirling Moss Collection)

Six minutes before the start of the race, I had a nasty surprise when I found that I could not select any gears. As the flag came down I managed to get away in second gear and, after a few difficult moments, everything seemed to be all right. I had a pit stop after seven laps for about 20 gallons of fuel and then came in again before the last lap because the car seemed to be holding back. I finished sixth, the first green car home, and I was very pleased about that. The engine was excellent and the brakes and road-holding were good, even though the car was still bottoming out slightly – but that was pretty usual at the Nürburgring.

231   4th

Grand Prix des Sables d'Olonne, Heat 1

Cooper-Alta MkII

9 August 1953, Sables d'Olonne, Nantes (F)

Race distance 45 laps of 1.86-mile circuit **Race time** 1h 7m 1.6s **Car no** 18 **Entrant** S.C. Moss

This weekend started on a bad note due to a gearbox fault that did not make itself apparent until our arrival at the circuit. Later, we found a quarter-inch nut bouncing around inside the 'box. We fitted bump stops to the suspension, which felt as though they were an improvement, but second gear began slipping towards the end of practice.

The first heat turned out to be a busy race. I started on the second row, made a bad start, but then was quickly up into second place. Due to that recurrent problem with second gear, I started to drop back slightly. Gradually it seemed to improve again but finally I dropped back to fourth at the finish, due to problems selecting both first and second gears, a minute behind Jean Behra's Gordini, 34 seconds behind Louis Chiron's Ferrari and 28 seconds behind Louis Rosier's OSCA. The car had also developed a fuel leak when the tank worked loose and its rev counter failed.

232   5th

Grand Prix des Sables d'Olonne, Heat 2

Cooper-Alta MkII

9 August 1953, Sables d'Olonne, Nantes (F)

Race distance 45 laps of 1.86-mile circuit **Race time** N/A **Car no** 18 **Entrant** S.C. Moss **Aggregate result** 3rd, 87 laps completed

I was on the second row of the grid again for the second heat, but made a slow start. After six laps I had no first gear again and after 10 laps there was also no second gear. I continued to finish in fifth place in the heat but third place on aggregate, with Rosier and Chiron respectively first and second on aggregate.

But for all the aforementioned problems suffered by the Cooper-Alta MkII in the two heats, together with the fact that the front wheels were locking and the engine was down on power, I felt could have won this race!

233   Retired

Charterhall, *Newcastle Journal* Trophy

Cooper-Alta MkII

15 August 1953, Charterhall, Scotland (GB)

Race distance 50 laps of 2-mile circuit **Reason for retirement** Fuel surge problems **Car no** 97 **Entrant** S.C. Moss

For this Formula 2 event we fitted fuel injection to the Alta engine, which gave terrific power, although initially we were troubled at being able to do only a single lap at a time due to oil overflowing from the cam cover. We also had a cracked magneto.

It was wet on race day. I made a good start to lead off the line but waved Ken Wharton past into the first hairpin due to my lack of practice. I came out of the corner about 70 yards behind his Cooper-Bristol but almost caught him up again 500 yards later – but then I encountered fuel surge problems and called it a day.

234   1st

Charterhall, 500cc Race

Cooper-Norton 500 MkVII

15 August 1953, Charterhall, Scotland (GB)

Race distance 20 laps of 2-mile circuit **Race time** 31m 23s **Race speed** 76.47mph **Car no** 98 **Entrant** S.C. Moss

The 500cc race produced a big dice from the start between Les Leston, Don Parker, Bob Gerard and me. My car was pulling 6,900rpm down the straight and I used this to good effect, pulling away from Parker to win by the best part of half a mile. The exhaust pipe worked loose, but it did not matter.

235   Retired

Charterhall, *Formule Libre* Race

Cooper-Alta MkII

15 August 1953, Charterhall, Scotland (GB)

Race distance 50 laps of 2-mile circuit **Reason for retirement** Carburettors **Entrant** S.C. Moss

I rounded off the day at Charterhall by switching the Cooper-Alta MkII back to carburettors for the *Formule Libre* race. I enjoyed quite a good tussle with Tony Rolt, who was driving Rob Walker's Connaught, until the carburettors went off tune and I pulled into the pits.

236 Retired

Goodwood 9 Hours

Jaguar C-type

22 August 1953, Goodwood, West Sussex (GB)

Race distance 9 hours on 2.4-mile circuit **Reason for retirement** Rear axle **Co-driver** Peter Walker **Car no** 1 **Entrant** Works

In practice, the track conditions were intermittently wet and we all lapped at around the 1m 46/47s mark as a result. At the start, I took the lead and held it for many laps, but then let Tony Rolt through, as arranged under team orders. All went well until about 11.10pm, with less than an hour go, when both our C-types suffered oil problems while running at the front and had to retire. Peter Whitehead, also in a C-type, continued to finish third behind two Aston Martins.

237 1st in class

RAC Tourist Trophy

Jaguar C-type

5 September 1953, Dundrod, Belfast, Northern Ireland (GB)

World Sports Car Championship, round 6

Organising club Royal Automobile Club **Race distance** 106 laps of 7.42-mile circuit **Race time** 9h 37m 39s **Race speed** 79.34mph **Fastest lap** 5m 7s, 86.96mph **Co-driver** Peter Walker **Car no** 7 **Entrant** Works

The Jaguar felt all right in practice, albeit down on revs. I set the fastest time in the first two practice sessions but the front hub bearings were wearing badly, causing a juddering through the steering wheel, and the car's back-end was twitchy. Although I was changing gear at 5,400rpm, I was seeing 5,900rpm on the clock by the end of the straight, where I was timed at 137.8mph.

The race itself was pretty straightforward, although at one point the C-type's bonnet broke loose and that lost me some time. However, in the end I was first in the 3-litre class and fourth overall. The car suffered a broken axle three laps from the finish, so I stopped just before the finishing line and waited by the side of the track until I could limp past the chequered flag in order to qualify as a finisher.

OPPOSITE *Heading for a finish at Monza in the Cooper-Alta, converted for the occasion to run on nitro-methane, which gave it a fantastic turn of speed on the straights.* (Rodolfo Mailander, Ludvigsen Library)

BELOW *The C-type's tattered radiator grille bears witness to the fact that the bonnet flew up during the Goodwood 9 Hours, although I eventually retired with rear axle problems.* (LAT)

238 13th

Italian Grand Prix

Cooper-Alta MkII

13 September 1953, Monza (I)

F1 World Championship, round 9

Race distance 80 laps of 3.92-mile circuit **Race time**
2h 51m 44.4s (70 laps) **Car no** 28 **Entrant** S.C. Moss

For this event, Alf Francis converted the Alta engine to run on nitro-methane, which dramatically increased its fuel consumption and made the performance fantastic – faster than the Ferraris, until the corners!

I lapped in 2m 6s, which was good enough for a place on the fourth row of the grid, about 3 or 4 seconds behind the Ferraris; the Gordinis were all slower than 2m 7s. On the evidence of the first practice session, it was clear that it would be necessary to change tyres during the race as well as to refuel. In the second practice session I did just a few laps to check how the car felt with the anti-roll bar removed, but as there was no difference we decided to refit it.

I made a good start to the race, running fifth on the first lap, and for the first 25 laps or so I chased Felice Bonetto's Maserati hard. The Cooper's speed across the start/finish line was about 135mph and where the concrete start-line apron changed to asphalt the car had developed the worrying habit of throwing its tyre treads after the transition from the cool concrete to the hotter asphalt. Each time I stopped for fresh rubber, the mechanics understandably took ages to undo the four wheel-securing nuts – we did not have quick-change 'knock-off' hubs fitted to the car – and so I steadily dropped back through the field.

Add to that the fact that the fuel tank had developed a leak, forcing me to stop four times instead of my scheduled three, and it was understandable that I was 10 laps behind Fangio's winning Maserati by the end of the race. At least the car had completed a race.

239 1st

Crystal Palace, London Trophy, Heat 1

Cooper-Alta MkII

19 September 1953, Crystal Palace (GB)

Race distance 10 laps of 1.39-mile circuit **Race time** 11m 48s
Race speed 70.68mph **Car no** 7 **Entrant** S.C. Moss

I struggled with quite a lot of understeer in practice for this event and eventually decided to race with the anti-roll bar removed. The car went all right and I won the first heat by 0.4 seconds from Tony Rolt in Rob Walker's Connaught. It is also worth mentioning that Bernie Ecclestone was driving a Cooper-Bristol in this race and, although he finished sixth, I lapped the future Formula 1 commercial rights holder before the finish.

240   1st

Crystal Palace, London Trophy, Heat 2

Cooper-Alta MkII

19 September 1953, Crystal Palace (GB)

Race distance 10 laps of 1.39-mile circuit **Race time** 11m 36.4s
Race speed 71.86mph **Car no** 7 **Entrant** S.C. Moss

I managed to win the second heat as well, this time by just over 2 seconds from Tony Rolt, even though the oil pressure was very low. It was good enough to give me a clear victory on aggregate.

241   2nd

Crystal Palace, Redex Trophy, Heat 2

Cooper-Norton 500 MkVII

19 September 1953, Crystal Palace (GB)

Race distance 7 laps of 1.39-mile circuit **Race time** 8m 32s
Entrant S.C. Moss

I made a very bad start in this race and the car generally felt off-form, but I managed second place behind Stuart Lewis-Evans.

RIGHT *Returning to my roots with an outing at Prescott in my 1,100cc Cooper-JAP.* (LAT)

242   Retired

Crystal Palace, Redex Trophy, Final

Cooper-Norton 500 MkVII

19 September 1953, Crystal Palace (GB)

Race distance 10 laps of 1.39-mile circuit
Reason for retirement Carburettor **Entrant** S.C. Moss

This race brought another disappointment because I made my second poor start of the day, but I worked my way up to third place, just behind Don Parker. Then the carburettor fell off and that was that.

243   1st in class

Prescott Hill Climb

Cooper-Alta MkII

20 September 1953, Prescott (GB)

Organising club Bugatti Owners' Club **Course length** 1,127yds **Best time** 46.48s **Car no** 93 **Entrant** S.C. Moss

Although I took part in many hill climbs during the early days of my career, this was my first visit to one for a long time. I won the Formula 2 class quite comfortably in my Cooper-Alta MkII.

244   2nd

Prescott Hill Climb

Cooper-JAP 1,100 MkVII

20 September 1953, Prescott (GB)

Organising club Bugatti Owners' Club **Course length** 1,127yds **Best time** 46.35s **Car no** 9 **Entrant** S.C. Moss

I used my Cooper-JAP to take part in the *Formule Libre* class and finished second.

245 — 2nd

Goodwood, Madgwick Cup

Cooper-Alta MkII

26 September 1953, Goodwood (GB)

Race distance 7 laps of 2.4-mile circuit **Race time** 11m 18.4s
Car no 7 **Entrant** S.C. Moss

In this relatively straightforward race I was beaten by Roy Salvadori's works Connaught A-type, which simply seemed to handle more predictably than my Cooper-Alta.

246 — 4th

Goodwood, Woodcote Cup

Cooper-Alta MkII

26 September 1953, Goodwood (GB)

Race distance 5 laps of 2.4-mile circuit **Race time** 8m 23.6s
Entrant S.C. Moss

It was obviously a bit much to expect the Cooper-Alta to square up effectively in this *Formule Libre* race against the ThinWall Special Ferrari and a couple of supercharged BRM V16s, but I hung on to finish fourth – possibly the best I could reasonably expect under the circumstances.

247 — Retired

Goodwood Trophy

Cooper-Alta MkII

26 September 1953, Goodwood (GB)

Race distance 10 laps of 2.4-mile circuit
Reason for retirement Magneto drive **Entrant** S.C. Moss

This was the last – and longest – of my three races in the Cooper-Alta MkII at Goodwood that day, and unfortunately I had to retire when the magneto drive failed.

248 — Retired

Goodwood, 500cc Race

Cooper-Norton 500 MkVII

26 September 1953, Goodwood (GB)

Race distance 3 laps of 2.4-mile circuit
Entrant S.C. Moss

And so to my last race of the day at Goodwood – I had to retire from this extremely short event with oil on the clutch. This had not been my most successful day's racing!

249 — 1st

Castle Combe, 500cc Race, Heat 2

Cooper-Norton MkVII

3 October 1953, Castle Combe, Chippenham, Wiltshire (GB)

Race speed 78.91mph **Fastest lap** 81.19mph (record)
Entrant S.C. Moss

I opened the meeting on a promising note with a strong run to victory, having no idea that this would be my final win of the 1953 season.

250 — Retired

Castle Combe, Joe Fry Memorial Race

Cooper-JAP 1,100 MkVII

3 October 1953, Castle Combe, Chippenham, Wiltshire (GB)

Category Formule Libre
Race distance 5 laps of 1.84-mile circuit
Reason for retirement Crash **Car no** 43 **Entrant** S.C. Moss

It was my idea to use my Cooper chassis fitted with a 1,100cc JAP twin for this *Formule Libre* event, although Alf Francis wanted me to use the Cooper-Alta because he thought the smaller Cooper-JAP might be vulnerable in a field of grown-up Formula 2 single-seaters.

Alf was proved absolutely correct. I went straight into the lead at the start but as I braked hard for Quarry corner I demonstrated, to my cost, that the little Cooper could stop much more effectively than Rob Walker's Connaught, which was sitting right on my tail driven by Tony Rolt.

Tony was taken by surprise and could not avoid running into me. I duly somersaulted off the road and was thrown out of the Cooper before it finished its crazy gyrations. I picked myself up and managed to stumble to the side of the track before I collapsed with a broken shoulder, damaged arm and twisted knee. Although I was back driving my Jaguar MkVII road car only five days after the shunt, it took 12 weeks for the fracture and muscle tissue to heal – which was all a bit tiresome.

RIGHT *This sequence shows the result of Tony Rolt's Connaught running into my Cooper-JAP in the Joe Fry Memorial at Castle Combe. I was fortunate to escape with nothing worse than a broken shoulder.* (Stirling Moss Collection)

1954

INTO THE BIG TIME

After the disappointments of 1953, particularly the Cooper-Alta fiasco, the racing world felt that I needed a much better season in 1954. I did not disagree!

Everyone knew that Mercedes-Benz was preparing to put together a Formula 1 team for 1954. Dad and Ken Gregory, my friend and manager, went over to visit Alfred Neubauer in Stuttgart to try to talk him into giving me a test run, with a view to driving for them. Neubauer's answer was that he knew about me and thought I was doing well but I had not been in a competitive car and, therefore, it would be too difficult for him to gauge my talents. His recommendation was that I should get a Ferrari or a Maserati, which would demonstrate whether I was up to scratch. Ferrari would not sell to privateers at that time, so a Maserati it had to be…

Mum, Dad and Ken had a meeting, the upshot of which was that they decided to underwrite the really frightening amount of £5,500 – the cost of buying a 250F Grand Prix car – although afterwards I was firmly told that the money would be coming out of my own bank account. Dad and Ken flew to Maserati and Signor Omer Orsi, the owner, agreed to sell them a car.

My mechanic, Alf Francis, then went over to Italy to help build the car. Alf knew that I preferred to drive with a straight-arm position but Maserati told him that that was not how they made the 250F. That evening he stayed on working late and moved the bulkhead chassis tube about six inches further forward from the position of the seat back and welded it into place. The next day, Medardo Fantuzzi, the body builder, came in and rolled the aluminium sheet around the repositioned tube and – *voila!* – I had my correct, relaxed driving position!

I was extremely worried about the raised expectations that people would have of me. As I would be running a competitive car, I would be expected to finish near the front of the field in all of the races I entered. It was a truly intimidating thought but, of course, no bad thing. Thanks to that Maserati 250F, the 1954 season became the crucial turning point of my career.

My real chance came at the Swiss Grand Prix, at the exceedingly difficult circuit in the Bremgarten Park. The first day of practice was very wet but, somehow, I managed to put my privately owned Maser on pole, ahead of all the factory Mercedes, including Fangio's, and the Ferrari and Maserati teams. That performance sealed my drive for Mercedes in 1955.

Someone once said that in 1954 I reached manhood at last. I think that is a very neat way of looking back on it all.

LEFT *Heading for the big time. At the wheel of my Maserati 250F, surely one of the most elegant Formula 1 cars of all time, during the* Daily Telegraph *Trophy at Aintree. This car was more crucial to my career progress than perhaps any other I ever drove.* (LAT)

251   15th

Monte Carlo Rally

Sunbeam-Talbot 90

18–25 January 1954, Monte Carlo (MON)

Co-drivers Desmond Scannell, John A. Cooper **Car no** 1

The 'old team' struggled a bit in this year's Monte and we could manage only a very disappointing 15th overall.

252   1st

Sebring 12 Hours

OSCA MT4

7 March 1954, Sebring, Florida (USA)

World Sports Car Championship, round 2

Race distance 12 hours of 5.2-mile circuit (170 laps)
Race speed 73.6mph **Co-driver** Bill Lloyd **Car no** 56
Entrant B. Cunningham

An invitation from the wealthy American privateer, Briggs Cunningham, led me to make my first visit to the United States at the start of 1954, at a time when Britain was still mired in the gloom of post-war austerity, and the idea of going to America seemed a really big deal for me.

The OSCA MT4 was a really lovely little car, but we were up against works entries from Aston Martin, Ferrari and Lancia. The Lancias, in particular, were in a class of their own and wiped the floor with the rest of us. But our little OSCA handled beautifully. Its brakes wore out quite quickly, but Bill Lloyd and I soon adapted our driving technique to throw it sideways at the corners to scrub off as much speed as we could.

Sebring itself, of course, was unlike anything else I had ever encountered. I had driven on aerodrome circuits in Britain, but nothing had prepared me for the width of the straights, some of which were very poorly marked out, let alone the parked aircraft in places along the way.

The race just fell into our hands after we got up to third place behind the two Lancias, and their bad luck was our good luck when they retired with mechanical problems while well ahead. We survived a slightly suspect clutch and a tremendous rain storm to take this totally unexpected win both outright and on handicap.

The OSCA was such a gem of a car that I suppose it will not surprise you to learn that I purchased one for myself a few years ago and still derive great pleasure from driving it in historic car racing. Mine is a 1956 FS372, a 1,500cc car with a desmodromic-valve head, which was designed by Ernesto Maserati in 1956. This does not give more power but offers a greatly increased rev range.

I was actually sailing back to Britain on the *Queen Elizabeth* after this race when I heard that my family had ordered the Maserati 250F. In those days, ship-to-shore communication was by means of radio telephone, a very hit-and-miss affair, and over the crackling line I could just about make out my father's voice telling me what he had planned and organised. I could hardly believe my ears.

After Sebring, I went on to Nassau in the Bahamas to nurse my wounds from the previous season. I chose Nassau because it was in the sterling area, where the Chancellor of the Exchequer's limit of £50 in foreign currency did not apply.

253   3rd

Oulton Park, British Empire Trophy, Heat 1

Leonard-MG

10 April 1954, Oulton Park, Cheshire (GB)

Race distance 20 laps of 2.23-mile circuit **Fastest lap** 1m 59s
Car no 7 **Entrant** L. Leonard

Lionel Leonard was a family friend and his business was importing tulip bulbs from Holland. He was a keen amateur racer, a rough-and-ready, get-up-and-at-'em kind of a chap, and he had an MG-engined special that he commissioned Cooper to rebody in the style of the Ferrari 166 Barchetta. He was

a great character and asked me to drive his car in the British Empire Trophy at Oulton Park. I finished third in the first heat.

254   Retired

Oulton Park, British Empire Trophy, Final

Leonard-MG

10 April 1954, Oulton Park, Cheshire (GB)

Race distance 32 laps of 2.23-mile circuit
Reason for retirement Engine **Car no** 7 **Entrant** L. Leonard

Unfortunately, I retired in the final. Lionel's car was nice enough, if a bit underpowered, and it wasn't the last we heard

of this smart little machine. He sold it to Cliff Davis, who rebuilt it around a Tojeiro chassis, and later AC bought the Tojeiro design – with Lionel's body style – as the basis for its Ace sports car, which eventually led to the legendary Shelby American Cobra. From little acorns…

OPPOSITE *Taking the chequered flag in the superb little OSCA at the Sebring 12 Hours during what was my first visit to the United States.* (Ozzie Lyons, Pete Lyons Collection)

ABOVE *The Leonard-MG was a neat little special built by a family friend who invited me to drive it in the British Empire Trophy at Oulton Park.* (LAT)

255   7th

Goodwood, 500cc Race

Beart-Cooper MkVIIA

17 April 1954, Goodwood, West Sussex (GB)

Car no 7 Entrant F. Beart

I finished in a rather disappointing note with seventh place in the Beart-Cooper 500 at Goodwood. I cannot recall much about the occasion apart from the fact that it seemed unusual to be at the popular Sussex circuit and competing in only a single race.

256   4th

Bordeaux Grand Prix

Maserati 250F

9 May 1954, Bordeaux (F)

Race distance 123 laps of 1.52-mile circuit
Race time 3h 6m 52.7s (121 laps) **Fastest lap** 67.67mph
Car no 7 Entrant S.C. Moss

This was my first race with the long-awaited Maserati 250F – the culmination of months of keen anticipation and expectation.

On 14 January 1954, we received a pro forma invoice from the Officine Alfieri Maserati laying out the terms of payment which – and I quote – were by 'irrevocable credit with Banca Commerciale Italiana of Modena, payable on presentation of delivery or shipping documents' for the amount of £5,275 in total, made up of £3,561 for the car (including engine) and £1,714 for the spares. The terminology seems quaint in retrospect, but Maserati agreed to supply under the terms of this agreement: 'One Maserati car type 250F/Formula 1 – new from works, body varnished in English green with red stripes round radiator complete with four tyres and

tool box. Equipment [includes] four front wheels, spare, 4 rear wheels, spare, 4 spare axle ratios.'

During this period Alf Francis, who went to Modena to supervise the car's manufacture, became something of an intermediary between me and Maserati, and there were many long 'phone calls between England and Italy discussing how to coax along the people there with little less of the *domani* attitude, while, of course, not wanting to offend them. Little things did cause offence, or so it seemed. When I suggested that we would supply the green paint for the car, they responded with, "We have any colour you want – our paints are very good, you know", so we let them get on with it and, in Alf's words, "That is why the Maserati raced in that rather peculiar, sickly shade of Adriatic sea green."

We had quite a fight with Maserati over my personal preferences – or, at least, Alf did on my behalf. The first thing was that I insisted on getting rid of the central throttle arrangement on my car. Maserati's chief mechanic, Guerrino Bertocchi, at one point remarked in exasperation, "I don't know who you people think you are," but Alf was well up to the task of fielding all these problems and did so in fine style.

The next thing was the driving position. I made it clear that I wanted to drive Farina-style, with my arms almost outstretched in front of me. The original Maserati driving position looked as if it had come from a London bus. As mentioned in the introduction to this chapter (page 141), Alf discreetly modified my car, moving the dashboard bulkhead forward a few inches so that the driving position was to my taste. It must have been a bit of a surprise for the team's body builder, Medardo Fantuzzi, when he came in the next day to finish fitting the bodywork to my car, but he must have done some quick improvisation and on-the-spot modifications.

RIGHT *Seventh place was a disappointing result in the Beart-Cooper 500 at the first Goodwood meeting of the year.* (LAT)

ABOVE *Driving my Maserati 250F, I finished third in the first heat of the BRDC International Trophy at Silverstone, but retired in the final with a broken de Dion tube.* (Tom March Collection)

My first race with the car, on the tight little Bordeaux circuit, was something of a learning curve. The conditions were damp at the start and I was feeling my way on the Dunlop tyres. Alf could see from the pit lane that I was not very happy and so, thinking on his feet, he nipped down to the Pirelli representative and asked if he could buy four tyres there and then. They were quickly fitted to the spare rims and I was called in for a wheel change.

Certainly the car was much better from that point onwards and I made up the best part of two laps to finish fourth behind Maurice Trintignant's Ferrari. It was quite a promising start.

257   3rd

Silverstone, BRDC International Trophy, Heat 1

Maserati 250F

15 May 1954, Silverstone (GB)

Organising club British Racing Drivers' Club
Race distance 15 laps of 2.9-mile circuit **Race time** 15m 32.5s
Car no 7 **Entrant** S.C. Moss

In the first practice session, I was second fastest behind José Froilán González's Ferrari, which was pretty satisfying, and then it rained for Friday's second practice session and I wound up qualifying third, behind González and Jean Behra's Gordini. I was also concerned that the brakes seemed to be losing their edge, so we

changed from the 'Frendo' (*sic*) linings that had been fitted by Maserati to another set of Ferodo linings. That was an immediate improvement.

In the first heat I finished third, after a careful run behind González and Prince Bira in his older Maserati A6GCM.

258   Retired

Silverstone, BRDC International Trophy, Final

Maserati 250F

15 May 1954, Silverstone (GB)

Organising club British Racing Drivers' Club
Race distance 35 laps of 2.9-mile circuit
Reason for retirement De Dion tube failure after 24 laps
Fastest lap 1m 52s **Car no** 7 **Entrant** S.C. Moss

I was on the third row of the grid for the final, but made a good start and was up to third by the end of the opening lap. I got the better of a dice with Jean Behra for second place and felt confident I would finish runner-up to González, but on lap 25 the Maserati's de Dion tube broke and I pulled up out on the circuit with a rear wheel askew.

259 3rd

Silverstone, Production Touring Car Race

Jaguar MkVII

15 May 1954, Silverstone (GB)

Organising club British Racing Drivers' Club
Race distance 17 laps of 2.9-mile circuit **Race time** 39m 36s
Race speed 75.39mph **Fastest lap** 2m 16s, 77.48mph (record, shared with Ian Appleyard and Tony Rolt) **Car no** 4
Entrant Works

Having won at Silverstone with the big Jaguar MkVII saloon in the two previous years, I was going for a hat trick in this race. Unfortunately, the starter motor jammed at the off, so I lost too much time to have a chance of catching Ian Appleyard and Tony Rolt, who finished one-two in their similar cars. Great fun!

260 1st

Silverstone, 500cc Race

Beart-Cooper MkVIIA

15 May 1954, Silverstone (GB)

Race distance 15 laps of 2.9-mile circuit **Race time** 31m 5s
Race speed 84.21mph **Entrant** F. Beart

The last race of the day was business as usual, I suppose you could say, with yet another satisfying run with the Beart-Cooper during a busy weekend at the 'Home of British Motor Racing'.

261 1st

Eifelrennen 500cc Race

Beart-Cooper MkVIIA

23 May 1954, Nürburgring (D)

Race time 58m 49.8s, 72.6mph **Entrant** F. Beart

This was another successful outing at the Nürburgring and I beat Les Leston home after an energetic battle.

BELOW *I had hoped to win the touring car race at the International Trophy for the third straight year with the Jaguar MkVII, but problems with the starter motor prevented me from challenging for victory.* (Tom March Collection)

262   1st

Aintree 500cc Race

Beart-Cooper MkVIIA

29 May 1954, Aintree, Liverpool (GB)

Race distance 10 laps of 3-mile circuit **Race time** 25m 22.8s
Race speed 70.92mph **Fastest lap** 2m 29.6s, 72.19mph
Car no 41 **Entrant** F. Beart

This was the first race meeting at Aintree, where a new motor racing circuit had been constructed. The cars ran in an anti-clockwise direction but this would be reversed for all subsequent meetings.

Such was the intensity of the rain that this 500cc race was more like a water-skiing event. I took the lead at the start and pulled steadily away to win by 22.8 seconds, which was pretty satisfying given the conditions.

263   3rd

Aintree 200, Heat 1

Maserati 250F

29 May 1954, Aintree, Liverpool (GB)

Race distance 17 laps of 3-mile circuit **Race time** 40m 12s
Car no 7 **Entrant** S.C. Moss

I had a bit of a disagreement with Alf over preparations for this race. I thought that Aintree would become the fastest circuit in the country, so I insisted on a change of axle ratio. Alf grumbled about this and it took 12 hours to complete.

I have to confess he was right. The ratio was too high and during first practice I was 6 seconds slower than Peter Collins in the ThinWall Special, so we had to revert to the Silverstone ratio – which meant more work. I finished third in my heat, although I was not too satisfied with the feel of the car.

264   1st

Aintree 200, Final

Maserati 250F

29 May 1954, Aintree, Liverpool (GB)

Category Formule Libre
Race distance 34 laps of 3-mile circuit **Race time** 1h 18m 48.4s
Race speed 77.7mph **Car no** 7 **Entrant** S.C. Moss

We fitted bigger chokes and jets to the carburettors for the final. The Maserati's performance was so much better that I was able to win from Reg Parnell's Ferrari by just under 50 seconds.

265   Unclassified

Rome Grand Prix

Maserati 250F

6 June 1954, Castelfusano, Rome (I)

Race distance 60 laps of 4.09-mile circuit
Reason unclassified Final drive failed 8 laps from end
Car no 10 **Entrant** S.C. Moss

After the Aintree race we really had to pull out all the stops to get down to Rome for the following weekend's event, a task that involved Alf and our other mechanic, Tony Robinson, in a marathon journey with the Maserati tucked up in its Commer transporter. Just from Calais to Turin took them 34 hours and they still had the best part of another 500 miles to cover to get to Rome.

The Castelfusano circuit was newly included on the calendar and involved a lot of guess-work for all the competitors when it came to axle ratios and so on. I ran second to Onofre Marimon's 250F from the start, but eight laps from the end the final drive failed.

RIGHT *Preparations for the Aintree 200 resulted in a disagreement with my mechanic Alf Francis and a lot of extra work!* (LAT)

Le Mans 24 Hours

Jaguar D-type

12/13 June 1954, Sarthe (F)

World Sports Car Championship, round 4

Race distance 24 hours of 8.38-mile circuit (2523.48 miles, 302 laps) **Reason for retirement** Brakes **Co-driver** Peter Walker **Car no** 12 **Entrant** Works

As I have said on many occasions, the D-type Jaguar was the ideal machine for Le Mans, although the C-type was a more versatile and user-friendly machine to drive on other circuits. Sharing with Peter Walker, I kept up with the leading 4.9-litre Ferraris in the opening phase, but shortly after I handed over to Peter the car was delayed by fuel-feed problems. Eventually, we dropped out with brake problems after I had experienced a very unsettling moment shooting up the escape road at the end of the Mulsanne straight when the car proved reluctant to slow down sufficiently!

OPPOSITE *Heading for third place with the Maserati 250F in the Belgian Grand Prix behind Fangio's works car and Maurice Trintignant's Ferrari.* (LAT)

BELOW *Leading the sprint across the road at Le Mans to my Jaguar D-type. On this occasion brake problems cost me a finish.* (LAT)

267   3rd

Belgian Grand Prix

Maserati 250F

20 June 1954, Spa-Francorchamps, Liège (B)

F1 World Championship, round 3

Race distance 36 laps of 8.77-mile circuit **Race time** 2h 46m 9s
Race speed 110.88mph **Car no** 22 **Entrant** S.C. Moss

This was a hugely memorable event because it was the race in which I scored my first ever World Championship points, with a third-place finish. I must say that initially I felt a little despondent because my 250F's engine, being a privateer version, could be run only to about 7,200rpm and I posted quite a slow time in first practice. Then Alf Francis informed me that Fangio had been using 8,000rpm on his works Maser engine, so I felt a little better.

Guerrino Bertocchi also urged us to try Pirelli tyres once again instead of our customary Dunlops, even going so far as to loan me a spare set from the works team. That certainly did the trick! I was able to slice 6 seconds a lap off my time without revving the car any more.

Initially I ran fifth in the race but I was up to fourth by half distance and eventually took the chequered flag third, albeit a lap behind Fangio's winning Maserati and with Maurice Trintignant second for Ferrari. I felt I was certainly getting the hang of it.

268   Retired

Reims 12 Hours

Jaguar D-type

4 July 1954, Reims (F)

Race distance 12 hours of 5.65-mile circuit (1,254.43 miles, 222 laps) **Reason for retirement** Broken driveshaft
Co-driver Peter Walker **Car no** 1 **Entrant** Works

We had chosen not to compete in the French Grand Prix so that we could be extra sure of our preparations for the British Grand Prix a fortnight later. However, I went to Reims to share a works Jaguar D-type in the 12-hour sports car race, which was due to finish at noon on the Sunday before the start of the Formula 1 race. I did, therefore, witness the Mercedes team's return to Formula 1 with Fangio and Kling, who dominated the French Grand Prix in their W196 streamliners.

The 12-hour race started at midnight in light drizzle and I was out in front straight away, leading past the pits at the end of the opening lap, ahead of the Cunningham shared by Briggs Cunningham and Sherwood Johnson. With little more than two laps completed I was already lapping the slower cars, sometimes a tricky task when you are relying on your headlights to pick out their profiles in the murk ahead of you.

With an hour gone, I was leading Umberto Maglioli's Ferrari by just 13 seconds and the pace was already proving too much for the Italian machine, which rolled into the pits to retire with a broken gearbox after only 25 laps. Just before 2am, I came into the pits again, losing six minutes or so while a couple of plugs were changed, and quite soon afterwards I handed the car over to Peter Walker. He stopped near Thillois with a broken driveshaft at around 4.40am and that was the end of our race.

This was one of only three races in which I competed with the D-type. The fact that I retired from all three of them probably rather coloured my feelings about this distinctive machine.

ABOVE *Making adjustments on the Alpine Rally to the cooling of our Sunbeam-Talbot Alpine. I became only the second person (after Ian Appleyard) to win a Gold Coupe des Alpes.* (LAT)

RIGHT *In the rain on the starting grid for the British Grand Prix at Silverstone. I was running second behind eventual winner José Froilán González when I retired with transmission trouble.* (LAT)

269 Coupe

Alpine Rally

Sunbeam-Talbot Alpine

9–16 July 1954

Event distance 2,290 miles **Co-driver** John Cutts
Car no 500 **Entrant** Works

The 17th Criterium Internationale des Alpes, as this event was formally titled, took place in the most appalling weather conditions in the history of the event, and 84 crews from nine countries battled against snow and rain in what should have been the height of the summer holiday season. I was again driving a Sunbeam-Talbot Alpine convertible with John Cutts as navigator and it was enormously satisfying to win a *Coupe des Alpes en Or* – the gold version – for my third straight unpenalised performance in this gruelling event. I was to remain only the second – and last – person to win a gold *Coupe*, Ian Appleyard having been the first.

British Grand Prix

Maserati 250F

17 July 1954, Silverstone (GB)

F1 World Championship, round 5

Race distance 90 laps of 2.927-mile circuit
Reason for retirement Transmission after 80 laps
Fastest lap 1m 50s, 95.793mph **Car no** 7 **Entrant** S.C. Moss

Even by this early stage in the season it seemed clear that Omer Orsi was impressed with the progress I had been making in my 250F and there were clear indications that he and his father had come to consider us as informal members of the factory team. This was underlined by the fact that Alf Francis, my mechanic, was permitted to prepare the car in the factory at Modena. In what we thought to be a clever political initiative, we also agreed to lend the car to the works so that Luigi Villoresi could drive it in the French Grand Prix, a move

that Alf advocated strongly because it might create a further sense of obligation towards us.

I was also told by Signor Orsi that I need not worry about running the engine up to 7,800rpm at Silverstone, rather than its customary 7,200rpm limit, because the factory would rebuild it if it failed. With all that in mind, I was feeling quietly confident as I went into my home Grand Prix at Silverstone.

It was important for me to deliver a strong showing in front of my supportive home crowd so it was satisfying to gain a position on the outside of the front row of the grid, alongside Fangio's Mercedes W196 streamliner in pole position, José Froilán González in the Ferrari 625 and Mike Hawthorn in another Ferrari. Karl Kling, clearly uncomfortable at Silverstone, could manage only the second row in his Mercedes. He and Fangio were finding that the all-enveloping bodywork of the silver cars made it difficult to place them accurately at Silverstone – which was just fine for me.

When the flag dropped at the start, I made the best use of a specially made low first gear provided by Maserati to sprint away in second place behind González. After 20 laps I was

running fourth behind González, Fangio and Hawthorn, and soon afterwards I got my head down to get past Mike for third place. Now it was a question of going all-out to catch Fangio, a task I achieved by lap 55, and by lap 60 I had settled in second place only 19 seconds behind González.

Then, with just 10 laps left to go, one of the Maserati's final-drive reduction gears came loose on its shaft and slid out of engagement. I could almost hear the gasp of dismay from the crowd as I coasted to a halt out on the circuit. It was one of the biggest disappointments of my career, particularly because Mike went through to finish behind González to make it a Ferrari one-two.

It had certainly been one of those days which demonstrated the user-friendly characteristics of the 250F. Yet it was still frustrating to be handicapped by the rev limit that private owners had to observe if they were not to incur significant bills for engine rebuilds.

Hopefully, it would not be long now before I would be taken under the wing of the factory and be free to use up to 8,000rpm in the heat of battle. The difference was huge and I looked forward to a time when I would no longer have to be footing the bills.

271   1st

Silverstone, 500cc Race

Beart-Cooper MkVIIA

17 July 1954, Silverstone (GB)

Race distance 17 laps of 2.94-mile circuit **Race time** 39m 33s
Race speed 75.49mph **Fastest lap** 2m 14s, 78.64mph **Car no** 7
Entrant F. Beart

It was pouring with rain for the final race on the British Grand Prix programme and I suppose it was some consolation that I managed to win convincingly in the Beart-Cooper.

From the start, I took the lead going towards the first corner and won by almost a minute from Reg Bicknell's Revis and Ivor Bueb's Cooper. That win went some way to making up for my disappointment with the Maserati in the British Grand Prix but, I must say, it was difficult to see that at the time.

BELOW *Splashing to victory in the 500cc race at the British Grand Prix meeting – but this was little consolation for my disappointment in the main race.* (LAT)

272   2nd

Caen Grand Prix

Maserati 250F

25 July 1954, Caen (F)

Race distance 60 laps of 2.18-mile circuit
Race time 1h 29m 4.2s **Fastest lap** 1m 25.7s, 92.4mph (record)
Car no 14 **Entrant** S.C. Moss

---

273   Retired

German Grand Prix

Maserati 250F

1 August 1954, Nürburgring (D)

F1 World Championship, round 6

Race distance 22 laps of 14.2-mile circuit
Reason for retirement Engine after 1 lap **Car no** 16
Entrant S.C. Moss/Works

---

274   2nd

Brands Hatch, *Daily Telegraph* International Challenge, Heat 4

Beart-Cooper MkVIIA

2 August 1954, Brands Hatch, Kent (GB)

Race distance 10 laps of 1.25-mile circuit **Car no** 27 **Entrant** F. Beart

---

275   2nd

Brands Hatch, *Daily Telegraph* International Challenge, Final

Beart-Cooper MkVIIA

2 August 1954, Brands Hatch, Kent (GB)

Race distance 40 laps of 1.25-mile circuit **Race time** 42m 19.4s
Car no 27 **Entrant** F. Beart

The weather for this race was cool and so overcast that plans for my parents and Ken Gregory to fly over to watch me compete had to be abandoned because their plane was grounded in England due to the poor conditions.

I qualified the 250F second behind Maurice Trintignant's Ferrari 625 and just ahead of Jean Behra's Gordini. Although I made a slowish start, I was leading Trintignant comfortably by the end of the opening lap, but unfortunately the handling deteriorated badly in the closing stages. As the fuel load in the tail tank was consumed and the car became lighter, so it became apparent that the rear shock absorbers were too stiff.

I was still leading by 8 seconds on lap 40, but Trintignant trimmed that advantage to 4 seconds by lap 44 and overtook me to take the lead a couple of laps later. I fought back and retook the lead on lap 51 but the Ferrari had the edge and, with only four laps left, Maurice squeezed past me again to win by 3.1 seconds.

On our arrival at the Nürburgring, the Maserati team manager Nello Ugolini invited me to join the factory team for the race and, of course, I was delighted to accept. My 250F was hand-painted red for the occasion, although it retained a distinctive green oval around its nose section.

Unfortunately, what should have been a happy weekend for Maserati was thrown into tragedy on the second day of practice when the team's pleasant Argentinian driver, Onofre Marimon, crashed on one of the tricky corners just before Adenau bridge and was killed. The team withdrew Luigi Villoresi as a mark of respect, leaving me as the sole representative of the Trident marque competing in this race.

I over-revved the engine in practice but the mechanics, despite their sorrow over Marimon's death, worked hard overnight to fit a new cylinder head for the race. Unfortunately, this was a bit of a wasted effort because the engine ran its bearings and I had to retire, after completing the opening lap in third place.

I came straight back from the Nürburgring overnight to compete in in some 500cc races in front of an estimated 40,000-strong Bank Holiday Monday crowd at the little Kent circuit, but in my heat I had to settle for second place behind Charles Headland's Martin-Headland.

It took me a few laps to battle through to second place behind Jim Russell's Cooper. Although I tried every trick in the book to catch him, Jim kept ahead and beat me by a fraction over 6 seconds.

276   1st

Oulton Park, Gold Cup

Maserati 250F

7 August 1954, Oulton Park, Cheshire (GB)

Race distance 36 laps of 2.76-mile circuit **Race time** 1hr 11m 27s **Race speed** 83.48mph **Fastest lap** 1m 56.8s, 85.11mph **Car no** 7 **Entrant** S.C. Moss/Works

Needless to say, my own 250F was pretty worn out after the rigours of Silverstone, Caen and the Nürburgring, so I appreciated the Maserati factory's gesture in making available one of the works cars for this important British non-championship event.

The car did not arrive in time for practice, so I had to start from the back of the 20-car grid. I was seventh, however, at the end of the opening lap, second on the third lap, and moved into the lead on the fourth lap. I managed to beat Reg Parnell's Ferrari 625 by more than a minute.

277   1st

Oulton Park, *Formule Libre* Race

Maserati 250F

7 August 1954, Oulton Park, Cheshire (GB)

Race distance 20 laps of 2.76-mile circuit **Race time** 39m 38s **Race speed** 82.91mph **Fastest lap** 1m 56.4s, 85.4mph (record) **Car no** 7 **Entrant** S.C. Moss/Works

Bob Gerard held the lead for the first five laps in his Cooper-Bristol, but then I went through into the lead and won easily, in the process setting a new Formula 1 record.

LEFT *I have always had a high regard for Oulton Park as a circuit and my win with the Beart-Cooper at the August meeting was particularly satisfying.* (LAT)

278   1st

Oulton Park, 500cc Race

Beart-Cooper MkVIIA

7 August 1954, Oulton Park (GB)

Race distance 27 laps of 2.76-mile circuit **Race time** 59m 43.8s **Race speed** 74.89mph **Car no** 7 **Entrant** F. Beart

This was my third race of the day and again I had to start from the back of the grid, but I overtook no fewer than 23 cars to complete the third lap in second place. After 10 laps I was more than half a minute in front of second-placed Jim Russell and by the end I was more than a minute ahead.

279   Retired

Pescara Grand Prix

Maserati 250F

15 August 1954, Pescara (I)

Race distance 16 laps of 15.84-mile circuit **Reason for retirement** Oil pipe **Car no** 18 **Entrant** Works/S.C. Moss

For this race on the spectacular Pescara road circuit, I was back behind the wheel of my own Maserati 250F, although by now it had been properly 'adopted' by the works and after Marimon's death I was now regarded as *de facto* team leader.

Although this was a non-championship race, I must say I felt pretty chuffed to qualify on pole position, 21 seconds ahead of Robert Manzon's Ferrari 625. I led easily from the start and was well ahead when, on the fourth lap, a steel feed pipe in the lubrication system fractured and started spraying oil into the cockpit. Rather than have the rear axle seize on this most demanding of high-speed circuits, I thought it prudent to stop. And I still think so!

280 Retired

Swiss Grand Prix

Maserati 250F

22 August 1954, Bremgarten (CH)

F1 World Championship, round 7

Race distance 66 laps of 4.52-mile circuit
Reason for retirement Oil pump after 21 laps **Car no** 32
Entrant Works/S.C. Moss

I n many ways this was the most significant race of my season. Not due to the disappointing outcome – another retirement – but because it was at this race that I think Alfred Neubauer, the Mercedes team manager, seriously began to sit up and take notice of my potential. In the first practice session it poured with rain and I set the fastest time ahead of all the Mercedes and Ferrari opposition. I think Neubauer was genuinely impressed and, if you like, put a tick on his mental card index labelled 'Moss'.

The race itself yielded another technical failure. Fangio started from the middle of the front row in his open-wheeled version of the Mercedes W196 between González, in pole position in the Ferrari, and me. As the Merc took an immediate lead, I slotted into third place behind González and that was the order in which we completed the opening lap.

Karl Kling was right behind me in the other W196 as we started the second lap but, trying to close the gap to my Maserati, he spun under braking at the hairpin and dropped to the back of the field. That at least took some pressure off me as I concentrated on my task to hunt down González for second place. On lap three, I managed to squeeze in front of the Ferrari to take second place and then tried my utmost to close the gap on Fangio. But the leading Mercedes edged away from me and, although I felt I had the legs of the rest of the field, I think second place would have been the best I could have hoped for.

Unfortunately, my Maserati's oil pressure began to fade and I had dropped back to fourth place by the time the oil pump drive sheared with 21 laps of the race completed. Nello Ugolini, Maserati's team manager, called in Harry Schell with the idea that I take over his car for the rest of the race, but, by the time he reached the pits, his engine also had no oil pressure left, so my work was clearly finished for the day.

281 10th

Italian Grand Prix

Maserati 250F

5 September 1954, Monza (I)

F1 World Championship, round 8

Race distance 80 laps of 3.92-mile circuit
Race time 2h 47m 53.7s **Car no** 28 **Entrant** Works/S.C. Moss

I nevitably there was a great sense of expectation at Maserati as we went into the Italian Grand Prix at Monza, although I certainly did not underestimate the challenge that awaited me against the streamlined Mercedes W196s. In addition, Lancia, which was running behind schedule with the development of its new D50 contender, agreed to release Alberto Ascari to drive for Ferrari in this event. It was clearly going to be a tough afternoon's work.

There had been only two weeks for Maserati to rebuild my engine for Monza and the 250Fs were also fitted with new tail-mounted oil tanks for this prestigious event. Detailed examination after the Swiss Grand Prix at Bremgarten confirmed that the oil tanks used at that race had been fitted with a revised filler-cap arrangement with a spring-loaded internal collar secured by a small nut. It turned out that this nut had vibrated loose on both cars, becoming sucked into the lubrication system and seizing the oil pumps. Changes were made for Monza.

Fangio qualified on pole with a lap in 1m 59.0s, followed by Alberto Ascari on 1m 59.2s and me on the outside of the front row on 1m 59.3s. At the start Kling burst through from the second row to snatch the lead from his team leader, Fangio, mid-way round the opening lap. I completed the first lap in fifth place, but on lap four the strain began to tell on Kling and he ran on to the grass at the tricky Curva Grande right-hander, dropping to fifth place in the process.

On the sixth lap, Ascari went ahead by a wheel from González, with Fangio third and my Maserati close behind him. At half distance I was still fourth, but only 2.1 seconds behind the race leader, Ascari, with Fangio and Villoresi running between us. Villoresi retired soon afterwards and I began to close in on Ascari and Fangio, hanging on in their slipstreams and then leapfrogging past them into Curva Grande.

Despite acknowledging signals from the pits to ease up, I seemed to be pulling effortlessly away from Fangio and was 20 seconds ahead of his Mercedes with 20 laps to run. Then, with just nine laps separating me from my first Grand Prix victory, the oil-pressure needle dropped off the bottom of the gauge and I was out of the race. I got out of the car and pushed it across the line to claim 10th in the official classification.

It was not until a little later that I heard some really touching news. Pirelli contacted me and said it would be paying me the full winner's bonus in appreciation of my effort. It was a not-inconsiderable amount of money, but, to me, it was the gesture that was more important.

RIGHT *Leading the Italian Grand Prix at Monza ahead of Fangio's Mercedes. It was a race I came oh-so-close to winning in my Maserati 250F, and it would have been my first Grand Prix victory. Pirelli even paid me the full winner's bonus.* (LAT)

282   18th

RAC
Tourist Trophy

Jaguar D-type

11 September 1954, Dundrod, Belfast,
Northern Ireland (GB)

World Sports Car Championship, round 5

Organising club Royal Automobile Club
Race distance 88 laps of 7.42-mile circuit **Fastest lap** 88.4mph
Co-driver Peter Walker **Car no** 20 **Entrant** Works

T his was a distinctly unmemorable race
for me and probably influenced my
lasting feelings about the D-type compared
with the C-type, which was always one of

my favourite cars. To be fair, the D-type
was not really in its element on the bumps
and changes of camber that abounded at
Dundrod, and was always more at home on
the smooth surface at Le Mans, which, of
course, it had been designed for.

We were never really on the winning pace
in this complex handicap race and eventually
the rear axle failed. I ended up pushing
the car across the finishing line with no oil
pressure to claim 18th place in the final
classification.

BELOW *Waiting in the rain to push my
Jaguar D-type across the finishing line after
a disappointing day in the Tourist Trophy at
Dundrod.* (LAT)

283   2nd

Goodwood,
500cc Race

Beart-Cooper MkVIIA

25 September 1954, Goodwood (GB)

Race distance 5 laps of 2.4-mile circuit **Race time** 8m 51s **Fastest
lap** 1m 43s, 85.88mph (record) **Car no** 37 **Entrant** F. Beart

I tried every trick in the book to beat Don
Parker in this first race of the day but if Don
did not want to be passed then he made it
pretty obvious. I am not sure I would call him
a dirty driver but there were times when his
obstructive tactics were not quite sporting.
I finished half a length behind him.

284 — 2nd

Goodwood, Sports Car Race

Lister-Bristol

25 September 1954, Goodwood (GB)

Race distance 5 laps of 2.4-mile circuit **Race time** 8m 46.6s
Fastest lap 1m 43.2s, 83.72mph **Car no** 87 **Entrant** Works

B rian Lister made it a particularly busy day for me at this Goodwood meeting with an invitation to drive his attractive little Lister-Bristol. It had a tendency to lift an inside-rear wheel under hard cornering and I was unable to keep up with Roy Salvadori in the Gilby Engineering Maserati, although I did finish the day with the fastest lap.

285 — 1st

Goodwood Trophy

Maserati 250F

25 September 1954, Goodwood (GB)

Race distance 21 laps of 2.4-mile circuit **Race time** 33m 3.2s
Race speed 91.49mph **Fastest lap** 1m 33s, 92.9mph **Car no** 7
Entrant Works/S.C. Moss

A fter those two highly promising Grand Prix outings at Bremgarten and Monza, it was good to be back at home for another series of national British races with which to round off the season and entertain my supportive fans. In the Goodwood Trophy, I qualified easily on pole position and, although Reg Parnell's Ferrari briefly headed me away from the line, I was in front before the end of the first lap and cruised away to an easy win.

286 — 3rd

Goodwood, Woodcote Cup

Maserati 250F

25 September 1954, Goodwood (GB)

Race time 15m 48s **Race distance** 10 laps of 2.54-mile circuit
Car no 7 **Entrant** Works/S.C. Moss

T his *Formule Libre* race finished off my busy day at Goodwood. Although my Maserati 250F simply did not have the power to match Peter Collins in the ThinWall Special or Ken Wharton in the supercharged BRM V16, I finished third and had the satisfaction of taking the chequered flag ahead of Mike Hawthorn in the Vanwall Special.

287 — 1st

Aintree, 500cc Race

Beart-Cooper MkVIIA

2 October 1954, Aintree, Liverpool (GB)

Race distance 17 laps of 3-mile circuit **Race time** 39m 38s
Race speed 77.53mph **Fastest lap** 2m 17.2s, 78.72mph (shared with Jim Russell) **Car no** 7 **Entrant** F. Beart

I went straight into the lead at the start of this race and won quite easily. It set the tone for the rest of the weekend at this popular new circuit that had been built on the outskirts of Liverpool as the northern equivalent of Goodwood.

288 — 1st

Aintree, *Daily Telegraph* Trophy

Maserati 250F

2 October 1954, Aintree, Liverpool (GB)

Race distance 17 laps of 3-mile circuit **Race time** 35m 49s
Race speed 85.43mph **Fastest lap** 2m 4.8s, 86.54mph (shared with Mike Hawthorn) **Car no** 7 **Entrant** S.C. Moss

T his was another fairly easy win for me from pole position, although Mike Hawthorn drove the Vanwall Special pretty well to finish second. I congratulated Tony Vandervell on his car's performance after the race, but it was to be a while yet before we could expect to see the Vanwall emerging as a potential winner.

BELOW *Ferodo made the most of my three victories at Aintree with this advertisement placed in the motoring press.* (Stirling Moss Collection)

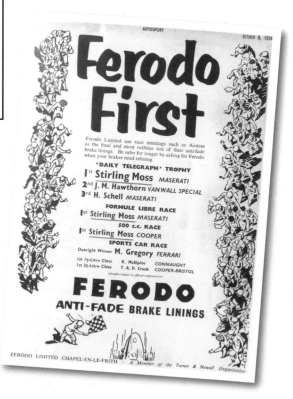

289   1st

Aintree, *Formule Libre* Race

Maserati 250F

2 October 1954, Aintree, Liverpool (GB)

Race distance 17 laps of 3-mile circuit **Race time** 35m 53.4s
Race speed 85.26mph **Fastest lap** 2m 0.6s, 89.55mph (record)
Car no 7 **Entrant** S.C. Moss

This race brought another easy win, this time ahead of Sergio Mantovani's Maserati 250F, with Ron Flockhart taking third place in the BRM.

290   1st in class

Montlhéry, Coupe du Salon

Connaught ALSR

10 October 1954, Montlhéry (F)

Race distance 24 laps of 3.9-mile circuit
Race time 57m 2.6s (22 laps) **Entrant** P. Bell

Entered by Peter Bell, the Connaught ALSR was a really nice little car and this was one of the two occasions that I competed in it. Staged to coincide with the Paris Motor Show, this sports car event was won by Jean Behra's Gordini and I finished 10th overall and first in the small-capacity 1.5-litre class.

LEFT *Leading Fangio's Mercedes in my Maserati during practice for the Spanish Grand Prix on the superb Pedralbes circuit in Barcelona. I retired with oil pump failure.* (Klemantaski Collection)

291   Retired

Spanish Grand Prix

Maserati 250F

24 October 1954, Pedralbes, Barcelona (E)

F1 World Championship, round 9

Race distance 80 laps of 3.93-mile circuit
Reason for retirement Oil pump after 20 laps **Car no** 8
Entrant Works/S.C. Moss

This was very much an anti-climax and a disappointing note on which to finish what had been such a promising season. Alf Francis was late arriving in Spain with my car and I took over the spare factory 250F for first practice, only to crash it when I got muddled up with the central throttle pedal arrangement and hit the wrong pedal.

I vowed that I would never again drive a car with a central throttle pedal. I qualified in the middle of the second row but retired after 20 laps with oil pump failure. But, as events would prove, my connections with Maserati were far from over.

292

Great American Mountain Rally

Sunbeam-Talbot Alpine

29 November 1954 (USA)

Event distance 1,100 miles **Co-driver** Ron Kessel
Entrant Works

This was very much in the nature of a promotional event for the Sunbeam-Talbot Alpine, which the Rootes Group had great hopes of selling in the USA. I must admit that my mind was a world away from this event because negotiations for me to join the Mercedes Formula 1 team were proceeding on the other side of the Atlantic.

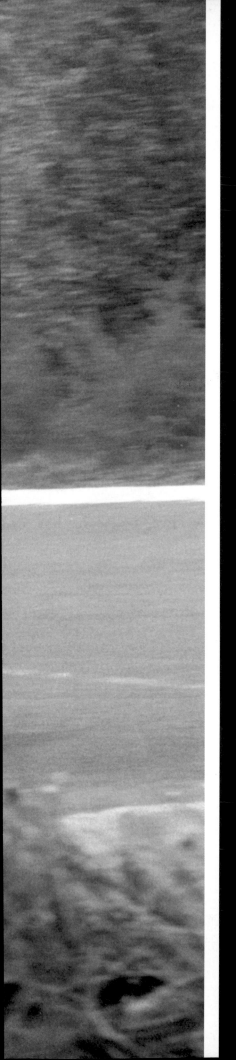

1955

LEARNING FROM THE MASTER

This was the year when I was finally invited to drive for a top-flight works Formula 1 team, in the form of Mercedes-Benz.

I was in New York when Ken Gregory 'phoned me on 22 November 1954 with news of a formal offer from Mercedes' Board of Directors in Stuttgart. I was on my way to drive a Sunbeam-Talbot Alpine in the so-called Great American Mountain Rally, which, as you can imagine, quickly dropped to quite a low priority in my mind.

I was really thrilled about the prospect of driving alongside Juan Manuel Fangio – my hero. I would also have the legendary Alfred Neubauer as my team manager and the equally celebrated Rudi Uhlenhaut as chief engineer. I was contracted to drive as Fangio's number two in all rounds of the Formula 1 World Championship, and in addition we were to undertake a full programme of sports car races in the 300SLR Roadster.

After the rally I flew to Cologne, where I was met by Mercedes personnel and whisked down to the Hockenheim circuit for my first test drive in one of the W196s, on 4 December. The car felt quite heavy compared to the Maserati 250F but the fuel-injected straight-eight engine was certainly most impressive. I was immediately impressed with the efficiency of the team, which seemingly had one's every need covered.

The season would turn out to be a huge turning point for me. Not only would I score a memorable first Grand Prix victory in the British race at Aintree but, navigated by my good friend Denis 'Jenks' Jenkinson, I also won the arduous Mille Miglia, which I rank pretty close to being the pinnacle of my achievements as a professional racing driver.

In addition to this, I retained my Maserati 250F as my new contract allowed me to continue driving in non-championship races that were not being contested by Mercedes, and I also raced a multitude of smaller cars in various other categories.

I retained Alf Francis to look after my Maserati and, although we continued our own experiments with disc brakes and fuel injection, I think it fair to say that the attitude of the Maserati factory towards us changed significantly. In fairness, one could hardly blame them. I had enjoyed factory-supported status and, now here was I, no longer just another privateer but moving in with the current World Champion, Juan Manuel Fangio, to the team that was most likely to cause Maserati competitive aggravation out on the circuits.

Even though I still had a burning desire to compete at the highest level at the wheel of a British Formula 1 car, there was no way I could even consider turning down the offer from Mercedes. It was the right thing to do and I never regretted the experience.

More than 50 years later, I felt great pride when, in 2009, the evocative Mercedes McLaren SLR Stirling Moss sports car was unveiled. My relationship with Mercedes has certainly stood the test of time.

LEFT *Driving for Mercedes-Benz in 1955 was a completely new experience for me with their high standards of detailed preparation and performance. Here I am drifting the W196 at high speed during the Belgian Grand Prix.* (LAT)

Argentine Grand Prix

Mercedes-Benz W196

16 January 1955, Buenos Aires (ARG)
F1 World Championship, round 1

Race distance 96 laps of 2.43-mile circuit **Race time** 3h 1m 51.6s (94 laps) **Car no** 6 & 8 (took over Hans Herrmann's car) **Entrant** Works

Mercedes really impressed me with its attention to detail. Everything was always covered – whether it was the mechanic who appeared, seemingly from nowhere, to give me a bowl of hot water, soap, flannel and towel after my first test in the W196 at Hockenheim or the fact that I was paid an extra dollar a day to ensure that my road car was kept clean, in line with the well-groomed Mercedes image. I made little secret of the fact that I pocketed the dollar and cleaned the car myself.

Initially, I thought I would have quite a formal relationship with the team manager, Alfred Neubauer, because his size and presence seemed rather intimidating, but it did not take long for me to break the ice and I quickly realised that behind that dominating façade was a character with a keen sense of humour.

For instance, on the long flight down to Buenos Aires for the opening Grand Prix of the season, we were in a noisy, cramped DC-6B airliner or some similar piston-engined machine. Suddenly there was a roar from Neubauer summoning Hans Herrmann and me to the back of the plane. The doors of the two toilets were very close together in a V-shaped lobby and he was pretending that his – admittedly vast – bulk had become trapped between them.

For this race, Fangio and Karl Kling had two new W196 chassis with a slightly shorter wheelbase, with Herrmann and I driving the longer 1954-specification cars. The heat was utterly stifling, in excess of 130 degrees Fahrenheit on the surface of the track, but Fangio seemed completely unaffected by it. Although Alberto Ascari's Ferrari led briefly in the early stages of the race, Fangio eventually surged through to take the lead and then dominated proceedings so convincingly that, late in the race, he was able to make a three-minute pit stop for fuel and a drink.

The heat was almost too much for me, although I was in trouble with a vapour lock, which eventually caused my car's engine to cut out. I managed to persuade the first-aid staff that I did not need an ambulance and walked back to the pits, whereupon Neubauer called in Herrmann and I took over his car to finish fourth.

Immediately after the race, when I was wiping my face with a rather dirty rag, someone offered me a very fine cotton handkerchief. I looked up to say 'thank you' and was staggered to see that it was none other than Juan Peron, the President of Argentina.

RIGHT *Pulling on my gloves in preparation for practice at the Buenos Aires autodrome.* (Klemantaski Collection)

BELOW *Rolling to a halt with vapour lock during my debut drive for Mercedes in the Argentine Grand Prix.* (Daimler Archives)

Mercedes-Benz W196

30 January 1955, Buenos Aires (ARG)

Category Formule Libre **Race distance** 30 laps of 2.92-mile circuit **Race time** 1h 12m 1.2s **Fastest lap** 2m 19.5s, 75.49mph (shared with Giuseppe Farina) **Car no** 6 **Entrant** Works

We stayed in Argentina for another fortnight to compete in the non-championship Buenos Aires City Grand Prix, which, being a *Formule Libre* event, enabled Mercedes to equip the W196s with the 3-litre engines that were being developed for the new 300SLR sports car.

This race was held over two heats on a slightly twistier variation of the Autódromo 17 October within the Parc Almirante Brown complex. The first heat settled down to a battle between Giuseppe Farina's Ferrari and the Mercedes of Fangio, Kling and me, but our special hard-compound Continental tyres – which were intended to be better in the terrific heat – provided extremely poor grip and this allowed Farina, on Pirellis, to ease away to a commanding victory, followed home by Fangio and me.

BELOW *The quartet of Mercedes W196s are pushed up to the starting grid in preparation for the start of the Buenos Aires City Grand Prix.* (Daimler Archives)

Mercedes-Benz W196

30 January 1955, Buenos Aires (ARG)

Category Formule Libre **Race distance** 30 laps of 2.92-mile circuit **Race time** 1h 11m 29.6s **Car no** 6 **Entrant** Works

After some attention was given to a slight brake-locking problem on my car, the Mercedes team had an easier time in the second heat.

At the start, Farina spun his Ferrari and came into the pits immediately to hand it

to José Froilán González. That left me second behind Fangio, but Maurice Trintignant was pushing me hard in his Ferrari and so I decided to take my chance and nip past Juan to take the lead. That is how we finished, with me taking second place on aggregate and Fangio winning thanks to his second places in both heats. It was certainly very satisfactory to have earned our first one-two finish so early in the season.

The standing team orders were that once a Mercedes, any Mercedes, held a lead of 30 seconds over the rest of the field, a sign reading REG – meaning 'regular' – would be hung out to indicate that we should hold our places.

ABOVE *I was quite happy with a strong sixth place in the 12-hour race at Sebring, sharing this Austin-Healey 100S with Lance Macklin.* (Ozzie Lyons, Pete Lyons Collection)

296   6th

Sebring
12 Hours

Austin-Healey 100S

13 March 1955, Sebring, Florida (USA)

World Sports Car Championship, round 2

Race distance 12 hours of 5.2-mile circuit (915.2 miles, 176 laps)
Co-driver Lance Macklin   **Car no** 44   **Entrant** Works

This was my second outing at Sebring, following my win in the little OSCA that I shared with Bill Lloyd 12 months earlier. My pal Lance Macklin had finished third in that event, sharing his Austin-Healey 100S with George Huntoon, and this year he invited me to join him in the car. It was prepared to a new, uprated 100S specification and Lance drove it down to Florida from New York. In practice, Lance and I were the quickest of the seven such cars fielded in this race.

I was proud of my Le Mans-style start at this event, moving up to second across the timing line from 33rd place in the row. We were class winners, and in the overall placings we were sixth behind a Jaguar D-type, two Ferraris and two Maseratis.

297   Retired

Goodwood, Sports Car Race

Beart-Rodger-Climax

11 April 1955, Goodwood, West Sussex (GB)

Race distance 5 laps of 2.4-mile circuit **Reason for retirement**
Broken throttle linkage after 2 laps **Car no** 54 **Entrant** F. Beart

There is little to say about this outing. I was lying sixth and leading my class after only two laps when the throttle linkage broke. The car was completely new and unpainted, having been completed at 6am that day. It was very disappointing indeed for the willing people who had put in so much effort.

298   3rd

Goodwood, Chichester Cup

Maserati 250F

11 April 1955, Goodwood, West Sussex (GB)

Category Formule Libre **Race distance** 7 laps of 2.4-mile circuit
Race time 11m 20s **Car no** 7 **Entrant** Stirling Moss Ltd

This was a good warm-up event to keep my hand in for the start of the European season. Peter Collins, in the 4.5-litre Ferrari, romped away with the race as we all expected him to, leaving me to battle for second place with Roy Salvadori in the Gilby Engineering 250F. Eventually I had to give best to Roy and settle for third place as the car was suffering from bad oversteer, although I was quicker in a straight line.

Following a test session at Silverstone to experiment with fuel injection and disc brakes, we did further work on these areas at Goodwood and I think the unwelcome amount of oversteer there may well have resulted from the abrupt arrival of the extra power when I got on the throttle coming out of the corners.

299   Retired

Goodwood, Glover Trophy

Maserati 250F

11 April 1955, Goodwood, West Sussex (GB)

Category Formule Libre **Race distance** 21 laps of 2.4-mile circuit **Reason for retirement** Fuel injection after 12 laps **Car no** 7 **Entrant** Stirling Moss Ltd

This was an extremely frustrating race. The SU fuel injection system we had fitted to my 250F relied entirely on atmospheric pressure, with metal diaphragms controlling the supply of fuel. One of the diaphragms developed a leak, so the mixture became progressively weaker and the engine eventually died completely, due to lack of fuel. So that was me finished.

300   4th

Bordeaux Grand Prix

Maserati 250F

24 April 1955, Bordeaux (F)

Race distance 123 laps of 1.52-mile circuit
Race time 2h 34m 36.9s (122 laps) **Fastest lap** 1m 20.9s, 67.67mph **Car no** 10 **Entrant** Stirling Moss Ltd

Immediately after Goodwood, I had to go to Italy to join Mercedes for Mille Miglia preparations, but Neubauer had agreed that I could fly back to Bordeaux to drive the Maserati in this non-championship race. I went really well and was harrying Jean Behra for the lead when the Moss jinx struck again – would you believe? – and one of the fuel tank retaining straps broke. I immediately pitted but it took over four minutes for Alf Francis to complete makeshift repairs so I could rejoin the race. I set a new lap record, trying to make up ground, but fourth place was still a bit of a disappointment.

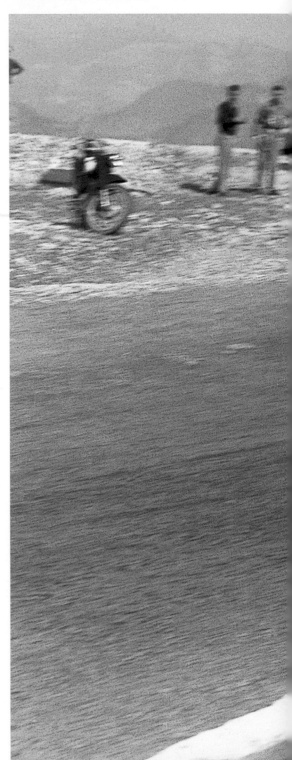

BELOW *At speed in the amazing Mercedes 300SLR which I drove to that win on the Mille Miglia with Denis Jenkinson at the average speed of 97.95mph.* (Klemantaski Collection)

301   1st

Mille Miglia

Mercedes-Benz 300SLR

1 May 1955, Brescia (I)

World Sports Car Championship, round 3

Race distance 1 lap of 992-mile circuit **Race time** 10h 7m 48s, 97.95 mph (record) **Co-driver** Denis Jenkinson **Car no** 722 **Entrant** Works

The Mille Miglia was the one race I felt genuinely scared of. I suppose that seems strange, bearing in mind that I raced at places such as the old Nürburgring and Pescara at a time when you could really cause yourself a lot of physical damage if you crashed badly, but I did not bat an eyelid at those two circuits. The Mille Miglia was different. I had driven in it with Jaguar on two previous occasions, each of which ended in disappointment. But I was determined that my outing in the Mercedes 300SLR – effectively a two-seater version of the W196 Grand Prix car but with a 3-litre engine – would be different.

ABOVE *The winning Mercedes 300SLR on the Mille Miglia starting ramp at Brescia.* (Daimler Archives)

I had been toying with the idea of taking a proper navigator, as opposed to a riding mechanic, and after I discovered that Denis Jenkinson – 'Jenks' – had been discussing the same subject with my Mercedes sports car team-mate, John Fitch, I really began to think through the whole project in more detail. John very kindly said he did not mind if 'Jenks' teamed up with me.

I had known 'Jenks', on and off, since I first started racing on the Continent because he was a leading member of the motorcycle racing fraternity, having partnered Eric Oliver 'in the chair' when they won the 1949 sidecar World Championship. He later became the respected Continental Correspondent of *Motor Sport* magazine but, of more importance as far as our planned outing in the Mille Miglia was concerned, 'Jenks' was someone who understood speed.

Central to our personal preparations was the roller map – affectionately known by some

of my more irreverent friends as 'the bog-roll holder' – on which 'Jenks' comprehensively logged every significant detail of the 1,000-mile run around Italy. The story of our preparations has been well told, including how we bounced off an army lorry on one occasion while practising in a 300SL road car, after which we received a personal apology from the local chief of police, who told us that these sorts of incidents were always happening and that he was fed up with the standards of driving in the military.

We also perfected a system of hand signals with which to communicate. Not only was it impossible to shout to each other above the noise of the Mercedes straight-eight when it was revving at 7,400rpm in fifth gear (about 180mph), but we also established that using an intercom system was a lost cause because we were concentrating so hard on our respective jobs that we had no spare brain capacity to deal with another task. Meanwhile, Mercedes had sited services depots for the cars in Ravenna, Pescara, Rome, Florence and Bologna.

The starting order from Brescia was determined by ballot *and engine size*. We drew 7.22am and so a red '722' was painted on the Mercedes SLR's bulbous silver bonnet. Unlike

the previous Mille Miglias I had contested, the weather was fine and, with 30 seconds to go before the start, I fired up the engine to the accompaniment of a fierce rasp from the side-exit exhausts and drove the car gently on to the starting ramp.

Initially we cruised at around 160–170mph down towards Verona, but nevertheless we were overtaken by Eugenio Castellotti's big 4.4-litre Ferrari quite early on in the proceedings. I was driving hard, but still leaving a bit of a margin and not going too close to the edge of the road at any point. Entering Padua, I made a slight slip when I locked up under braking and slid wide, nudging the 300SLR's nose into a straw bale, but the car bounced off without any obvious damage.

For many miles I kept Castellotti in sight, although I was wondering just how much punishment the Ferrari would be able to take, as it was being hurled from kerb to kerb with blue smoke pouring from its inside rear tyre under harsh acceleration. Through the Ravenna control we went, noticing with little surprise that Castellotti's Ferrari was stationary having its wheels changed, then it was flat out towards Pescara with the shimmering blue Adriatic on our left. At one point 'Jenks' signalled the approach of a blind brow that the 300SLR could easily take without my lifting from the throttle. But we were going quite a bit faster than we had been during practice and the car took off like an aeroplane. We could not have been airborne for more than a couple of seconds, but at the time it seemed like an eternity.

Going into Pescara, I brushed some straw bales, nearly pitching us across the road and into the pumps on a filling station forecourt, but I just held control and within another couple of minutes we were through the time control and slowing to enter the Mercedes pit area. The car was refuelled, the tyres checked, we were handed a slice of orange and a peeled banana, and then it was off over the mountain leg to Rome. Only a single 15-litre churn of fuel was used to ensure that we would not suffer fuel surge in the mountains. I have to confess that, coming out of Pescara, I made another slip and slid through another line of straw bales, thankfully emerging unscathed on the pavement behind, whereupon I selected first gear and immediately shot off again.

By the time we reached Rome I was absolutely bursting for a comfort break. Once they had stamped our route card at the control, I accelerated the short distance to the Mercedes service area, where I braked to a standstill and hopped out of the car to relieve myself. Meanwhile 'Jenks' was handed a piece of paper on which was written 'Moss, Taruffi, Herrmann, Kling, Fangio'. We were in the lead, a hugely satisfying achievement, although there was a nagging worry in the back of my mind because there was an old legend that 'he who leads at Rome is never first home'.

After just 64 seconds we were roaring out of Rome, with a new set of tyres, a full tank of fuel, a clean screen and the oil checked, heading for the hills once again. As we climbed the Radicofani pass, however, one of the 300SLR's front brakes began to grab and I spun to a halt while entering a sharp left-hander. The car stopped with its tail lodged in a shallow ditch. Fortunately, I could select first gear and, with a bit of jiggling backwards and forwards, was able to extricate the car and continue the race.

We were still in the lead when we had the card stamped at Florence, so now I got my head down, determined to cover the next leg

over the Raticosa and Futa passes in just an hour. Unbeknown to us, and concealed by a crowd of people, Fangio's 300SLR had limped into the Florence control to have an injector pipe repaired. Kling had already crashed and, later, we saw Herrmann's car parked on the side of the road, so we were, in effect, Mercedes' last hope. We arrived at Bologna firmly in the lead and with the 300SLR still running perfectly, so now all that was left was the sprint back up the Po valley, through Cremona, and on to Brescia. Looking back, the one thing I find hardest to believe is that we averaged 165.5mph from Cremona to Brescia, just over 83 miles, and that included stopping at the time control.

For the last few miles into Brescia, 'Jenks' put away the route map after signalling the last marker point on the route and we tore past the line to finish first in this epic motor race. After a slightly nerve-racking wait to hear how Taruffi had done, the news was finally confirmed to us that we had won. Remarkably, the car's bonnet had never been opened from start to finish, except to check the oil, and we ran from Rome back to Brescia on only 42 gallons of fuel while averaging 100mph.

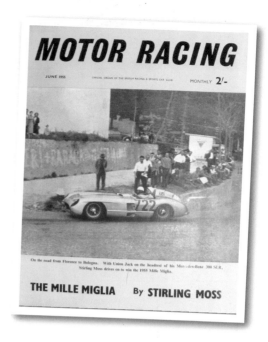

ABOVE *My story of the race appeared in* Motor Racing *magazine.* (Stirling Moss Collection)

BELOW *Celebrating victory with 'Jenks'. On his right is chief engineer Rudi Uhlenhaut and on my left Mercedes director Dr Fritz Nallinger.* (Daimler Archives)

302　Retired

Silverstone, BRDC International Trophy

Maserati 250F

7 May 1955, Silverstone (GB)

Race distance 60 laps of 2.92-mile circuit **Reason for retirement** Engine after 10 laps **Car no** 7 **Entrant** Stirling Moss Ltd

This was another disappointing outing back behind the wheel of my own Maserati. After only 10 laps of this prestigious event at Silverstone, the engine seized solid and I abandoned the car out on the circuit.

When Alf stripped down the engine later, it became clear that a cylinder liner had dropped by a fraction of an inch when the car had overheated on the first day of practice. From then on the water system kept pressurising and the engine ran hotter and hotter. We just had not been able to pinpoint the problem at the circuit.

303　Last

Silverstone, Sports Car Race

Beart-Rodger-Climax

7 May 1955, Silverstone (GB)

Race distance 40 laps of 2.92-mile circuit **Car no** 37 **Entrant** F. Beart

This was the second of my two outings in the Beart-Climax and not much improvement on the previous race in the Maserati. Everything seemed to go wrong. The ignition played up and the catch on the driver's door broke, allowing the door itself to drop down and dangle at the side of the car as I limped home in last place.

BELOW *Variety is the spice of life. Struggling through a difficult race at Silverstone with the Beart-Rodger-Climax sports car.* (LAT)

304　9th

Monaco Grand Prix

Mercedes-Benz W196

22 May 1955, Monte Carlo (MON)

F1 World Championship, round 2

Race distance 100 laps of 1.95-mile circuit **Reason for retirement** Engine (but classified 9th) **Car no** 6 **Entrant** Works

This was the first European round of the Formula 1 World Championship, but it was not a success. Fangio and I were driving a couple of short-wheelbase versions of the W196 and I qualified on the outside of the front row. We built up a commanding lead until, at half distance, Fangio suffered an engine failure and I inherited the lead. Then, with only 18 laps to the finish, my car also suffered an engine breakage and I was out as well. I pushed the car over the line to be classified in ninth place.

On closer examination it emerged that an adjusting screw in the valve gear had broken and punched a hole in the cam box, allowing oil to spew out over the exhausts. All in all, it had been quite a race, what with Alberto Ascari skidding into the harbour in his Lancia D50. He emerged unscathed, only to be killed at Monza a few days later testing a Ferrari sports car. The race itself was won by Maurice Trintignant in a Ferrari 625. You could say that he avoided problems and just plodded along to win after the quicker cars packed up.

My own Maserati was due to be driven in this race by my old friend Lance Macklin but he was unable to qualify, just missing the cut for the 20th and last place on the grid.

I pointed out to Rudi Uhlenhaut, the chief

ABOVE *Rounding the old Gasworks hairpin at Monaco in the Mercedes W196. I was leading only to suffer an engine failure on the 82nd lap.* (Klemantaski Collection)

engineer, that my 250F was the only car at Monaco fitted with disc brakes and he accepted my invitation to drive a few laps in it. He did so and acquitted himself very respectably indeed. Driving for Mercedes certainly gave me a great sense of assurance and security in the knowledge that an engineer of his calibre and versatility was responsible for the cars' technical development.

307 Withdrawn

Le Mans 24 Hours

Mercedes-Benz 300SLR

11/12 June 1955, Sarthe (F)

World Sports Car Championship, round 4

Race distance 24 hours of 8.38-mile circuit (2,569.6 miles, 307 laps) **Reason for withdrawal** Accident **Car no** 19 **Entrant** Works

For this race the Mercedes 300SLRs were fitted out with the fantastic hydraulically activated air brake, mounted full-width across the cars' tails. This not only assisted braking, but reduced wear on our drum brakes and helped with rear aerodynamic down-force, enhancing the grip from the rear tyres. After seeing how

305   2nd

Eifelrennen

Mercedes-Benz 300SLR

29 May 1955, Nürburgring (D)

Race distance 10 laps of 14.2-mile circuit **Race time** 1h 44m 53s
Fastest lap 10m 10.8s, 83.516mph **Car no** 3 **Entrant** Works

ABOVE *The Eifelrennen turned into a promotional event for Mercedes on their home turf, the 300SLRs finishing first, second and third.* (Daimler Archives)

This was a relatively minor sports car race at the Nürburgring that also served, in part, as a shake-down for the upcoming Le Mans 24 Hours. I finished second between Fangio and Kling, much to the delight of the usual capacity crowd drawn to the Eifel circuit.

306   2nd

Belgian Grand Prix

Mercedes-Benz W196

5 June 1955, Spa-Francorchamps, Liège (B)

F1 World Championship, round 4

Race distance 36 laps of 8.77-mile circuit
Race time 2h 39m 37.1s **Car no** 14 **Entrant** Works

In practice I tried a short-wheelbase W196, to the Argentina specification, and Fangio had a go in a longer, 'medium-wheelbase' version with outboard front brakes, but he eventually decided to race one of the inboard-braked long-wheelbase versions.

I qualified third fastest for a place on the front row, behind my team leader, pole position going to the Lancia D50 of Eugenio Castellotti. I think we were all rather surprised by Castellotti's sheer speed in the first practice session, although Fangio and I were pretty confident that we could have bettered the Lancia's time, but the bad weather on the second day of practice meant that we had to settle for second and third places.

At the start, Fangio and I got the jump on Castellotti and quickly began to pull away from the pursuing pack. Fangio eventually opened a lead of about 13 seconds over me, although I pulled that back slightly in the closing stages. Johnny Claes drove my Maserati on this occasion but suffered an engine failure in practice and did not start.

effective the air brake was in slowing the car at the end of the Mulsanne straight, I must say that I found myself wishing, in retrospect, that I had had it for the Mille Miglia.

There were some changes to the Mercedes driver line-up for Le Mans. While I was paired with Fangio, Karl Kling drove with André Simon, a pleasant chap but something of a journeyman. The other pairing was John Fitch and the 49-year-old Pierre Levegh, who had almost won the race single-handed in 1953, driving an elderly Talbot.

The race was billed as a major duel between Jaguar and Mercedes and, from the very start, Fangio was locked in a battle for the lead with Mike Hawthorn's D-type. Such was their ferocious pace that just after 6pm on the Saturday evening they were coming up to lap Kling and Levegh in the other two 300SLRs.

At precisely 6.20pm, as they came up to complete their 35th lap, Hawthorn's intention was to go into the pits. Still out on the circuit and obviously not wanting to lose any time if he could avoid it, he drove past Lance Macklin's Austin-Healey and then pulled across to the right in front of him. Macklin, in turn, edged across to the left to make sure he could still see the road ahead.

Tragically, Levegh was coming up fast, immediately behind Lance. He ran into the back of the Austin-Healey and was launched into the air. His 300SLR completely broke apart when it hit part of the side of an underpass. Levegh was killed outright. The engine broke loose and scythed through the crowd in the public enclosure.

It was the worst accident in the history of motorsport and more than 80 spectators were killed. This was obviously an extremely difficult situation, which called for careful and reasoned thinking. Realistically, as a driver, I was in no position to influence the situation, so I simply got on with my job, taking over from Fangio in the leading SLR and extending our lead progressively at the head of the field. However, John Fitch convinced Neubauer to call the Mercedes directors at their homes.

As a result, early on Sunday morning, the Daimler-Benz board of directors sent word that the cars should be withdrawn from the race. At that stage, Fangio and I were four laps in the lead. I disagreed with this decision and no evidence has subsequently emerged to change my viewpoint. All we did was hand Jaguar an easy victory, which some people feel to this day was not really deserved.

BELOW *The confined and narrow pit straight at Le Mans that was the scene of the sport's greatest disaster in 1955.* (LAT)

308   2nd

Dutch Grand Prix

Mercedes-Benz W196

19 June 1955, Zandvoort, Haarlem (NL)

F1 World Championship, round 5

Race distance 100 laps of 2.61-mile circuit **Race time** 2h 54m 24.1s **Race time** 89.64mph **Car no** 10 **Entrant** Works

Inevitably, after the tragedy at Le Mans, there were weeks of reflection and analysis. The French Grand Prix was cancelled and all circuit racing in Switzerland was banned, with immediate effect. The next race to be held was the Dutch Grand Prix.

Mercedes had also faced some penetrating questioning from the German media. In fact,

I understand that the Chairman of the Board, Dr Fritz Könecke, suggested to the Technical Director of the Racing Department, Professor Fritz Nallinger, that it might be wise for the team to miss the next race of the season, at Zandvoort. Nallinger, very boldly and, I thought, bravely, made it clear that he felt that this would be a mistake because some would see it as a tacit admission of liability.

As it turned out, of course, we went to Zandvoort, where we qualified first, second and third. I was in the middle of the front row between Fangio, who took pole, and Kling. I messed up my start slightly, allowing Luigi Musso's Maserati briefly to get between us as we sprinted away from the grid. I quickly got ahead of him and thereafter took up station a few lengths behind Fangio. We finished in one-two formation a lap ahead of the field. Not for nothing did the two of us become known as 'the train'.

309   1st

British Grand Prix

Mercedes-Benz W196

16 July 1955, Aintree, Liverpool (GB)

F1 World Championship, round 6

Race distance 90 laps of 3-mile circuit **Race time** 3h 7m 21.2s **Race speed** 86.468mph **Fastest lap** 2m 0.4s, 89.7mph (record) **Car no** 12 **Entrant** Works

For years, people have debated whether Fangio gifted me this race, but I do not think any of us, me included, will ever be quite certain. I know I qualified on pole and was driving well that day but, boy, the Old Man hung on no matter how fast I drove.

Years after the race, I asked if he let me

OPPOSITE *Shadowing Fangio closely in the Dutch Grand Prix, illustrating why we were referred to as 'the train'. Neubauer was a bit cross with me on this occasion as my engine had ingested quite a lot of sand.* (LAT)

ABOVE *In the pits at Aintree prior to the start of the 1955 British Grand Prix.* (Tom March Collection)

RIGHT *Fangio keeping just ahead of me in the early stages of that memorable race in front of my home crowd at Aintree.* (Tom March Collection)

ABOVE *Celebrating with Fangio. I admired him more than any other driver I encountered.* (LAT)

RIGHT *Job done! Taking the chequered flag by less than a length from Fangio at Aintree in 1955.* (Daimler Archives)

win. "No," he said. "It was your day." He was the sort of person who would think, "A win for Stirling in his own GP would be good for him." You decide.

At the start, Fangio sprinted into the lead. On the third of the 90 laps I went through into the lead when he was having a problem passing a backmarker. I can tell you that for the rest of the race I went as fast as I damned well could. As I came round the final corner, I pulled over and waved him by, realising that there was no way he could get past unless he had a lot more power than me, which I was sure he had not.

I kept my nerve and just made it to the line first, officially winning my maiden *grande épreuve* victory by the slender margin of two-tenths of a second. It was also a race that delivered a remarkable one-two-three-four grand slam, with Kling and Taruffi following us home to complete a truly memorable day.

Further back down the grid was the Moss Maserati, again driven by Lance Macklin. After its disappointing run of results thus far that year, my father suggested that we change its colour, reasoning that, "After three blow-ups, it's about time we had some colour other than green."

He eventually settled on a rather ghastly shade of grey, but when Alf Francis arrived with it at Aintree, John Morgan, the Secretary of the British Automobile Racing Club, was so horrified that he asked Alf to repaint it in some shade of green. Not that repainting it did much good to its fortunes. Lance crossed the finishing line in eighth place, but was too far back to be officially classified after an excursion into the straw bales at Tatts corner.

310   1st

Lisbon, Civil Governor's Cup

Porsche 550 Spyder

24 June 1955, Monsanto Park, Lisbon (P)

Race distance 25 laps of 3.35-mile circuit **Race time** 1h 2m 36.3s **Race speed** 80.99mph **Fastest lap** 2m 25.84s, 83.53mph **Car no** 3 **Entrant** Works

311   2nd

Swedish Sports Car Grand Prix

Mercedes-Benz 300SLR

7 August 1955, Kristianstad (S)

Race distance 32 laps of c4-mile circuit **Race time** 1h 18m 14s **Fastest lap** 2m 24.5s (shared with Fangio) **Car no** 2 **Entrant** Works

312   3rd

Snetterton, Redex Trophy

Maserati 250F

13 August 1955, Snetterton, Norwich (GB)

Race distance 25 laps of 2.71-mile circuit **Race time** 50m 26s **Fastest lap** 1m 56s, 83.79mph **Car no** 12 **Entrant** Stirling Moss Ltd

Just as my Mercedes contract permitted me to race my Maserati 250F in events not contested by the Mercedes team, so I was free to compete in other sports cars when the 300SLRs were not racing. The week after the British Grand Prix, I tried a Porsche for the very first time, having been invited to drive a 550 in a national sports car race in Portugal. It was a well-balanced little machine and, although I got left at the start of the race with too much wheel-spin, I managed to climb through the field to win.

This was the 300SLR's first race since the Le Mans tragedy and produced a disciplined one-two finish, with me following Fangio around to team orders. We both had cars fitted with the air brake for better stability under braking.

My biggest problem arose when a stone smashed my goggles and left me with blood dripping down my face for the rest of the race. After it was over, I had to attend a local hospital, where a surgeon carefully removed splinters from my left eye.

I had a rather disappointing outing in this non-championship race, which resulted in a Vanwall one-two, with Harry Schell ahead of Ken Wharton. I do not think there was anything specifically wrong with the Maserati apart from the fact that Alf Francis and I agreed that we had fitted the wrong axle ratio. I had to fight really hard to beat off a challenge from a very well-driven Cooper-Bristol with an Australian new boy behind the wheel. His name was Jack Brabham – we would hear a lot more about him in the years to come.

313 Retired

Goodwood
9 Hours

Porsche 550

20 August 1955, Goodwood, West Sussex (GB)

Race distance 9 hours of 2.4-mile circuit (1193 miles,
309 laps) **Reason for retirement** Collision after 237 laps
Co-driver Huschke von Hanstein **Car no** 34 **Entrant** Works

When I drove the Porsche 550 in Lisbon, I formed the impression that it would be an ideal car in which to contest the Goodwood 9 Hours, another race in which Mercedes would not be competing. I arranged with Huschke von Hanstein of Porsche to share one of the cars with him, and it looked very promising from the start of the race. After seven of the nine hours, we were well on course to win our class, but shortly after I took over Tony Crook spun his Cooper-Bristol on oil spilled by another competitor and I could not avoid running into him. End of story.

RIGHT *The Connaught ALSR was a very nice little car, but perhaps a little short on power.* (LAT)

LEFT *I had a lot of fun with this Standard 10 saloon at Oulton Park, but preferred my own Morris Minor!* (LAT)

314   7th

Oulton Park, *Daily Herald* Trophy

Connaught ALSR

27 August 1955, Oulton Park, Cheshire (GB)

Race distance 80 laps of 2.76-mile circuit **Race time** 2h 44m 56.4s (78 laps) **Race speed** 78.34mph **Car no** 14 **Entrant** P. Bell

This was my second drive in Peter Bell's Connaught ALSR – a very nice car. I won my class and finished seventh overall.

315   2nd in class

Oulton Park, *Sporting Life* Trophy

Standard 10 saloon

27 August 1955, Oulton Park, Cheshire (GB)

Race distance 15 laps of 2.76-mile circuit **Race time** 14 laps in 36m 56.2s **Race speed** 62.79mph **Car no** 23

I drove a loaned Standard 10 in this minor race. I liked Standards and, for road use, I owned a Standard 8, into which Alf Francis had fitted a well-tuned 10-spec engine. It was a nice enough little car but it never really handled as well as my previous car – a Morris Minor.

316   Retired

Aintree, *Daily Telegraph* Trophy

Maserati 250F

3 September 1955, Aintree, Liverpool (GB)

Race distance 17 laps of 3-mile circuit **Reason for retirement** Engine failure 4 laps from end **Car no** 7 **Entrant** Stirling Moss Ltd

I was beginning to wonder whether my Maserati had picked up something of a jinx when I failed to finish yet another race in it, this time at Aintree, where I had earlier had so much satisfaction winning the British Grand Prix. From the start I lay second behind Reg Parnell in one of the Connaught streamliners and he held me at bay for 13 laps before my engine blew up, with just four laps to go. Roy Salvadori scored a lucky win in the Gilby Engineering 250F after the Connaught also blew its engine in the closing stages of the race.

317 Retired

Italian Grand Prix

Mercedes-Benz W196

11 September 1955, Monza (I)

F1 World Championship, round 7

Race distance 50 laps of 6.214-mile circuit
Reason for retirement Engine after 27 laps
Fastest lap 2m 46.9s, 134.029mph (record)
Car no 16 **Entrant** Works

Even before we arrived at Monza, we knew that Mercedes would be pulling out of Formula 1 at the end of the season but we understood that it would continue its sports car racing programme with the 300SLRs. Certainly, there was no sign of any reduction in the team's efforts as we prepared for the Italian Grand Prix at Monza, for which two all-new streamlined long-wheelbase W196s had been specially built.

By the end of practice, Fangio had secured pole position at the wheel of the streamliner with the latest aerodynamic bodywork. I was alongside him in a similar car, but fitted with the slightly taller 1954 bodywork. Then came Taruffi and Kling in open-wheelers.

After the start, I took up station behind Fangio and all seemed to be going to plan until lap 19, when his car kicked up a stone that smashed the aero-screen on the front of my cockpit. I came straight into the pits, where – and I should have not been surprised by this – the mechanics had a replacement to hand and fitted it in a matter of 36 seconds. I drove really hard to make up lost ground and on lap 27 was poised to move up into sixth place when a piston failed. My last Grand Prix at the wheel of a Mercedes had come to an end.

LEFT *A rare shot from the top of the banking at Monza with all four Mercedes W196s in the frame during the opening laps of the 1955 Italian Grand Prix. Fangio and I lead in the two streamliners pursued by Taruffi and Kling in a couple of open-wheelers.* (Klemantaski Collection)

BELOW *Bringing to an end a great Formula 1 partnership. Monza was my final Grand Prix at the wheel of a works Mercedes.* (LAT)

RAC Tourist Trophy

Mercedes-Benz 300SLR

17 September 1955, Dundrod, Belfast, Northern Ireland (GB)

World Sports Car Championship, round 5

Race distance 84 laps of 7.4-mile circuit **Race time** 7h 3m 11s
Race speed 88.32mph **Co-driver** John Fitch **Car no** 10
Entrant Works

This race took place on my 26th birthday and Mercedes was anxious to add to its points tally in the World Sports Car Championship. I was paired with John Fitch, Fangio was with Kling, and Wolfgang von Trips was with André Simon in the third car.

I went straight into the lead at the start, pulling away from Mike Hawthorn, who was driving extremely well in the Jaguar D-type and was locked in a battle with Fangio for second place. I was approaching the time for my first scheduled refuelling stop when an almighty flapping and banging at the rear of the car signalled that the 300SLR had burst its right-rear tyre. Even though I was doing around 130mph at the time, I did not hit anything. When I came into the pits, the ragged edges of the rear wing were cut away by the mechanics and then John resumed the chase. Now Desmond Titterington took the lead in the Hawthorn Jaguar, well ahead of Kling, and I was a long way back in third.

I knew I had to pile on the pressure and, as rain began to fall, I caught and passed Kling with relative ease to take second place. Then I settled down to nibble away at the leading D-type's advantage. At the 50-lap mark Des handed the car back to Mike, so I was only 25 seconds behind. I took the lead from Mike five laps later and gradually pulled away. It was hard work, but my third victory in the RAC Tourist Trophy at Dundrod was cemented when Mike's hard-pressed Jag blew up on the penultimate lap.

BELOW *Heading to victory in the Tourist Trophy despite rear body damage caused by a flailing tyre tread.* (LAT)

RIGHT *My mother cuts my 26th birthday cake as John Fitch and I talk to photo-journalist Bernard Cahier.* (LAT)

Oulton Park, Gold Cup

Maserati 250F

24 September 1955, Oulton Park, Cheshire (GB)

Race distance 54 laps of 2.98-mile circuit **Race time** 1h 44m 5.4s **Race speed** 85.94mph **Fastest lap** 1m 52.3s, 87.81mph (record) **Car no** 4 **Entrant** Stirling Moss Ltd

This was quite a race with which to round off my Formula 1 season. I was driving a factory Maserati because by now they could see the possibility that I might be in a position to join their works team for 1956. There was an excellent entry, including Luigi Musso in the other works Maserati, two Lancia-Ferraris, a couple of Vanwalls and a full array of the regular privateers.

I qualified second behind Mike Hawthorn's Lancia-Ferrari, but we were beaten away from the start by Eugenio Castellotti in the other Lancia-Ferrari from the outside of the front row. I took the lead mid-way round the opening lap and stayed there all the way to the finish.

320   1st

Targa Florio

Mercedes-Benz 300SLR

16 October 1955, Piccolo Madonie, Sicily (I)

World Sports Car Championship, round 6

Race distance 13 laps of 44.7-mile circuit **Race time** 9h 43m 14s **Race speed** 59.8mph **Fastest lap** 43m 7.4s, 62.25mph (record) **Co-driver** Peter Collins **Car no** 104 **Entrant** Works

The Mercedes management made a late decision to contest the Targa Florio and I was on holiday on the French Riviera when the message came that I should make my way to Sicily for this race, which could enable the team to clinch the World Sports Car Championship along with its Formula 1 title, which Fangio had won.

On my recommendation, the team had contracted Peter Collins to drive with me, and I had also put in a good word for Des Titterington, who lined up with John Fitch while Fangio and Kling again drove together. I was suffering very badly with a bout of 'flu and hardly slept the night before the race. However, I did manage to build up a minute's lead on the opening lap of this 44.7-mile circuit and extended that to over five minutes after three laps.

Unfortunately, just as I had done on the Mille Miglia, I had a moment when I lost control, possibly on stones or gravel, and shot off the road, landing upright and with the wheels still all pointing in the right direction but about 12 feet below the road. With the help of some willing locals who managed to manhandle the car back on to the road, the 300SLR, amazingly, was still game for the challenge. I had lost about 12 minutes with this unscheduled detour and was now back in fourth place.

Back at the pits, the team had given me up for lost, but Peter was ready and waiting to take over when I arrived in the battered car. He managed to graze a wall during his three-lap stint, but he was leading when he brought it back in for me to take over for the final five-lap run to the finish – and another remarkable victory.

321   6th

Nassau, Governor's Trophy

Austin-Healey 100S

9 December 1955, Windsor Field, Nassau (BA)

Race distance 30 laps of 3.5-mile circuit **Entrant** Works

This was an enjoyable diversion that was very much in the nature of a fun outing. The Austin-Healey 100S was a nice little car but powered by a very humble engine indeed. Mine was capable of pulling only 4,400rpm in top on the 'Nassau Mile', the longest straight on the Windsor Field circuit.

322   Retired

Nassau Trophy

Austin Healey 100S

9 December 1955, Windsor Field, Nassau (BA)

Race distance 60 laps of 3.5-mile circuit **Reason for retirement** Top wishbone on lap 13 **Entrant** Works

This was my second outing of the day in the Healey 100S but it came to an unwelcome and unexpected end when a top suspension wishbone broke.

OPPOSITE TOP *Pressing on hard in my tattered 300SLR on my way to victory in the Targa Florio.* (Daimler Archives)

OPPOSITE BOTTOM *Frantic pit stop as I vacate the cockpit and hand over to Peter Collins.* (Daimler Archives)

BELOW *In the Bahamas with (from left) Lance Macklin, Roy Jackson-Moore, Lady Greta Oakes, Donald Healey and Sir Sydney Oakes.* (Bahamas News Agency, Terry O'Neil Collection)

1956

TEAM LEADER AT LAST

In 1956, I switched to the Maserati factory team after also testing the Vanwall, Connaught and BRM. In a sense, you could say this represented another significant turning point in my international racing career. On the one hand, you could argue that I had come of age when I won the British Grand Prix at Aintree in the Mercedes, but then I remained officially the number two driver to Juan Manuel Fangio. At Maserati, I was contracted as the official number one driver and all the relevant contractual paperwork reflected that reality.

My contract was typed rather chaotically and amusingly, on official Officine Alfieri Maserati SpA headed paper. It read, 'Stirling Moss Ltd undertakes that Mr Stirling Moss will participate during the year 1956 in the capacity of official first driver for the Officine Alfieri Maserati or other company controlled by it. In all Formula 1 races and international sports car races in which Maserati intend to enter'. Crucially, the contract contained the explanatory phrase, 'The position of official first driver shall mean choice of cars and the right to all the usual privileges of a first driver, and that the appropriate team directions will be given in every race to ensure that these rights are observed'.

I was paid £500 per race for all rounds of the Formula 1 World Championship in which I competed, £300 for any other Formula 1 races, and 60 per cent of bonus monies. In international sports car races, for which starting money was paid, I would receive 60 per cent of that, plus all the bonus payments. For sports car races for which no starting money was paid, I would get all my travelling expenses plus 60 per cent of all prize and bonus monies.

As far as my sports car programme was concerned, I was free for Le Mans, the Tourist Trophy, Rouen, Oulton Park, Sebring and a sixth race to be agreed, so I was able to sign a contract with Aston Martin to fill in the gaps in my diary.

This was also the year that I first drove the Vanwall and I won my first race at Silverstone with it. Later in the year, I tested it again at Silverstone and Oulton Park. Undoubtedly, the car was quick and I suggested quite a few improvements.

Before the new season started, I received an invitation to take my faithful 250F out to New Zealand for the non-championship race at the Ardmore circuit, near Auckland. This involved Alf Francis loading it as deck cargo on a ship for the long journey to the other side of the world. Alf followed just before the end of November, taking a five-week voyage via the Panama Canal on the Royal Mail liner *Rangitata*. Nearer the date of the race I flew out, an experience that took the best part of three days. It was a successful trip. I won the race, then flew home, leaving Alf to sell the Maserati locally. I told him not to accept less than £3,500 but, surprisingly, there were no takers. Considering it had cost only a little over £5,000 two years earlier, that Maserati had certainly earned its keep. But, it would have been a bargain.

The car came back to Britain and I lent it, in the main, to my old friend Lance Macklin and to Mike Hawthorn, although I did have a couple of outings in it as well.

LEFT *My return to the Maserati fold was as number one driver in their works team rather than as a paying privateer. Winning the Monaco Grand Prix was certainly one of the highlights of my season.* (LAT)

323   1st

Ardmore, Sports Car Handicap

Porsche 550

7 January 1956, Ardmore, Auckland (NZ)

Race distance 15 laps of 2.1-mile circuit **Race time** 29m 49.6s
Car no 10 **Entrant** Works

---

324   1st

New Zealand Grand Prix

Maserati 250F

7 January 1956, Ardmore, Auckland (NZ)

Race distance 100 laps of 2.1-mile circuit
Race time 2h 32m 43.1s **Race speed** 78.4mph
Fastest lap 1m 28s (record) **Car no** 7 **Entrant** Stirling Moss Ltd

---

325   Retired

Argentine Grand Prix

Maserati 250F

22 January 1956, Buenos Aires (ARG)

F1 World Championship, round 1

Race distance 98 laps of 2.43-mile circuit
Reason for retirement Engine failure after 81 laps **Car no** 2
Entrant Works

My visit to Ardmore was something of a winter holiday trip and it was also the first time I had been to New Zealand. I found it to be the most beautiful country in the world, with extremely nice people as well. If I did not have to live in London, New Zealand is the place I would choose.

This was only my third drive in a Porsche at that point in my career, and I had to travel a very long way to participate! Thanks to the apparent generosity of the handicappers, I had a relatively easy run to a convincing win, even though I was the 'limit' man (ie,

the fastest). Although the Porsche's clutch was slipping and its brakes were not very convincing either, I stil managed to come home first.

This race brought me an easy win from pole position. The race pace was quite moderate and I never used more than 7,000rpm at any time. About 20 laps from the end a fuel pipe split and six laps from home I had to make a stop for another 10 gallons of fuel to be added, but I kept my lead. I rounded off a pleasant day by going to a local speedway meeting and then to the Auckland Car Club dance.

Having started the season with a gruelling trans-Pacific flight to New Zealand, I now had to deal with the complicated business of getting to Buenos Aires for the opening round of the Formula 1 World Championship and my first race as the works Maserati team leader.

I flew back across the Pacific to Los Angeles, via San Francisco, and then went up to Las Vegas on a TWA Convair with Masten Gregory. While there, we saw Frankie Laine perform at the Desert Inn. Then I flew on to New York and back to Buenos Aires via Santiago in Chile, where they ripped me off to the tune of £4 10s – about £40 in today's money – for a visa just to allow me into the country for a five-hour stop-over.

Eventually I arrived at the airport in Buenos Aires at the same time as most of the Ferrari and Maserati team members. First practice was not too successful, although I managed to post a better time than the other Maserati drivers – Carlos 'Charlie' Menditéguy, Jean Behra and José Froilán González. Juan Manuel Fangio in the Lancia-Ferrari D50 was next in the pecking order.

LEFT *I won the New Zealand Grand Prix at Ardmore in my own Maserati 250F, which we had shipped out from England by boat with Alf Francis accompanying it.*
(Bruce McLaren Trust)

Fangio eventually took pole posiiton and I started from a disappointing seventh place, on the outside of the second row. I had been forced to qualify in the spare 250F as my assigned race car suffered an engine failure while being warmed up immediately before the final practice session, but for the race my original car was ready again with its motor rebuilt, though hashed up. Although I managed to lead, I was eventually passed by Fangio and then by Behra. My car's engine had been smoking for quite a long time before it finally gave up the ghost with piston failure only 17 laps from the end of the race.

I finished an unmemorable day with a trip to hospital for an X-ray to my foot because it had been run over by my race car as we were pushing it out to the starting grid. Just how stupid could I be?

326   1st

Buenos Aires 1,000kms

Maserati 300S

29 January 1956, Buenos Aires (ARG)

World Sports Car Championship, round 1

Race distance 1,000kms of 2.43-mile circuit (106 laps)
Race time 6h 29m 37.9s **Race speed** 96.11mph (record)
Co-driver Carlos Menditéguy **Car no** 31 **Entrant** Works

Apart from the Maserati Birdcage, the Maser 300S was possibly my favourite of all the front-engined sports cars I drove during my career. After the disappointment in the Grand Prix, I was happy to pair up

with 'Charlie' Menditéguy and we won quite decisively. Fangio took over Eugenio Castellotti's Ferrari but could not catch me and, when his car broke, we were left a clear two laps in front of the Ferrari of Phil Hill and Olivier Gendebien.

327   2nd

Buenos Aires City Grand Prix

Maserati 250F

5 February 1956, Mendoza (ARG)

Race distance 60 laps of 2.6-mile circuit
Race time 1h 53m 17.5s **Car no** 2 **Entrant** Works

After the two races in Buenos Aires, we were off to the Plaza Hotel at Mendoza, in the foothills of the Andes, for the second Formula 1 race to be held in Argentina. In practice, Fangio took pole in the Lancia-Ferrari with Luigi Musso second, me third and Eugenio Castellotti fourth. In the race I came through to second place 25 seconds behind Fangio.

The following morning I was off to Santiago, where I caught a DC-7B to Lima, then I flew on through Miami to New York, where I switched to a TWA Constellation for the flight on to London, via Gander in Newfoundland. Mum met me at Heathrow airport.

LEFT *With Fangio after the race, and José Froilán González jokingly signalling to me that I should slow down during the 1956 Buenos Aires 1,000kms sports car race.* (Stirling Moss Collection)

MOSS DEFEATS FANGIO AFTER 20-LAP DUEL

During his off-duty spell, González signals piano! piano! to Moss, now well in the lead

Sebring 12 Hours

Aston Martin DB3S

24 March 1956, Sebring, Florida (USA)

World Sports Car Championship, round 2

Race distance 12 hours of 5.2-mile circuit (1008.8 miles, 194 laps) **Reason for retirement** Engine **Co-driver** Peter Collins **Car no** 26 **Entrant** Works

BELOW *I used Roy Salvadori's Aston Martin DB3S, an elegant-looking car, to win the sports car race at Goodwood at Easter.* (LAT)

I had tested a works Aston Martin DB3S at Goodwood in February on my return from Argentina and it was then that I agreed to drive for David Brown's team when my commitments to Maserati allowed me to do so. I accepted a signing-on fee of £50, which you would have to say was very modest indeed, even by the standards of the time.

Sebring was the first of the six races that season in which I would drive the DB3S and, given that there was a seven-week break between the Mendoza Formula 1 race and the sports car race on the bumpy aerodrome in Florida, I took the opportunity of stopping off in Nassau in the Bahamas on my way to the USA for some swimming, water-skiing and general relaxation.

For the Sebring race I was partnered with Peter Collins but, while Mike Hawthorn managed a best practice lap of 3m 28s in his Jaguar D-type and Fangio set 3m 33s in his Ferrari, I was disappointed to record only 3m 34.1s. Given that we had calculated that the brakes would last no more than eight hours, and the tyres no more than two, obviously I did not start the race exactly bursting with confidence.

At the Le Mans-style start, I made a good getaway and managed to hold second place between Hawthorn and Fangio, running three seconds a lap faster than I had managed in practice. About 90 minutes after Pete took over from me, however, the engine broke.

329   1st

Goodwood, Sports Car Race

Aston Martin DB3S

2 April 1956, Goodwood, West Sussex (GB)

Race distance 15 laps of 2.4-mile circuit
Race speed 89.18mph **Fastest lap** 1m 35s, 90.95mph
Car no 59 **Entrant** Works

330   1st

Goodwood, Glover Trophy

Maserati 250F

2 April 1956, Goodwood, West Sussex (GB)

Race distance 32 laps of 2.4-mile circuit **Race time**
48m 50.4s **Race speed** 94.35mph **Fastest lap** 1m 30.2s,
95.79mph (record) **Car no** 1 **Entrant** Works

ABOVE *Giving Archie Scott-Brown a lift home after I had won the Glover Trophy in my works 250F.* (LAT)

I used Roy Salvadori's Aston Martin DB3S to win this short race quite easily. It was a bad day, with Tony Dennis killed when he crashed his D-type and A.P.O. Rogers killed in the Sun-Pat Special. I drove back to London immediately after dinner.

I practised my own Maserati to start with, but then switched to the factory car, in which I was 0.9 seconds quicker. Mike Hawthorn led off the line in the BRM, but I was soon up into second place, behind Archie Scott-Brown's Connaught, which stayed ahead for quite a few laps. Archie was driving very well but I eventually passed him and, a lap later, his Connaught seized up. I won easily, with the Connaughts of Roy Salvadori and Les Leston the only other cars on the same lap as me at the finish.

336   2nd

Silverstone, Sports Car Race

Aston Martin DB3S

5 May 1956, Silverstone, Northamptonshire (GB)

Race distance 25 laps of 2.9-mile circuit **Race time** 46m 47s
Car no 21 **Entrant** Works

Practice for this race started with a rather ticklish problem. Roy Salvadori's Aston Martin DB3S proved to be a couple of seconds a lap faster than my car. When I asked if I could exercise my privilege of being number one driver and try his car, I was told, rather sheepishly, that it was not actually a works car at all and that Roy in fact owned it. I must say I thought it was a bit daft for a works team to be selling its best car, but these things did happen.

In the race I made a fabulous start but moved over and waved Roy's quicker car past on the approach to Stowe, where we made slight contact. Mike Hawthorn and Des Titterington also went by in their Jaguars, but Roy later drove Des off the road and Mike retired with seized steering. I finished second behind Roy. Quite a race!

337   1st

Silverstone, BRDC International Trophy

Vanwall

5 May 1956, Silverstone, Northamptonshire (GB)

Organising club British Racing Drivers' Club
Race distance 60 laps of 2.9-mile circuit **Race time** 1h 44m 53s
Race speed 100.47mph **Fastest lap** 1m 43s, 102.3mph (shared with M. Hawthorn) **Car no** 3 **Entrant** Works

I suppose it was always in the back of my mind that I would like to be asked to drive the Vanwall. Not because it had yet been developed into a car capable of winning consistently but because you just knew that Tony Vandervell was serious about his motor racing and would not rest until he was successful.

In November 1955, when I was still trying to decide what to do for the following Formula 1 season, Vanwall, Connaught and BRM had each provided me with a car to test at Silverstone. All had their merits but the Vanwall was the one that really impressed me. But at that time Maserati had the definite edge and I told Tony Vandervell that I would be pleased to drive for him in the future if other commitments permitted.

Over the winter, Colin Chapman and Frank Costin reworked the original Vanwall concept and I gave the revised car its first race outing in this International Trophy race. The car was not quite ready when I got to Silverstone for first practice on the Thursday but, in second practice, I qualified on pole position, ahead of my team-mate Harry Schell, Fangio's Lancia-Ferrari and Mike Hawthorn's BRM. Despite a change to softer dampers, the car was still not perfect but it was good enough to get the job done.

In the race I had a bad start but the Vanwall felt fabulous and I was able to pass Fangio any time I liked. I did 14 laps at 1m 43s, which was only a second away from my pole-winning best. About eight laps into the race I could smell oil fumes in the cockpit, so I backed off but still managed to win comfortably from the Connaughts of Archie Scott-Brown and Des Titterington. A good result, particularly because Tony Vandervell paid me £1,500 for my trouble.

338   1st

Monaco Grand Prix

Maserati 250F

13 May 1956, Monte Carlo (MON)

F1 World Championship, round 2

Race distance 100 laps of 1.95-mile circuit
Race time 3h 0m 32.9s **Race speed** 64.943mph
Car no 28 **Entrant** Works

Maserati produced a car fitted with a four-speed gearbox specially for this race and my team-mate Cesare Perdisa's car was rigged up with a right-hand throttle arrangement like mine – rather than Maser's traditional central throttle – in order to provide for the possibility of my needing to take it over during the course of the race.

Fangio was a little quicker than me in practice, but I had an excellent start and led the race all the way to finish, easily ahead of Peter Collins, Fangio and Behra. About 20 laps before the end I hit Perdisa up the rear due to his braking on the straight. Apart from that, it was a very straightforward race and was my first *grande épreuve* win for the Maserati team.

339   1st

Crystal Palace, London Trophy, Heat 1

Maserati 250F

21 May 1956, Crystal Palace, London (GB)

Category Formule Libre
Race distance 10 laps of 1.39-mile circuit **Race time** 11m 17s
Race speed 73.91mph **Fastest lap** 79.4mph **Car no** 80
Entrant Stirling Moss Ltd

This was a Whit Monday national-level race that I won easily in my own Maserati 250F, although I was asked not to push too hard so as to make a bit of a race of it with Paul Emery's Emeryson to keep the crowd entertained.

OPPOSITE *On my way to victory at Monaco. Short-sleeved cotton polo shirt to keep cool, no face mask, open-face helmet – things were so very different in the 1950s.* (Klemantaski Collection)

340   1st

Crystal Palace, London Trophy, Heat 2

Maserati 250F

21 May 1956, Crystal Palace, London (GB)

Category Formule Libre
Race distance 10 laps of 1.39-mile circuit **Race time** 11m 13.4s
Race speed 74.31mph **Fastest lap** 79.94mph **Car no** 80
Entrant Stirling Moss Ltd

A fter again dicing with Emery, I won the second heat to take overall victory on aggregate.

341   2nd

Crystal Palace, Anerley Trophy

Cooper 'Bobtail' MkII

21 May 1956, Crystal Palace, London (GB)

Race distance 10 laps of 1.39-mile circuit **Race time** 11m 15s
Car no 22 **Entrant** Stirling Moss Ltd

I n the third of my four races at Crystal Palace that day, I simply could not find a way past Les Leston's Cooper 'Bobtail' because there was just not enough room to find a gap on this very tight circuit.

342   1st

Crystal Palace, Norbury Trophy

Cooper 'Bobtail' MkII

21 May 1956, Crystal Palace, London (GB)

Race distance 10 laps of 1.39-mile circuit **Race time** 11m 2.4s
Race speed 75.55mph **Fastest lap** 1m 4.8s, 77.22mph (record)
Car no 22 **Entrant** Stirling Moss Ltd

T his was another 10-lapper to round off the day at Crystal Palace, this time with another win in my own Cooper 'Bobtail'.

343   1st

Nürburgring, ADAC 1,000kms

Maserati 300S

27 May 1956, Nürburgring (D)

World Sports Car Championship, round 4

Race distance 44 laps of 14.2-mile circuit
Race time 7h 43m 54.5s **Race speed** 80.59mph
Co-drivers Jean Behra, Harry Schell and Piero Taruffi
Car no 5 & 6 **Entrant** Works

First practice for this gruelling event took place in the pouring rain, but the rest of the weekend was quite dry. I made a good start to lead in the Maserati 300S for the first six laps, after which I handed over to my co-driver Jean Behra, who kept the lead by almost a minute.

OPPOSITE *Taking the chequered flag to win the Nürburgring 1,000kms race in the Maserati 300S that I shared with Jean Behra and took over from Harry Schell and Piero Taruffi after our original machine hit trouble.* (LAT)

Unfortunately a rear spring broke, so the Maserati team manager, Nello Ugolini, transferred us to the sister car, which had been driven up to that point by Harry Schell and Piero Taruffi. Behra gave the car back to me for the final 12-lap stint just under one and a half minutes behind Fangio's Ferrari, but I managed to pull out all the stops and caught up to 35 seconds adrift with six laps to go. Then Fangio made a 25-second final refuelling stop and I went through into the lead, which I held all the way to the chequered flag.

344   3rd

Belgian Grand Prix

Maserati 250F

3 June 1956, Spa-Francorchamps, Liège (B)

F1 World Championship, round 4

Race distance 36 laps of 8.77-mile circuit
Race time 2h 43m 16.9s **Fastest lap** 4m 14.7s, 124.015mph
Co-driver Cesare Perdisa **Car no** 30 & 34 **Entrant** Works

ABOVE *I had a busy Belgian Grand Prix at Spa-Francorchamps. After my 250F stopped out on the circuit having lost a rear wheel, I ran back to the pits to take over Cesare Perdisa's similar car and managed to finish third.* (LAT)

On the Thursday before this race, I caught a plane from Heathrow to Brussels, then spent four hours at the airport waiting to pick up journalist Alan Brinton for the road journey to Spa. The works 250Fs had a new, more aerodynamic nose section, with top ducting for the hot air from the radiators. I tried both the fuel-injected and carburated engine set-ups and decided to race with the Weber carburettors because, although there was not much to choose between their performance, the injected set-up used more fuel.

I qualified in the middle of the front row between the Lancia-Ferraris of Fangio and Pete Collins. Although I made a good start and held the lead for a few laps, Fangio's Lancia-Ferrari was quicker and there was no way I could hold him off for long. I was running an easy second when my car's left-rear hub shaft snapped, shedding the wheel, hub and brake drum, leaving me at the wheel of a Formula 1 tricycle.

I managed to gather everything up and skid to a halt without hitting anything, then sprinted back to the pits, where I took over Cesare Perdisa's car to finish third. Fangio eventually retired with engine trouble, leaving Pete to finish first ahead of his team-mate for the weekend, Paul Frère, the respected Belgian journalist and semi-professional racer.

345 2nd

Monza, Supercortemaggiore Grand Prix

Maserati 300S

24 June 1956, Monza (I)

Race distance 100 laps of 6.21-mile circuit (1,000kms) **Race time** 5h 7m 40.7s **Co-driver** Cesare Perdisa **Entrant** Works

In the three-week break following the Belgian Grand Prix, I did a couple of days' intensive testing at Monza with the Maserati team before returning to the track for this important Italian national sports car event. I made a fair start in the 300S, but on the second lap the propshaft broke. I later took over Perdisa's car – yet again! – and was only 17 seconds behind the winner at the finish.

346 Retired

Reims 12 hours

Cooper 'Bobtail' MkII

1 July 1956, Reims (F)

Race distance 12 hours of 4.99-mile circuit (1,227.12 miles, 246 laps) **Reason for retirement** Overheating **Fastest lap** 2m 45.5s **Co-driver** Phil Hill **Car no** 8 **Entrant** Stirling Moss Ltd

Up to this point in the season, the 'Bobtail' had hardly been an unqualified success and, when I discussed with Alf Francis what we should do with it, all he could suggest was "sell it". While I was away at my next event, Alf got Jack Brabham to test it at Brands Hatch and they discovered that the chassis had been somehow misaligned in the building jig, upsetting the handling as the front leaf spring bottomed out against the damper brackets.

Once that was sorted out, I entered it at Reims with Phil Hill as my co-driver. I led for the first half hour, but the engine began to run rough, then to overheat. Shortly after I handed it over to Phil, he had to retire the car.

347 5th

French Grand Prix

Maserati 250F

1 July 1956, Reims (F)

F1 World Championship, round 5

Race distance 61 laps of 5.16-mile circuit **Race time** 2h 35m 1.5s (59 laps) **Car no** 2 & 6 **Entrant** Works

I knew from my experience with the 250F at Spa-Francorchamps that I was just not fast enough on the straights, so for Reims the team produced a streamlined version of the car with all-enveloping bodywork. Unfortunately, this was not the answer at all. It seemed to me that Jean Behra had the best car that weekend, qualifying ahead of me in the middle of the third row. I was two seconds slower than him and six seconds slower than Fangio, who was on pole.

I made a good start but the car was just hopeless. Eventually my gear lever snapped off at the base, so poor old Perdisa was flagged in yet again to give up his car. When I climbed aboard I found that the cockpit was awash with oil. I finished in fifth place, which was pretty lucky under the circumstances.

RIGHT *Smiling at the trackside photographer in the French Grand Prix at Reims. The 250F was simply hopeless on this occasion and I could only battle home fifth.* (LAT)

348   2nd

Rouen, Sports Car Race

Aston Martin DB3S

8 July 1956, Rouen-les-Essarts (F)

Race distance 50 laps of 4.07-mile circuit **Race time** 2h 10m 35s **Car no** 14 **Entrant** Works

This sports car race, which supported the Rouen Grand Prix, was one where I was specifically not contracted to drive for Maserati, even though the works team was competing, so on this occasion I was racing against them, for Aston Martin. But the DB3S was really not very good that day, juddering and oversteering alarmingly in the fast corners. I shared the second row with Pete Collins, in the other Aston, and, although I had a good start, the car felt bad from the word 'go' and I ran fourth for a while. Later in the race, Jean Behra's Maserati broke a suspension damper and Cesare Perdisa's sister car suffered clutch failure, leaving me to have a big dice with Eugenio Castellotti's Ferrari – I was only 3.9 seconds behind at the end.

349   Retired

British Grand Prix

Maserati 250F

14 July 1956, Silverstone (GB)

F1 World Championship, round 6

Race distance 101 laps of 2.93-mile circuit
Reason for retirement Rear axle after 94 laps
Fastest lap 1m 43.2s, 102.104mph **Car no** 7 **Entrant** Works

After two disappointing races at Spa and Reims, Maserati decided to shelve its experiments with fuel injection and concentrate on making the carburettor set-up work as efficiently as possible. This time everything went well. I started from pole position ahead of Fangio's Lancia-Ferrari, Mike Hawthorn's BRM and Pete Collins' Lancia-Ferrari.

The speed of the BRMs off the line was remarkable. Mike sprinted straight into the lead, with Tony Brooks catapulting through into an immediate second place before the field even got to Copse corner. With only 10 laps completed, Mike was eight seconds ahead of Tony and me, and we were running nose to tail as we battled for second place.

By lap 16 I was through into the lead, opening a 4-second advantage over Mike by lap 20, but he retired soon afterwards and Roy Salvadori moved up to second place in his Gilby Engineering 250F. After 68 laps I had to relinquish the lead when I made the first of three pit stops for fuel, due to a split tank. Finally, when I was running second to Fangio's Lancia-Ferrari, I had to retire when the back axle broke.

350   1st

British Grand Prix, Sports Car Race

Maserati 300S

14 July 1956, Silverstone (GB)

Race distance 25 laps of 2.93-mile circuit **Race time** 46m 44s
Race speed 93.94mph **Fastest lap** 1m 49s, 96.67mph
Car no 27 **Entrant** Works

Tony Brooks did not compete in the Aston Martin DB3S because he had been thrown from his BRM in a fiery crash during the Grand Prix earlier in the day, so all I had to do in this race was beat Roy Salvadori. The Maserati 300S went really well. I qualified on pole, set the fastest race lap and led from start to finish, a result that went a little way towards making up for my disappointment in the day's main race.

LEFT *In the crowded Silverstone pit lane during a disappointing British Grand Prix weekend. That's John Bolster in the background wearing his trademark deerstalker and talking into his radio microphone.* (LAT)

351   1st

Bari,
Sports Car Race

Maserati 300S

22 July 1956, Lungomare della Fiera (I)

Race distance 36 laps of 3.41-mile circuit
Race time 1h 30m 52.4s **Race speed** 81.82mph
Fastest lap 2m 28.9s **Car no** 42 **Entrant** Works

I flew out to Rome from Heathrow on BEA, then on to Bari for another Italian national race in the Maserati 300S. Ferrari did not compete because it was putting all its efforts into preparing for Le Mans, so this event was something of a Maserati demonstration run. I won easily from Behra, Perdisa and Taruffi.

352   2nd

Le Mans
24 Hours

Aston Martin DB3S

28/29 July 1956, Sarthe (F)

Race distance 24 hours of 8.38-mile circuit (2,497 miles, 299 laps) **Race speed** 104.04mph **Co-driver** Peter Collins
Car no 8 **Entrant** Works

From the outset I felt Pete Collins and I were going to have our hands full when it came to fighting the Jaguar D-types at Le Mans with our Aston Martin DB3S.

Light drizzle was falling as we all lined up opposite our cars for the traditional start, and I quickly sprinted across to lead the pack away up to the first right-hander under the Dunlop bridge. The Jaguar's superior aerodynamics, however, gave Mike Hawthorn a decisive edge on straight-line speed and he came past me to take the lead before we got to the end of the Mulsanne straight, and on the second lap Ron Flockhart also passed me in the Ecurie Ecosse D-type.

However, it was destined to be a poor

weekend for the works Jaguars. On the second lap, the D-types of Paul Frère and Jack Fairman were eliminated in a multiple pile-up at the Esses, together with Alfonso de Portago's Ferrari. Then Mike pitted with fuel-injection problems early on, so with an hour of the race gone I was in second place, just 2 seconds behind Flockhart.

I briefly took the lead at the first round of refuelling stops, but relinquished it when I came in to hand over to Pete. As the evening drew in, the drizzle turned into heavy rain and Pete began to slice into the Ecurie Ecosse D-type's advantage, eventually going through to take the lead. A dice with the D-type continued through much of the night, but in the early morning Pete lost second gear and dropped one and a half

ABOVE *Not too many races were held on trolley-bus routes, even in the 1950s. Happily services had been suspended for long enough for me to win at Bari with the Maserati 300S!* (LAT)

OPPOSITE *Peter Collins and myself shared the Aston Martin DB3S at Le Mans, but we just could not quite get on terms with the winning Ecurie Ecosse D-type in the closing stages of the race.* (Klemantaski Collection)

laps as a result. We did everything we could to make up ground thereafter, but the deficit was too big and we finished just over a lap behind the winning Jag.

353   2nd

Nürburgring, Sports Car Race

Maserati 150S

5 August 1956, Nürburgring (D)

Race distance 7 laps of 14.16-mile circuit
Race time 1h 13m 29.8s **Fastest lap** 10m 13.3s, 83.2mph
Car no 32 **Entrant** Works

I had a bad start in this sports car race, a supporting event to the German Grand Prix, and ran fourth in the early stages. An initial misfire seemed to cure itself and I battled with Roy Salvadori's Cooper 'Bobtail' for second place behind Hans Herrmann's Porsche, getting the upper hand over Roy by 11 seconds at the finish, even though his Cooper was capable of taking 250 yards off my Maserati under braking at the end of the straight on each lap.

354   2nd

German Grand Prix

Maserati 250F

5 August 1956, Nürburgring (D)

F1 World Championship, round 7

Race distance 22 laps of 14.173-mile circuit
Race time 3h 39m 30.1s **Car no** 7 **Entrant** Works

On the Wednesday before the German Grand Prix I met my Canadian girlfriend, Katie Molson, at Le Bourget airport, near Paris, and at 3pm we set off by road to the Nürburgring in my Mercedes 220, arriving in Adenau at 9pm.

I qualified on the outside of the front row, behind the three Lancia-Ferraris, with a lap of 10m 3.4s, some 8 seconds slower than Fangio in pole position. Interestingly, after the Saturday practice session I did a lap of the 14-mile circuit in my Mercedes 220, four-up in the pouring rain, in 14m 18s, which I thought was pretty respectable.

Pete Collins took an immediate lead from the start in his Lancia-Ferrari, with Fangio second and me getting the jump on Castellotti to run third. By the time we got to Schwedenkreuz on the opening lap, Fangio and I had gone past Pete into first and second places, but by the end of the first lap the Lancia-Ferraris were first and second again, with Fangio steadily pulling away from the rest of us.

Pete challenged Fangio hard, but eventually retired with a split oil tank. He took over de Portago's car and had got back up to fourth when he spun off. I finished second, but there was no way the Maserati could live with Fangio's Lancia-Ferrari on this occasion. Juan did a lap 11 seconds faster than Hermann Lang's old Mercedes circuit record, dating from 1939, just to rub home his advantage.

355   Retired

Swedish Sports Car Grand Prix

Maserati 300S

12 August 1956, Rabelov, Kristianstad (S)

World Sports Car Championship, round 5

Race distance 153 laps of 4.04-mile circuit **Reason for retirement** Caught fire in pits, brake pipe failure **Co-drivers** Jean Behra, Harry Schell and Luigi Villoresi **Car no** 8 **Entrant** Works

For this race I flew from London to Malmo via Copenhagen, then drove to Kristianstad in a borrowed Sunbeam Rapier. I qualified the Maserati 300S on pole position for the race, with Jean Behra as my co-driver. The team also brought the first of its 4.5-litre V8-engined 450S machines but it was not raced, although Harry Schell briefly drove it in practice.

I tailed Pete Collins' Ferrari in the opening stages but took the lead when he stopped to hand over to Olivier Gendebien. Behra took over from me but at his first refuelling stop the car caught fire because the fuel tank had been over-filled. I switched to Schell's car and continued in fifth place until a brake pipe broke and I had no other option but to retire.

RIGHT *The start at the Nürburgring with three Lancia-Ferraris ahead of my Maserati on the outside of the front row. I finished second, but Fangio was in a class of his own and I simply could not match his speed on this occasion.* (Klemantaski Collection)

356 1st

Oulton Park, *Daily Herald* Trophy

Aston Martin DB3S

18 August 1956, Oulton Park, Cheshire (GB)

Race distance 40 laps of 2.76-mile circuit **Race time**
1h 26m 3.8s **Race speed** 76.99mph **Fastest lap** 2m 6.8s,
78.39mph **Car no** 8 **Entrant** Works

It was pouring with rain so hard on the morning of this race that there was quite a debate among the organisers and competitors over whether it should be cancelled. I was on pole position, heading an all-Aston front row with Tony Brooks and Roy Salvadori alongside me. I made a good start and led all the way to the finish.

357 1st

Oulton Park, *Sporting Life* Trophy

Cooper 'Bobtail' MkII

18 August 1956, Oulton Park, Cheshire (GB)

Race distance 10 laps of 2.76-mile circuit **Race time** 21m 53.2s
Race speed 75.69mph **Fastest lap** 2m 8.5s, 77.41mph
Entrant Willment

For this race, I got talked into driving the Willment team's Cooper 'Bobtail', which was usually raced by Les Leston. I qualified on the third row, but was up to second mid-way round the opening lap and then took the lead from Mike Hawthorn's Lotus Eleven coming up to the line. Thereafter, I led all the way to the finish.

Mike was lucky to get away with a shunt when he tangled with Roy Salvadori and got thrown out of his car, after which Roy withdrew from the race.

358 1st

Italian Grand Prix

Maserati 250F

2 September 1956, Monza (I)

F1 World Championship, round 8

Race distance 50 laps of 6.21-mile circuit
Race time 2h 23m 41.3s **Race speed** 129.73mph
Fastest lap 2m 45.4s, 135.5mph **Car no** 36 **Entrant** Works

Fully realising that they would have to pull something pretty dramatic out of the bag for Monza, Maserati built two new 250F chassis – for Behra and me – with offset propshafts, which enabled the driving position, and therefore the centre of gravity, to be considerably lowered, improving the handling.

Even so, the Lancia-Ferraris proved formidable in practice. Fangio again qualified on pole, almost a second faster than his team-mates, Eugenio Castellotti and Luigi Musso, who lined up beside him on the front row of the grid. I was on the outside of the second row, alongside Taruffi's Vanwall and Behra in the other Maserati. It was raining on race morning but the weather gradually cleared up in time for the start at 3pm.

I made a good start but the Lancia-Ferraris quickly asserted themselves in the first four places, although, happily for me, this turned out to be short-lived. On the fifth lap, both Castellotti and Musso paid the price for pushing too hard too soon and their rear tyres started throwing treads. That left me in the lead from Harry Schell's Vanwall and Fangio. We became locked in quite a battle and with 15 laps gone I was only 0.6 seconds ahead of Harry. Four laps later Fangio stopped his Lancia-Ferrari with damaged steering but Pete Collins generously relinquished his sister car to the World Champion. Harry retired after 28 laps, from which point I built up a one-minute lead until I ran out of fuel and had to be pushed into the pit lane by Luigi Piotti's private 250F. I resumed still in the lead and won by five seconds from Fangio.

359

Monza record attempts

Lotus Eleven

3 September 1956, Monza (I)

Records achieved 50kms, 135.54mph; 50 miles, 132.77mph

I accepted an invitation to have a go at the International Class G 1,100cc records. This had been scheduled to take place in October but was brought forward to the day after the Italian Grand Prix. The record attempt certainly looked promising but the punishing banking proved too much for the Lotus's chassis frame, which broke, but not before we had clinched the 50km record at 135.54mph and the 50-mile one at 132.77mph.

ABOVE *Being pushed by fellow 250F driver Luigi Piotti towards the pit lane after I ran short of fuel on my way to victory in the Italian Grand Prix at Monza.* (LAT)

RIGHT *I stayed at Monza after the Grand Prix to drive this streamlined Lotus Eleven in a record run.* (LAT)

360   2nd

Tour de France

Mercedes-Benz 300SL

17–23 September 1956 (F)

Result 7,405.73 points **Event distance** 3,000 miles
Car no 149 **Co-driver** Georges Huel
Entrant Stirling Moss Ltd

361   1st

Grand Prix of Caracas

Maserati 300S

4 November 1956, Caracas (VE)

Race distance 85 laps of 2.5-mile circuit **Race time**
2h 31m 49.8s **Race speed** 84.33mph **Fastest lap** 1m 39.7s,
84.53mph **Car no** 27 **Entrant** Works

This was one of two outings I had in the Tour de France in my own gullwing Mercedes 300SL, a terrific road car for a terrific event that involved a succession of rally stages, circuit races and hill climbs. For much of the event I was handicapped by a misfire, without which I think I could have beaten the eventual winners, 'Fon' de Portago and Ed Nelson in a Ferrari 250 Europa.

This was my first trip to Caracas and I flew there via New York – another really long haul in the piston-engined airliners of the time. I qualified on pole and led from the start but 'Fon' de Portago got his Ferrari ahead of me on the seventh lap. I regained the advantage eight laps later and stayed in front to the finish to win from Fangio, also in a Ferrari, and de Portago.

362   1st

Australian Tourist Trophy

Maserati 300S

25 November 1956, Albert Park (AUS)

Race distance 32 laps of 3.13-mile circuit **Race time**
1h 3m 24.2s **Race speed** 94.63mph **Fastest lap** 1m 55.8s
(record) **Car no** 7 **Entrant** Works

My first visit to Australia meant another long trans-Pacific flight, to Sydney, followed by a four-hour hop in an elderly Dakota to Melbourne. I was loaned a Humber Snipe as my personal road car for the duration of my stay in this convivial city that I would come to know and like very much over the years. My visit was made all the more

interesting by the fact that Melbourne was hosting the Olympic Games at the time.

The race, held at the Albert Park circuit, much of which is still used for today's Australian Grand Prix, proved to be uneventful. I took the lead from the start in the Maserati 300S and won by almost a lap from my team-mate Jean Behra, also in a 300S.

363   1st

Australian Grand Prix

Maserati 250F

2 December 1956, Albert Park (AUS)

Race distance 80 laps of 3.13-mile circuit
Race time 2h 36m 15.4s **Race speed** 95.9mph
Fastest lap 100.26mph (record) **Car no** 7 **Entrant** Works

There were no fewer than 28 competitors in this race, including three local drivers with private Maserati 250Fs: Reg Hunt, Jack Brabham and Stan Jones, whose son Alan would go on to win the Formula 1 World Championship in a Williams 24 years later. As far as I was concerned, this entertaining non-championship race was as rewarding for me as the previous weekend's sports car race had been. I started from pole, set the fastest race lap, led all the way and won ahead of Behra.

364   1st

Nassau Trophy

Maserati 300S

9 December 1956, Windsor Field (BA)

Race distance 60 laps of 3.5-mile circuit **Race time** 2h 10m 57s, 96.21mph **Car no** 30 **Entrant** Bill Lloyd

OPPOSITE *Chatting with Harry Schell and 'Fon' de Portago alongside my Mercedes 300SL in which I finished second to their Ferrari in the Tour de France.* (LAT)

ABOVE *This was Olympic year in a Melbourne and I won the Grand Prix quite easily ahead of Jean Behra. Here I negotiate Jaguar Corner as the marshals clear up debris from an accident involving local driver Kevin Neal.* (LAT)

This race in the Bahamas was a pleasant interlude in the sunshine to round off a busy season. I was only 18th in the Le Mans-style starting line-up, but I was soon battling for the lead in a Maserati 300S loaned from Bill Lloyd, the works cars having been sold to local drivers in Australia. Masten Gregory's Ferrari was second ahead of Fon de Portago.

1957

FINDING A BRITISH WINNER

Despite having finished second in the Formula 1 World Championship with the Maserati 250F, for the 1957 season I was still extremely keen to find a British car that would be a consistent winner.

After my victory with the Vanwall at Silverstone in the International Trophy race the previous year and a subsequent test session with the car, I felt that the team owner, Tony Vandervell, really meant business. Admittedly, that success at Silverstone was not over a full Grand Prix distance, but there was really no doubt that the Vanwall cars were fast – and they were certainly the fastest 'green' Formula 1 cars that I had driven up to that point. I did have a few misgivings, however, as the cars had still not proved to be totally reliable.

Despite my reservations, I decided to accept Tony Vandervell's offer to drive for the team in 1957 and I would win two Grands Prix – the British and the Italian – during the year. My team-mate for the season was to be Tony Brooks, a man I regard as 'the greatest unknown driver of all time' and who remains a good friend to this day.

As with my previous contracts, I would be free to drive for other teams in Formula 1 races where Vanwall was not fielding a car, although, as it turned out, I exercised this privilege only at the start of the year for the two Formula 1 races in Argentina, where I joined Juan Manuel Fangio and Jean Behra for guest outings with the Maserati squad.

On the sports car front, I remained contracted to Maserati, which was now fielding the fearsome 450S V8 on a regular basis. This machine gave me the briefest of my Mille Miglia outings in what turned out to be the final running of this classic Italian road race. Only seven miles after the start the brake pedal snapped off, which was both frightening and frustrating.

I competed in fewer races during 1957, just 22 compared with 39 in 1956. The main reason was that I was concentrating on the *grandes épreuves* counting for the World Championship, at the expense of many of the non-championship Formula 1 and sports car events in which I had regularly taken part in previous years.

LEFT *The 1957 season brought with it the welcome prospect of a British Formula 1 car that might enable me to win Grands Prix from the front at long last. The Vanwall might not have had the rakish good looks of the 250F or the technical innovation of the Mercedes W196, but it was a winning machine – as I demonstrated in the British Grand Prix.* (Tom March Collection)

Argentine Grand Prix

Maserati 250F

13 January 1957, Buenos Aires (ARG)

F1 World Championship, round 1

Race distance 100 laps of 2.43-mile circuit **Fastest lap** 1m 44.7s, 83.581mph **Car no** 4 **Entrant** Works

---

I flew down to Buenos Aires via Miami from Nassau in the Bahamas, where I had decided to build a house. On the morning of first practice, I attended the official Rootes Group launch of the Hillman Minx on to the Argentinian market, and then it was out to the circuit to sample one of the three new lightweight 250Fs the team had produced for Juan Manuel Fangio, Jean Behra and me.

The car felt good in practice and I qualified on pole position in dry but windy conditions, lapping in 1m 42.s, which was 0.9 seconds quicker than Juan and 1.4 seconds ahead of Behra. I had a fair start but the throttle broke after only 300 yards and I lost eight laps in the pits while the mechanics completed the necessary repairs. Although I had been ordered not to beat Fangio, this delay was a pity because I would have achieved an easy second place, even though the new 250F was difficult to handle on a full fuel load.

366   2nd

Buenos Aires 1,000kms

Maserati 450S & 300S

20 January 1957, Costanera (ARG)

World Sports Car Championship, round 1

Race distance 98 laps of 6.29-mile circuit **Race time** 6h 11m 53.4s **Fastest lap** 3m 36s, 106mph **Co-drivers** Juan Manuel Fangio, Jean Behra and Carlos Menditéguy **Car no** 2 & 31 **Entrant** Works

---

BELOW *Manhandling the Maserati 450S I shared with Fangio in the Buenos Aires 1,000kms, held on the lurid Costanera road circuit.* (LAT)

We started practice for this sports car race at the Costanera circuit on the Wednesday and my first impression was that it was bumpy, poorly marked and extremely dangerous. I shared the 450S with Fangio and it certainly felt extremely quick indeed. In fact, after Fangio managed one lap at an average speed of 114mph, even the organisers began to feel nervous and decided to install a makeshift chicane on the main straight to slow the cars down a bit.

Fangio qualified the 450S on pole, but I took the start, got away cleanly and pulled out a 20-second lead over Masten Gregory's 3.5-litre Ferrari, which he was sharing with Cesare Perdisa and Eugenio Castellotti. I handed over to Fangio after two hours and all went well until the clutch and gearbox failed, and we were out.

With 33 laps to go, however, I took over the Behra/Menditéguy 300S, which was now running third, some two and a half minutes behind the Ferrari of Alfonso de Portago and Castellotti. I started lapping almost 10 seconds a lap faster than the second-placed Ferrari and caught it before the end, finishing about a minute and a half behind them.

The following day I flew over to Uruguay in a Sunderland flying boat, enjoying a very pleasant flight from up in the cockpit. Then I returned to Buenos Aires to prepare for the following weekend's City Grand Prix, our third race in Argentina in as many weeks.

367 12th
Buenos Aires City Grand Prix, Heat 1

Maserati 250F

27 January 1957, Buenos Aires (ARG)

Race distance 30 laps of 2.92-mile circuit **Car no** 4 **Entrant** Works

368 6th
Buenos Aires City Grand Prix, Heat 2

Maserati 250F

27 January 1957, Buenos Aires (ARG)

Race distance 30 laps of 2.92-mile circuit
Co-driver Carlos Menditéguy **Car no** 4 **Entrant** Works

Conditions for this two-heat event were unbearable, with 80 per cent humidity and a track temperature of 156 degrees Fahrenheit, and I also woke on race morning feeling dizzy because of two sleeping pills I had taken the previous evening.

In the first heat I made a good start, running third, and then worked my way up to the lead. But the car was sliding all over the place, possibly because we were using 16-inch wheels or because the tar was loosening up in the heat, and eventually a brake locked as well. I was too tired to fight the car any longer, so I stopped and ended up classified 12th.

In the second heat I took over Carlos Menditéguy's car for five laps and was about to lap Perdisa when I spun, caught out again by that wretched central throttle pedal. We were classified sixth, which gave me sixth place on aggregate. That night I was completely unable to sleep and I remember ordering cornflakes at 4.45am.

BELOW *My exhaustion during the Buenos Aires City Grand Prix was well documented by the popular press, both in Argentina and back home in Britain (Stirling Moss Collection)*

ABOVE *I raced on some pretty wild circuits, but few came close to the Malecon Highway track at Havana. I drove a tired old Maserati 200S from the start, then switched to a rather better 300S, but both failed to finish.* (LAT)

369 Retired

Cuban Grand Prix

Maserati 200S & 300S

25 February 1957, Malecon Highway (CU)

Race distance 90 laps of 3.47-mile circuit
Reason for retirement Engine after 22 laps
Fastest lap 2m 36.2s **Car no** 6 **Entrant** Ettore Chimeri/Pines

I flew to Havana via New York and Miami only to discover that, due to a dock strike in New York, a large number of cars destined for this race in Cuba on the Malecon street circuit had simply not arrived. The organisers had to scramble around trying to get together a makeshift field of cars and drivers, and the race was delayed by a day.

I was given a Maserati 200S owned by Ettore Chimeri and found that it did not handle at all well. The circuit was also just awful, particularly when it was wet during practice. I made a bad start to the race but pretty much recovered the lost ground by the time I got to the first corner and ran second for 12 laps until Fangio overtook me. Then at 17 laps, while I was still running third, an oil leak caused the Maser's engine to seize. I hung about and took over Harry Schell's private Maserati 300S, which had been elevated to third place after my car's retirement, but then a valve broke and that was the end of my day.

370 2nd

Sebring 12 Hours

Maserati 300S

24 March 1957, Sebring, Florida (USA)

World Sports Car Championship, round 2

Race distance 197 laps of 5.19-mile circuit (1022.4 miles)
Race time 2 laps behind **Co-driver** Harry Schell **Car no** 20
Entrant Works

I spent more time in Nassau working on the house before returning to Florida for the Sebring race. Practice took place on the Thursday and Friday before the race on the Saturday, but it was wet on the second day so I had to rely on my Thursday time, which earned me fourth place on the grid. The car felt bad even though its braking performance was quite reasonable, but basically it was just too heavy.

I ran second to Fangio's 450S in the opening stages of the race. I had planned to do a five-hour opening stint but after just over four hours I handed over to Harry Schell for 20 laps. I then did another three hours, Schell another hour, and then I took over and finished the race, still in second place.

BELOW *Working hard in the cockpit of the works Maserati 300S I drove to second place at Sebring, sharing with Harry Schell.* **(LAT)**

371   3rd

Syracuse Grand Prix

Vanwall

7 April 1957, Sicily (I)

Race distance 80 laps of 3.47-mile circuit
Fastest lap 1m 54.3s, 107.64mph (record)
Car no 20 **Entrant** Works

On the Thursday before the race, I caught a charter flight from Lydd Airport, Kent, which went direct to Catania in Sicily via a refuelling stop in Nice. From Catania it was a two-hour drive to Syracuse, where I was scheduled to have my first outing of the new season with the Vanwall team.

Jean Behra was fastest in his Maserati during the first day's practice but I was only 0.7 seconds behind him in the Vanwall practice car, which had a difficult feel to its throttle and was over-geared to the tune of 600rpm. On Saturday the gear ratios were improved and I was able to pull 7,500rpm in fifth gear, although the engine was misfiring slightly at the top end.

I qualified third, behind the Ferraris of Peter Collins and Luigi Musso, but made a bad start, dropping to sixth on the opening lap. By the end of the second lap, however, I was in the lead with Tony Brooks briefly second in the other Vanwall before Collins overtook him. I opened up a lead of 35 seconds in 32 laps, but then an injector pipe broke and I lost four laps in the pits having it repaired.

I resumed seventh but, despite not having fourth gear by this stage, I set a new lap record and caught up to third behind Collins and Musso by the end. I reckon I drove a good race and could easily have won but for the problems with the car. Tony drove very well until a water pipe broke and forced him to retire.

372 Retired

Goodwood, Glover Trophy

Vanwall

22 April 1957, Goodwood, West Sussex (GB)

Race distance 32 laps of 2.4-mile circuit
Reason for retirement Throttle **Car no** 7 **Entrant** Works

This was a really disappointing day. I qualified on pole for this traditional Easter Monday fixture, with Tony Brooks alongside me. I made a good start and led for 13 laps but then the throttle broke. In the following week's *Autosport* the editorial was devoted to a few sharp comments on the improvements Vanwall – and our rivals, BRM, come to that – needed to effect if they were unable to keep the cars in one piece for a short 77-mile sprint race at Goodwood. I must say

that I found it difficult to question the logic of their argument.

On a brighter note, during the week immediately following the Goodwood meeting, Katie Molson and I formally announced our engagement.

373 Retired

Mille Miglia

Maserati 450S

12 May 1957, Brescia (I)

World Sports Car Championship, round 3

Race distance 1 lap of 992 miles **Reason for retirement** Broken brake pedal **Co-driver** Denis Jenkinson **Car no** 537 **Entrant** Works

The Maserati 450S was a stunningly quick car and I thought this time there was a possibility of matching my 1955 winning performance. On the Thursday

before the start, 'Jenks' – Denis Jenkinson – and I were off at 5.15am for a two-hour blast in the 450S as far as Padua and then back to Brescia. On the Saturday we were up at 4.50am and went off for another practice session, going just beyond Padua and back via Cremona in time to get back for breakfast at 8.30am. In the evening we tested the car on the *autostrada* and it felt fabulous.

On race morning, we were up at 4.30am to take our starting slot at 5.37am. Three and a half minutes and 12kms later our Mille Miglia ended abruptly when the brake pedal broke at speed. We were both unharmed, but there were some anxious moments while I tried to slow down the car through the gears from about 130mph. We trickled back to Brescia where, despite our disappointment, you just had to feel sorry for the Maserati mechanics, who were mortified when we appeared unexpectedly.

Just 20-odd miles from the finish, poor 'Fon' de Portago and Ed Nelson were killed in their Ferrari, along with 12 spectators, in an accident that spelled the end of this fabulous event for good.

LEFT *In the pits during the Glover Trophy at Goodwood, where the Vanwall failed to finish this short race due to throttle problems.* (LAT)

RIGHT *Preparing for my shortest-ever Mille Miglia in company with my co-driver Denis Jenkinson. 'Jenks' would subsequently become a lifelong friend.* (Klemantaski Collection)

374 Retired

Monaco Grand Prix

Vanwall

19 May 1957, Monte Carlo (MON)

F1 World Championship, round 2

Race distance 105 laps of 1.954-mile circuit

Reason for retirement Crash on lap 4 **Car no** 18 **Entrant** Works

ABOVE *My Vanwall lined up on the outside of front row at Monaco. Fangio's Maserati is on pole position with Peter Collins's Ferrari 801 between us.* (LAT)

RIGHT *Leading the opening lap at Monaco before a brake problem pitched me into a major accident at the chicane, as reported – somewhat hysterically! – in the magazine article below.* (Klemantaski Collection)

Tony Vandervell was understandably pretty disappointed with his team's performances at Syracuse and Goodwood, so he adopted our suggested modifications for Monaco. They included more steering lock, better low-speed torque and shortened nose sections, which would make the front of the cars less vulnerable to damage in close traffic.

In first practice, I shunted at the chicane and the impact buckled the chassis. The following day my car did not feel too good, so

I took over Tony Brooks's car – with my engine installed in it – and qualified on the outside of the front row, alongside Fangio's Maserati and Pete Collins's Ferrari 801. I could not improve my time in the third and final session because there was too much oil on the circuit and the car felt down on power.

Despite all this I made a good start to lead for the first three and a half laps. Then, when I braked for the harbour-front chicane, the car simply did not stop and I had no choice but to go straight on into the pole-and-sand barrier, breaking both the Vanwall's nose and my own, as well as bruising my elbow. The car was pretty well wrecked and both Mike Hawthorn and Pete crashed their Ferraris in the general mayhem that ensued. Clever old Fangio dodged through to win, with Tony finishing second to score Vanwall's first championship points of the season.

MIRACLE ESCAPE FROM A DEATH CRASH

His front brakes gone, his speedometer reading 100 miles an hour, Stirling Moss stared death in the face!

STIRLING MOSS just made the sharp curve when he felt his front brakes give way. He tested the rear brakes gently — they were barely holding, and his speed was well over 100! England's most famed sports car driver had only seconds to make a decision—to send his hurling Vanwall against the sandbag barrier or crash into the nearby Mediterranean. The first might mean death by fire. The second a watery grave. It was a wretched spot!

Leaning clear of wreckage, Moss (top foto) sees other racers hurtling down upon him. Before his escape, Moss poses below with fiancée Katie Molson.

375 5th

Nürburgring, ADAC 1,000kms

26 May 1957, Nürburgring (D)

Maserati 450S & 300S

World Sports Car Championship, round 4

Race distance 44 laps of 14.15-mile circuit **Race time** 1 lap behind **Fastest lap** 9m 49.96s, 86.43mph **Co-drivers** Juan Manuel Fangio, 'Paco' Godia and Horace Gould **Car no** 1, 2 & 4 **Entrant** Works

I drove straight to the Nürburgring from Monaco, stopping off at Mercedes in Stuttgart to collect my Mercedes 220 road car.

I was down to share the Maserati 450S with Fangio and I set the second-fastest time in wet conditions during the first session, 16 seconds slower than Tony Brooks managed in the Aston Martin DBR1/300 in the dry. On the Friday, I tried both the 450S and the 300S, finding that the smaller-engined car did not handle very well though it was certainly fast.

On race morning I was up at 7.30am, thanks to the general noise surrounding the hotel. At the Le Mans-style start, the 450S would not fire up and I lost about a minute getting it to start. Nevertheless, I was up to first place after eight laps and, three laps later, had pulled out a lead of about 30 seconds when a half-shaft broke and the left-rear wheel parted company from the car, leaving me to spin to a stop. I returned to the start-line and Fangio took over the other 450S, but the oil tank in that car broke loose after another six laps. The mechanics sort-of fixed it and I took over for two more laps, but it was to no avail and I retired the car.

That was not the end of my afternoon, however, as I took over Francesco Godia's 300S, which he was sharing with Horace Gould, and went like the proverbial to climb back through the field to fifth place, after which Fangio took over and held the position to the finish.

LEFT & ABOVE *The Maserati 450S Zagato was developed specially for Le Mans, in part at my behest, I have to confess. It really was a terrible piece of equipment and I was almost relieved when it retired with transmission failure. Vision was a problem as the wipers lifted off the screen and heat within the car misted up the glass on the inside…* (LAT)

376 Retired

Le Mans 24 Hours

Maserati 450S Zagato

22/23 June 1957, Sarthe (F)

World Sports Car Championship, round 5

Race distance 24 hours of 8.38-mile circuit (2,732.23 miles, 327 laps) **Reason for retirement** Transmission **Co-driver** Harry Schell **Car no** 1 **Entrant** Works

This was a genuinely bad car, even though I suppose I have to take a slice of responsibility for being the one who suggested that Maserati should design an aerodynamic coupé body for the 450S, primarily for Le Mans. With Medardo Fantuzzi, the usual body builder, overwhelmed with work, Maserati commissioned Zagato to build the Frank Costin-designed bodywork in two weeks flat.

The whole build process was a typically Italian last-minute panic and they omitted or messed up a number of crucial elements, including leaving off the full-length undertray that Costin had specified in his original design. The car looked awkward and was a real handful.

Cooling the cockpit turned out to be a nightmare and the air-flow over the windscreen continually lifted the wipers clear of the screen at high speed. When I braked, the wipers would make enough contact to smear the screen, but that was about all. Add to that the fact that there was no demisting and you start to get the picture.

The race turned out to be a fiasco as well. As at the Nürburgring, the car would not start after my sprint across the road, so I was slow away, but I was up to third by the time we got out on to the Mulsanne straight. Soon I was up to second but having to drive out of my skin to keep pace with Mike Hawthorn's leading Ferrari.

After an hour Jean Behra came shooting past in the open 450S, by which time my wretched coupé was vibrating badly, its cockpit full of heat and fumes. I handed it over to my co-driver, Harry Schell, but he managed just three more laps before an oil pipe broke. After this was repaired I rejoined, only for a rear universal joint to seize. End of story.

British Grand Prix

Vanwall

20 July 1957, Aintree, Liverpool (GB)

F1 World Championship, round 5

Race distance 90 laps of 3-mile circuit **Race time** 3h 6m 37.8s
Race speed 86.8mph **Fastest lap** 1m 59.2s, 90.6mph (record)
Co-driver Tony Brooks **Car no** 18 & 20 **Entrant** Works

After Le Mans I had gone down to La Napoule, near Cannes, for a short break with my fiancée Katie. I was messing around in the surf trying to mono-ski backwards when a spray of water shot straight up my nose as I attempted, too cleverly, to make a sharp turn. That ended up with my suffering from an unpleasant sinus infection, which necessitated a spell in the London Clinic and hardly impressed Tony Vandervell when it became clear that I would have to miss the French Grand Prix at Rouen and the non-championship race at Reims.

Tony Brooks was also unfit for these races, having up-ended his Aston at Le Mans, so Roy Salvadori and Stuart Lewis-Evans stood in for us. In fact, Stuart did such a superb job that he was recruited as the full-time third driver for the Vanwall team.

Fortunately, I recovered in time for the British Grand Prix at Aintree, where we were clearly going to have strong opposition from Maserati, with Fangio and Behra faster than the Vanwalls on the first day's practice. Even though I was still feeling the after-effects of the sinus problem, I managed to qualify on pole position, right at the end of the session. I tried Tony's car in practice, as well as mine, on a 'just-in-case' basis as Tony was still badly bruised, and we arranged that he would relinquish his car to me if such a strategy was required because he was unsure whether he would be well enough to drive competitively for the full 90-lap distance.

After making a fair start, I was second into the first corner and led the race by the end of the opening lap. I pulled away steadily, but at about the 25-lap mark the Vanwall began to misfire. I stopped to have an earth wire ripped out and rejoined in seventh place, but the car was still misfiring so I brought it into the pits again two laps later. Tony was immediately signalled to come in, which he did, and I took over his car. I resumed in ninth place, but was quickly up to seventh. Meanwhile, Behra led by over a minute.

I passed Fangio for sixth place on lap 34, then I closed in on Musso and overtook him for fifth place on lap 40, and then I got past Collins for fourth place on lap 46. Then came a slice of good fortune. Just as I passed Stuart Lewis-Evans's Vanwall for third place, the clutch disintegrated on Behra's leading Maserati and Hawthorn's second-placed Ferrari suffered a punctured tyre running over the debris. With 20 laps to go, Stuart and I in our green Vanwalls were running one-two, although I would soon be left alone at the head of the field, after Stuart stopped on the circuit with throttle problems.

I took no chances in the closing stages. I even made a precautionary late stop to top up with fuel. The car did not miss a beat and, after 90 laps, I finally saw the chequered flag in the British Grand Prix at Aintree for the second time in my career. And it was my first time in a British car! However, Tony and I had to share the points, four each, in our tally for the World Championship.

LEFT *I take a swig of water as Tony Brooks (left) relinquishes his Vanwall cockpit to me and the car is topped up with fuel for the run to victory in the British Grand Prix at Aintree.* (LAT)

RIGHT *Being congratulated on my victory by Aintree's owner, Mrs Mirabel Topham. Earl Howe, President of the BRDC (centre), looks on.* (LAT)

OVERLEAF *Another great achievement accomplished. Taking the chequered flag in my home Grand Prix at the wheel of a British car.* (LAT)

German Grand Prix

Vanwall

4 August 1957, Nürburgring (D)

F1 World Championship, round 6

Race distance 22 laps of 14.17-mile circuit
Race time 3h 35m 15.8s **Car no** 10 **Entrant** Works

O n the Thursday before the race, I met up with my fiancée Katie, Mum and Dad at Heathrow airport, then Katie, Alf Francis and I flew to Le Bourget, where I had left my Mercedes 220 so that we could drive straight on to the Nürburgring. After the six-hour drive, we arrived to discover that we had no room – the guys who should have made our reservations had let us down.

The Nürburgring was always going to be a bit of a contrast compared with the smooth circuit of Aintree. Our cars were bouncing around a lot and the gap between second and third gears was too wide for my liking. And the taut suspension was hopeless on a track like this. In the opening stages my car felt really awful, jumping everywhere and really tiring me out. The brakes were also poor at the beginning but improved a bit as the race wore on.

I finished a disappointing and disappointed fifth. Fangio was in a class of his own, winning comfortably in his Maserati 250F.

BELOW *My Vanwall could only make the second row of the grid for the German Grand Prix at the Nürburgring and fifth place was a poor reward for a difficult race.* (LAT)

Swedish Sports Car Grand Prix

Maserati 450S & 300S

11 August 1957, Rabelov, Kristianstadt (S)

World Sports Car Championship, round 6

Race distance 145 laps of 4.04-mile circuit **Race time** 6h 1m 1.1s **Race speed** 97.88mph **Car no** 7 & 9 **Co-drivers** Jean Behra, Harry Schell, Jo Bonnier and Giorgio Scarlatti **Entrant** Works

T he Friday of this race weekend was Maserati team manager Nello Ugolini's birthday as well as first practice day. Driving 450S versions, Jean Behra and I both managed to lap in 2m 22.5s, and Harry Schell was a tenth slower, his time being equalled by Pete Collins in the

4.1-litre Ferrari. My 450S felt better in Saturday practice and I think I could have managed a faster time.

I started the race well and by the time we reached the two-hour mark I was leading from Jean by 5 seconds. At my first stop I handed over the car to Harry, then I took Jean's car when he stopped, maintaining his lead. In a bid to beat Ferrari in the World Sports Car Championship, our aim was to keep them out of the top five at all costs. So our next move was for me to hand back the 450S to Jean and to take over the best-placed 300S. This car immediately developed gearbox trouble, but we plugged on as best we could. Although I ended the day sharing both the win and third place, Ferrari finished second and fourth, so the championship seemed to be theirs.

However, Maserati was given another chance when the previously cancelled Venezuelan Grand Prix at Caracas was reinstated at the end of the season. Good luck – and bad – as it would transpire.

380   1st

Pescara Grand Prix

Vanwall

18 August 1957, Pescara (I)

F1 World Championship, round 7

Race distance 18 laps of 15.89-mile circuit **Race time** 2h 59m 22.7s **Race speed** 95.695mph **Fastest lap** 9m 44.6s, 97.87mph (record) **Car no** 26 **Entrant** Works

With the Dutch and Belgian Grands Prix cancelled in the aftermath of the Mille Miglia tragedy, the Italians were permitted to add the Pescara race to the World Championship schedule. Ferrari sent only a single car for Luigi Musso, owing to the controversy still raging about the Mille Miglia, but Maserati sent a three-car team. Not only was the Pescara circuit extremely exhilarating to drive, but it had a straight long enough to play to the Vanwall's aerodynamic strengths.

I flew to Rome from London airport on the Thursday before the race, then drove for three and a half hours to Pescara in a Fiat 1100, completing three laps of the circuit before I got some food and turned in for the night.

Practice took place on the Saturday and I found that my Vanwall was perfectly geared, pulling 7,200rpm, which was about 173mph in top along the long straight. It did wander around badly, however, so I tried Stuart Lewis-Evans's car, which felt a lot better, perhaps due to being fitted with Armstrong dampers. I also did a few laps in Tony Brooks's car, which felt good but was prone to overheating.

I qualified on the front row between Fangio's pole-winning Maserati and Musso's Ferrari. There were still some mechanics on the grid when the start flag went down and Musso was away like a rocket, but Fangio made a bad start in his Ferrari and I was right with him as we tore away into the distance. Unfortunately, Brooks had the wretched misfortune to suffer an engine failure on the opening lap, but on lap two I managed to force my way past Musso to take the lead.

From then on it was plain sailing and I led all the way to the finish, despite a brief pit stop to top up with oil. I used no more than

ABOVE *Heading for victory in the Pescara Grand Prix, one of the few circuits on which the Vanwall's aerodynamics really paid off.* (LAT)

7,000rpm in top gear and lifted off many times to preserve the engine. It was certainly very satisfying to finish the race three minutes ahead of Fangio, who was followed in third place by his team-mate Harry Schell.

You might think today's generation of Formula 1 drivers has a tendency to sprint flat out to the local airport to catch a plane home almost immediately the chequered flag has fallen, but Pescara in 1957 was just the same. After a quick bite to eat we were off to Rome, but our little Fiat blew a head gasket on the way and we had to hire a taxi – at the enormous cost of 10,000 Lire – for the balance of the journey. Our BEA flight was cancelled, so we took an Alitalia flight an hour later, eventually taking off at 4.30am.

Bonneville record attempts

MG EX181

23 August 1957, Bonneville, Utah (USA)

Times 1km, 254.64mph; 1 mile, 245.11mph; 5kms, 243.08mph; 5 miles, 235.59mph; 10kms, 224.7mph

In the three-week break between the Pescara race and the Italian Grand Prix at Monza I went to the Bonneville Salt Flats, where I broke five 1,500cc class world records in the MG EX181 record car. The most worring aspect of this exercise was the fact that the front bodywork of the car was secured by Dzus fasteners and that, if anything happened, I would not be able to get out.

OPPOSITE TOP
Posing alongside the MG EX181 record-breaker on the salt flats at Bonneville. (Brian Moylan Collection)

OPPOSITE BOTTOM
Three Vanwalls buttoned up the first three places on the grid for the Italian Grand Prix. I won the race, to my great satisfaction. (LAT)

RIGHT *I had another outing in the Tour de France in 1957, finishing third in my Mercedes 300SL Gullwing.* (LAT)

382 1st

Italian Grand Prix

Vanwall

8 September 1957, Monza (I)

F1 World Championship, round 8

Race distance 87 laps of 3.57-mile circuit Race time 2h 35m 3.9s Race speed 120.275mph Car no 18 Entrant Works

The entire race weekend unfolded sensationally well for us. I was fastest in Friday practice, but then Stuart Lewis-Evans performed brilliantly on the Saturday to take pole 0.8 seconds quicker than me. With Tony Brooks qualifying third, the Italian fans had to put up with the sight of three green British Vanwalls in one-two-three formation on the front row, the only blob of red in that sea of green being Fangio's Maserati on the outside of the grid in fourth place.

On this occasion, our Vanwalls completely outclassed the Ferraris. It came down to a straight fight with Maserati. I made a good start and played around a bit in the leading bunch during the opening phase. I must confess that my heart skipped a beat on the 13th lap when the gearbox started jamming but after four anxious laps it somehow righted itself. Tony's throttle began to stick, so he made a precautionary pit stop and I therefore led again from Stuart. Then his car's steering tightened and he too pulled in to investigate.

By lap 40 I was nearly 18 seconds ahead of Fangio and, when he stopped to change tyres, I opened my advantage to almost a full lap. Barring mechanical failure, I now had the race in the bag. Just as at Pescara, I made a precautionary stop 10 laps from the end, topping up the oil and fitting new rear tyres, and before I knew it there was the chequered flag waiting for me as I accelerated the Vanwall out of the last corner.

For the third consecutive year I was runner-up to Fangio in the drivers' World Championship, but, of even more significance to me, I had won at this shrine to Italian motor racing at the wheel of *una macchina Inglese* – and that was the most important achievement of all.

383 4th

Tour de France

Mercedes-Benz 300SL

15–21 September 1957 (F)

Event distance 3,800 miles Co-driver Peter Garnier Car no 175 Entrant Stirling Moss Ltd

I flew to Nice to meet *The Autocar*'s Peter Garnier, who had driven there in my gullwing Mercedes 300SL. After scrutineering, I drove out to the La Turbie hill climb with Peter for a little unofficial pre-event practice and got hit with a hefty speeding fine from a local *gendarme*.

We ran seventh in the early stages of this six-day event but this year our road car was simply not quick enough to get on terms with the Ferrari GTs, which were much faster than they had been the previous year. Despite this, and the fact that the Merc developed an unwelcome habit of consuming a gallon of water every 100 miles, we moved up to fourth overall and held it to the end.

384 Did not start

Moroccan Grand Prix

Vanwall

27 October 1957, Ain Diab, Casablanca (MO)

Race distance 55 laps of 4.75-mile circuit
Reason did not start Withdrew from event
Car no 20 **Entrant** Works

385 Retired

Venezuelan Sports Car Grand Prix

Maserati 450S

3 November 1957, Caracas (VE)

World Sports Car Championship, round 7

Race distance 1,000kms of 6.17-mile circuit (101 laps)
Reason for retirement Crash **Fastest lap** 3m 38.5s, 101.71mph
Car no 2 & 4 **Entrant** Works

I was fastest in first practice but then was laid low by Asian 'flu for the rest of the weekend and was unable to compete. I recovered sufficiently to catch a 'plane from Casablanca to Paris on the morning of the race, arriving at London airport at 8.10pm. Just to cap everything, I got home without my luggage because Air France very helpfully left it in Paris

What a race this turned out to be! I qualified my 450S on pole ahead of the sister car of Jean Behra, but I lost a minute at the start. It took me an hour to make up the lost time, and after a further hour and a quarter I had built up a lead of 1m 52s on the rest of the field. By this time Masten Gregory had rolled his 450S, thankfully without injury.

Then an American amateur driver by the name of Joseph Hap Dressel, driving an AC Ace-Bristol, pulled right on to my racing line as I came up to lap him. I could not avoid hitting him and the impact was massive. His car somersaulted into a telegraph pole, breaking into two pieces, while my Maserati spun to a stop up the road.

Back in the pits, Harry Schell brought in the other 450S to hand over to Behra and it burst into flames during refuelling. Jean's hands were burned, so I took over – only to find that the seat was still smouldering. I had to come straight back in and hand the car back to Harry while I had my wounds attended to. To complete Maserati's day from hell, Jo Bonnier's 300S lost a wheel just as it was being overtaken by Schell's 450S and the two cars collided. They were both written off but the drivers had lucky escapes.

BELOW *Relaxing in Nassau with Reg Parnell (left) and John Wyer of Aston Martin.* (LAT)

ABOVE *At the wheel of Jan de Vroom's Ferrari 290S with which I won two races at Nassau just before Christmas.* (Terry O'Neil Collection)

386   24th

Nassau Tourist Trophy

Aston Martin DBR2

3 December 1957, Oakes Field (BA)

Race distance 60 laps of 5-mile circuit **Race time** 96.21mph **Car no** 30 **Entrant** Works

This was my first outing in a 3.7-litre Aston Martin DBR2, although a DBR2 had first raced earlier in the year at Le Mans, with Peter and Graham Whitehead driving. In the first of my two outings with the car in the Bahamas, an ignition fault cost 17 minutes, dropping me to 24th place.

387   4th

Governor's Trophy

Aston Martin DBR2

3 December 1957, Oakes Field (BA)

Race distance 30 laps of 5-mile circuit **Car no** 1 **Entrant** Works

Unfortunately after this race we loaned the DBR2 to Ruth Levy for the ladies' race and she ended up wrecking it.

388   1st

Nassau Sports Car Race

Ferrari 290S

8 December 1957, Oakes Field (BA)

Car no 105 **Entrant** Jan de Vroom

After the Aston was wrecked by Ruth Levy, the US fraternity got their heads together and arranged for me to borrow a 3.5-litre V12 Ferrari 290S owned by a Dutch amateur with the splendid name of Jan de Vroom. I won quite easily.

389   1st

Nassau Trophy

Ferrari 290S

8 December 1957, Oakes Field (BA)

Fastest lap 1m 5.4s, 101.603mph **Car no** 105 **Entrant** Jan de Vroom

Despite bad brakes and a poor start, I managed to get through into the lead after changing tyres and won again in the Ferrari 290S, with Carroll Shelby second, Phil Hill third and Jo Bonnier fourth.

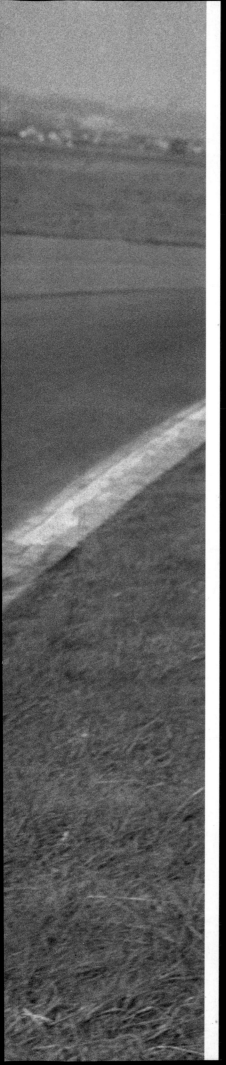

1958

NEARLY MADE IT!

The 1958 season was one of huge diversity and interest for me. I re-signed with Tony Vandervell to drive for the Vanwall team at £1,000 for each grande épreuve contested and I had sports car contracts for certain races with both Maserati and Aston Martin. I also had an agreement that, whenever I was not driving for Vanwall, I could race Rob Walker's Cooper, which I could also use in Formula 2 events.

Little did I know it at the time, but this was to be the start of a very close personal and professional relationship with Rob Walker that would last until the end of my career, and a friendship that would endure until his death in 2002. He and his wife, Betty, were utterly charming and generous-minded people and were always fun to be with. It is a measure of the man that the word 'Gentleman' was written as his profession in his passport, and this is exactly what he was in both senses of the word.

Rob and I never had any written contract. We did not even have a handshake, let alone a verbal agreement. It just was not necessary.

Motor racing was Rob's life – and his hobby. He was never a team manager in the conventional sense; he was very much the patron. By this time Alf Francis worked for him and Rob basically left Alf and me to decide which races we wanted to do. When I asked Rob if I could do a certain race, his reply would always be, "If Alf will do it, then you can do it". Rob would always give me the pit signals and I would decide my strategy accordingly.

My first really big success with the RRC Walker Racing Team came in the very first race of the 1958 season, when I drove the 2-litre Cooper-Climax to victory in the Argentine Grand Prix at Buenos Aires, a race that Vanwall, naturally, was not contesting.

This was a hugely satisfying and tactical victory for me. Not only was it the Cooper Car Company's first Formula 1 victory but it was also the first grande épreuve ever to be won by a rear-engined Formula 1 car. It was also an extremely challenging race in such heat and afterwards I was over the moon, my adrenalin flowing freely. It felt so good because I had managed to outwit all the other entries, using tactics and guile, and, at the same time, I had managed my tyre wear so carefully that by the end of the race even one more mile would have been impossible – in fact my front tyres had worn past the white breaker strip and were actually through some of the canvas carcass as well.

This was a very high note on which to start a season, but it was also the start of a very bad period in motor racing as far as deaths on the circuit were concerned. It was also an exceptionally disappointing year for me personally as I missed out in my battle for the World Championship with Mike Hawthorn by a single point, although I won a further three *grandes épreuves* in the Vanwall.

All in all, I drove in 38 races during 1958, with 14 retirements and 18 wins – not a bad record, I suppose.

LEFT *The 1958 season marked the start of my fruitful and enjoyable association with Rob Walker. Here I am at the wheel of his Cooper-Climax on the way to victory in the Aintree 200 non-championship Formula 1 race.* (LAT)

390　1st

Argentine Grand Prix

Cooper-Climax

19 January 1958, Buenos Aires (ARG)
F1 World Championship, round 1

Race distance 80 laps on 2.43-mile circuit **Race time** 2h 19m 33.7s **Race speed** 83.604mph **Car no** 14 **Entrant** R.R.C. Walker

Adapted from a Formula 2 machine, the little Cooper was propelled by a 1,960cc version of the twin-cam, four-cylinder Climax engine. Granted, we were down on power compared with the front-engined Maserati 250Fs and new Ferrari Dino 246s, but we had the potential to run through the 80-lap race without making a refuelling stop. The problem was going to be tyre wear.

Dunlop advised us that, in the gruelling conditions, our tyres would last only 30 to 40 laps, about half the race distance, but a tyre change would cause an insuperable delay because the Cooper wheels had four-stud attachments rather than the traditional 'knock-off' spinners. I thought about this long and hard, and then told Alf that I was going to have to run the race non-stop – no new tyres and no refuelling. But we just had to make the others *think* that we were going to make that time-consuming pit stop. I duly went around the paddock complaining to the other drivers, telling them, "Well, it's all right for you. My car is very quick, but we're going to have to throw away three minutes in the pits."

In order to conserve my tyres, I did only three laps in practice and started from seventh place on the grid, having lapped 2 seconds slower than Fangio's pole position time in his Maserati. I had a problem with blurred vision in one eye, caused by Katie accidentally poking me in the eye when we were fooling around together, as a result of which I had to drive wearing an eye patch. On

reflection, I am amazed that I was allowed to do so. Perhaps this would not have been allowed if the race organisers had appreciated just what tactics the Walker team was going to deploy once the race was underway.

Once the race started I soon worked my way through to fourth place behind Fangio and Jean Behra in their Maseratis and Mike Hawthorn in the Ferrari. Then the gearbox momentarily jammed in second and I was just about to come into the pits when it miraculously freed up. It later emerged that the clutch had broken but a stone had become jammed in the interlock mechanism, enabling me to continue driving with an inoperative clutch.

I drove as gently as I dared, letting the car run as wide as possible out of the corners to minimise tyre wear, and trying to use the slipstreams of other cars on all the straight bits. Slowly, I edged

BELOW *In Rob's Cooper heading for that memorable victory in the Argentine Grand Prix, the first* grande épreuve *victory for a Cooper and also for a rear-engined car.* (LAT)

my way through the field. I overtook Behra and Hawthorn, and then, when Fangio pitted for fuel on lap 35, I went through into the lead, which quite soon became a very comfortable lead of a minute.

Alf started giving me signals from the pits that suggested he was counting me down to a pit stop for tyres. Of course, I realised that he was just trying to mislead the other teams so that they would continue to relax, waiting for me to come in for a long pit stop. With about 20 laps to go, the penny dropped in the Ferrari team that they were being duped, and Luigi Musso, in second place, started to pile on the pressure just as I saw the first signs of potential trouble with my tyres.

First the tread wore away so the tyres looked pretty much like slicks. A few laps later, I could see the white breaker strip that appears as a warning between the rubber and the carcass. At first there was just the odd spot of white going round but, as the tyres wore further, the spots became continuous white lines. A few laps later, the lines gave way to the canvas, which then grew hairs and flashed round. This was becoming a real concern because I realised that either front tyre, or even both of them, could easily burst.

So here I was, leading the Argentine Grand Prix outright, with relatively few laps to go and a damned Ferrari catching me very fast. By now I was using as little steering as possible, letting the car ride up and over the low chamfered kerbs on to the grass to cool and save tyre wear. I finished just 2.7 seconds ahead of Musso's Ferrari – and that was after over two hours of racing.

I am not sure if that was brave or stupid. Mind you, only a very fine line divides the two!

ABOVE *I really enjoyed my drive to third place with Jean Behra in the Buenos Aires 1,000kms, sharing the Porsche 500 RSK.* (Porsche)

This race was held on one of the longer circuit combinations within the Parc Almirante Brown, including a section on the fast dual carriageway adjacent to the autodrome's entrance. I had originally planned to share a Maserati 300S with Jean Behra, but that machine almost literally fell apart with a broken crankshaft after only two laps of practice and arrangements were made for us to switch to the Porsche. I cannot say I was too bothered about this because the Maserati felt really terrible.

By contrast, the little air-cooled Porsche, with its seemingly unburstable engine, felt terrific. I qualified sixth fastest, 4 seconds quicker than Behra could manage in it. We ran as high as second at one point and made the 3-litre Ferrari drivers – winners Pete Collins and Phil Hill and second-placed Olivier Gendebien and Luigi Musso – work harder for their success than they would have liked. We also won our class by miles. A good result.

392   Retired

Buenos Aires City Grand Prix, Heat 1

Cooper-Climax

2 February 1958, Buenos Aires (ARG)

Race distance 30 laps of 2.9-mile circuit **Reason for retirement** Collision on lap 2 **Car no** 18 **Entrant** R.R.C. Walker

This race was a pretty brief affair for me because I was punted off the circuit by local driver Jesus Iglesias in the pouring rain at the first corner. The car was too badly damaged for me either to continue the race or to take part in the second heat later in the day.

393   1st

Cuban Grand Prix

Ferrari 335S

23 February 1958, Havana (CU)

Race distance 500km of 3.5-mile circuit **Race time** 12m 59.3s (5 laps, race stopped because of crash) **Car no** 4 **Entrant** NART

For this race in Cuba, Luigi Chinetti's North American Racing Team entered me in a Ferrari Tipo 335S 4.1-litre V12.

The most worrying aspect of the weekend was the risk of being kidnapped by Fidel Castro's rebels and this resulted in some of us drivers being assigned personal bodyguards. That was all very well, but mine kept knocking on my bedroom door, all through the night,

and saying, "Moss, are you there?" to which I would repeatedly reply, "Yes, okay." I did not get much sleep.

Fangio, of course, was the main target and in fact he was kidnapped, missing the race as a result. Katie and I were with him when he was abducted from the Lincoln Hotel. He told the kidnappers, "Look, you must not take Moss. He has his new wife on honeymoon with him and she will be very frightened." He said he was well treated and was released after the race, the organisers having paid a substantial ransom for him.

I had been fastest in practice and took the lead away from the start, followed by Masten Gregory in a big Ferrari. As it was a 500km race, I did not really want to be followed all the time, so we passed back and forth.

At one point on the circuit there was a pretty rough, fragile-looking pedestrian bridge. After a few laps it collapsed, no doubt because

it was too crowded with spectators, and when Masten and I arrived at the chaos someone showed us a red flag. This, of course, means 'stop the race' – and should be shown only by the Clerk of the Course. I realised that there was no way the Clerk of the Course could have got to the wreckage of the bridge before we did, so I followed Masten very slowly back to the finish and then, 50 yards from the line, dropped the Maser into second gear and gunned it, so that I crossed the line just in front of Masten.

Of course, he complained. "I was in the lead when the race was stopped and should be first. And you, Stirling, second." I called Masten over and said, "Look, leave it as it is, me first and you second, and we will split the prize money 50/50." Otherwise the matter would have had to go before the FIA and goodness knows when we would have got our money.

394 Retired

Sebring 12 Hours

Aston Martin DBR1

22 March 1958, Sebring, Florida (USA)

World Sports Car Championship, round 2

Race distance 200 laps of 5.2-mile circuit
Reason for retirement Transmission **Fastest lap** 3m 20.3s, 93.6mph (record) **Car no** 24 **Co-driver** Tony Brooks
Entrant Works

My decision to return to Aston Martin for the 1958 season was prompted in part by the dominant victory achieved by Tony Brooks and Noel Cunningham-Reid in the 1957 Nürburgring 1,000kms race with the DBR1. Sebring was my first race for the team this season and I was immediately impressed by the car's ability to soak up the bumps and by how very much superior it was to the DB3S, which I had experienced during my previous stint with Aston. That said, the DBR1 had a terrible gearbox but, by the end of practice, I had managed to clip a full second off Behra's lap record, achieved in a Maserati 450S.

I led from the start and, as the race approached the two-hour mark, I was a lap ahead of Roy Salvadori's sister car and Mike Hawthorn's Ferrari. Then a tyre blew, which cost us three minutes, and Tony Brooks took over. When he handed the car back to me after four hours, we were a lap and 10 seconds behind the Ferrari. I managed to pull back about 14 seconds of that deficit, but then the gearbox broke.

395 1st

Sussex Trophy

Aston Martin DBR2

7 April 1958, Goodwood, West Sussex (GB)

Race distance 21 laps of 2.4-mile circuit **Race time** 33m 37.4s
Race speed 89.94mph **Fastest lap** 1m 33.4s, 92.5mph (sports car record) **Car no** 102 **Entrant** Works

Aston Martin made a last-minute entry for the 3.8-litre DBR2 for this race. I took the lead at the Le Mans-style start but Archie Scott-Brown in the Lister-Jag came tanking past me on the opening lap. He was driving extremely well, as he always did, particularly at Goodwood, and it took me until the start of the eighth lap to catch and pass him again. Archie then retired with a steering problem a couple of laps later and thereafter I had a reasonably easy run to victory, ahead of Pete Collins in the new 2-litre V6 Ferrari.

396   Retired

Goodwood, Glover Trophy

Cooper-Climax T43

7 April 1958, Goodwood, West Sussex (GB)

Race distance 42 laps of 2.4-mile circuit **Reason for retirement** Broken con-rod **Fastest lap** 1m 28.8s, 97.3mph (shared with Mike Hawthorn) **Car no** 7 **Entrant** R.R.C. Walker

Jean Behra led in the BRM from the start but then smacked firmly into the chicane, wrecking his car. I stalled at the start, but climbed through to second place behind Mike Hawthorn's Ferrari before the Climax engine in my Cooper broke a con-rod and I stopped out on the circuit.

397   1st

British Empire Trophy, Heat 3

Aston Martin DBR2

12 April 1958, Oulton Park, Cheshire (GB)

Race distance 20 laps of 2.76-mile circuit **Race time** 87.53mph **Race speed** 87.53mph **Car no** 76 **Entrant** Works

This was something of a repeat of the Goodwood performance, with Archie Scott-Brown's Lister-Jaguar grabbing an immediate lead at the start and me getting past him after 10 laps as he began to slow, and then retired with steering problems. I finished ahead of Tony Brooks in the other Aston DBR2, with Bruce Halford's Lister following us home in third.

RIGHT *A frustrating moment when I stalled Rob's Cooper on pole position for the Glover Trophy at Goodwood. A broken con-rod thwarted my chances of making amends.* (LAT)

398 1st

British Empire Trophy, Final

Aston Martin DBR2

12 April 1958, Oulton Park, Cheshire (GB)

Race speed 87.45mph **Race distance** 25 laps of 2.76-mile circuit
Fastest lap 1m 50.8s, 89.70mph (record, shared with Graham Hill) **Car no** 76 **Entrant** Works

I led the final from start to finish with Tony Brooks second and Archie Scott-Brown third. Archie had been switched into Bruce Halford's Lister after the problems with his own car during the heat.

BELOW *From pole position I won the British Empire Trophy with team-mate Tony Brooks, who qualified alongside me, in second place.* (LAT)

399 1st

Aintree 200

Cooper-Climax T45

19 April 1958, Aintree, Liverpool (GB)

Race distance 67 laps of 3-mile circuit **Race time** 2h 20m 47s
Race speed 85.66mph **Car no** 7 **Entrant** R.R.C. Walker

I qualified Rob Walker's Cooper on pole, ahead of Roy Salvadori's works car and Jean Behra's BRM P25, and led from the start. But towards the end of the race, while I was having difficulties with both the clutch and engine overheating, I had my hands really full with a challenge from Jack Brabham. He tried to get around me on the last corner of the final lap but ran wide, just as he had done earlier in the race. I floored the throttle and just made it to the line 0.2 seconds ahead of him.

400 Retired

Silverstone, BRDC International Trophy

Cooper-Climax T45

3 May 1958, Silverstone (GB)

Organising club British Racing Drivers' Club **Race distance** 50 laps of 2.9-mile circuit **Reason for retirement** Gearbox **Car no** 7 **Entrant** R.R.C. Walker

This race at Silverstone was an embarrassing repeat of my earlier Goodwood experience. My Cooper stalled on the front row of the starting grid and I faced the prospect of battling through the pack. That recovery went quite well and I was up to fifth place by lap 18, when the gearbox casing split and I coasted into the pits to retire.

401 Retired

Silverstone, Sports Car Race

Aston Martin DBR3/300

3 May 1958, Silverstone (GB)

Race distance 25 laps of 2.9-mile circuit
Reason for retirement Engine **Car no** 12 **Entrant** Works

For this race Tony Brooks and I, in the works Aston Martins, were ranged against the lighter and more nimble Lister-Jaguars, so it was no surprise that Archie Scott-Brown in the works Lister and Masten Gregory in the Ecurie Ecosse entry headed the starting line-up. Tony was driving one of the 3.9-litre DBR1s and I had one of the short-stroke 3-litre DBR3/300s.

Archie led from the start but Masten eventually overtook him to win. I ran as high as fourth, close behind Hawthorn's Ferrari, but when my engine began to tighten I pulled off before something broke.

402 Retired

Targa Florio

Aston Martin DBR1

11 May 1958, Piccolo Madonie, Sicily (I)

World Sports Car Championship, round 3

Race distance 13 laps of 44.74-mile circuit
Reason for retirement Transmission **Fastest lap** 42m 17.5s, 63.33mph **Co-driver** Tony Brooks **Car no** 100 **Entrant** Works

I had been so impressed by the handling and ride of the Aston Martin DBR1 over the bumps and ruts of the Sebring aerodrome circuit that I talked team manager John Wyer into entering one for the Targa Florio. I flew to Sicily via Modena, where I tried out the new 3-litre V12 Maserati, then started my preparations for the race by driving three laps of the 45-mile circuit in a rented Fiat 1100.

The car – not the Fiat! – clearly had potential, but about 12 miles into the race I made a mistake and hit a rock at the side of the road. I had to change the left-rear wheel, which lost me more than a minute. After about 25 miles the crankshaft damper came loose and set up an unnerving vibration that shook the whole car. I made a lengthy pit stop, then resumed, only for the gearbox to break on the fourth lap.

403 Retired

Monaco Grand Prix

Vanwall

18 May 1958, Monte Carlo (MON)

F1 World Championship, round 2

Race distance 100 laps of 1.95-mile circuit
Reason for retirement Valve-gear failure after 38 laps
Car no 28 **Entrant** Works

For 1958 the Formula 1 technical regulations had been changed to ban alcohol fuels, substituting instead 130-octane AvGas petroleum. The reason that Vanwall had missed the Argentine Grand Prix was that it wanted to retune and develop its engines before the start of the European season, so Monaco was the first *grande épreuve* in which Vanwall competed.

The race weekend was awful. My engine popped and banged and the car's front end juddered unnervingly. As my status as number one driver gave me the right to choose the equipment I used, I was a little disappointed when Tony Vandervell and the team manager, David Yorke, turned down my request that my engine should be fitted to Tony Brooks's car for me to drive in the second day's practice – so I had to put up and shut up!

Things were not helped by the fact that I was not feeling particularly well for much of the weekend and, thanks largely to oil on the circuit, could qualify no higher than the third row of the grid. In the early stages of the race I ran third, then moved up to second behind Mike Hawthorn's Ferrari and managed to squeeze past him on lap 32. Disappointingly, my tenure of the lead lasted only until lap 38, when my engine suffered valve-gear failure.

ANOTHER VICTORY FOR BP

Moss wins Aintree "200" using BP Energol and BP Fuel

LFFT I featured prominently and regularly in BP's promotional material through much of my career. (Stirling Moss Collection)

404   1st

Dutch Grand Prix

Vanwall

26 May 1958, Zandvoort, Haarlem (NL)

F1 World Championship, round 3

Race distance 75 laps of 2.61-mile circuit **Race time**
2h 4m 49.2s **Race speed** 93.93mph **Fastest lap** 1m 37.6s,
96.101mph **Car no** 1 **Entrant** Works

After the disappointment of Monaco, this proved to be the tonic the whole Vanwall team needed. Stuart Lewis-Evans took pole and the three Vanwalls were ranged across the front row of the grid. I got away to an excellent start, with Lewis-Evans running second, ahead of Harry Schell's BRM and Tony Brooks in the third Vanwall.

From the word 'go' my car felt really good, although it was weaving slightly in the gusty cross-winds that were always such a feature of this circuit. After about 50 laps, I lapped Mike Hawthorn, who really seemed to be having

an uncomfortable ride in the Ferrari. I never thought he looked particularly relaxed behind the wheel but on this occasion he was really hunched up and looking as though he was having a real struggle with the car's handling.

It was a good day for British motorsport as I crossed the line to score my third *grande épreuve* victory in a Vanwall, this time for the full quota of World Championship points. The BRMs of Schell and Behra were second and third, with Roy Salvadori fourth in a Cooper.

405   1st

Nürburgring, ADAC 1,000kms

Aston Martin DBR1

1 June 1958, Nürburgring (D)

World Sports Car Championship, round 4

Race distance 44 laps of 14.15-mile circuit **Race time** 7h 23m
33s **Race speed** 84.26mph **Fastest lap** 9m 43s, 87.55mph
Co-driver Jack Brabham **Car no** 1 **Entrant** Works

For this race I shared the Aston Martin DBR1 with Jack Brabham and led from the start, opening out a lead of a minute by the time I handed the car over to him after 10 laps. Unfortunately, Jack, largely through his lack of familiarity with the circuit, lost all that and more to drop back to third.

Then I took over again and by lap 22 was back in the lead, this time by two minutes. Jack drove from lap 25 to 30, then I took over again and, in total, I drove 36 of the race's 44 laps. I enjoyed every minute of it, but it took me a week to recover (longer than it took to recover from winning the Mille Miglia). It taught me a lesson and I vowed not to drive such a large percentage of an endurance race again.

RIGHT *Swooping down over Adenau Bridge at the Nürburgring on my way to victory in the 1,000kms race in the Aston DBR1.* (LAT)

BELOW *An all-Vanwall front row at Zandvoort for the Dutch Grand Prix, with me in the middle. I felt extremely confident and won quite easily.* (LAT)

Belgian Grand Prix

Vanwall

15 June 1958, Spa-Francorchamps, Liège (B)

F1 World Championship, round 5

Race distance 24 laps of 8.76-mile circuit
Reason for retirement First-lap error **Car no** 2 **Entrant** Works

The start of this race turned out to be very badly organised. All the competitors were directed to the wrong side of the grid, with pole on the left instead of its correct position on the right, as Mike Hawthorn correctly pointed out. The front-row starters were swapped around, but not the remainder of the grid.

It was a very hot day and we were held too long on the grid, with the result that several cars were already overheating, including Peter Collins's Ferrari. I shot off cleanly and immediately began to pull away from the pack. By the time I went through Stavelot for the first time I had a lead of more than 200 yards. I was up to maximum revs in fourth gear, then pulled for fifth and went straight back on to the throttle – but I was in neutral. The engine disintegrated and I was extremely embarrassed about what was one of the biggest disappointments of my career.

407 Retired

Le Mans 24 Hours

Aston Martin DBR1

21/22 June 1958, Sarthe (F)

World Sports Car Championship, round 5

Race distance 24 hours of 8.38-mile circuit (2,548.81 miles, 305 laps) **Reason for retirement** Engine after 30 laps **Co-driver** Jack Brabham **Car no** 2 **Entrant** Works

Le Mans was a race that was never particularly kind to me and the 1958 event was no exception. I was again sharing the car with Jack Brabham but he never had the chance to drive in the race. I led for the first two hours and was over a minute and a half ahead of Mike Hawthorn's Ferrari when the engine blew up at Mulsanne, just after 6.10pm.

OPPOSITE *My Vanwall leading the pack through Eau Rouge at the start of the Belgian Grand Prix. It didn't last long as I missed a gear on the opening lap and the engine blew up!* (Klemantaski Collection)

BELOW *Another engine failure came at Le Mans after I was leading for the first two hours in the Aston DBR1. I was well ahead of Mike Hawthorn's Ferrari at the time.* (LAT)

408 — 4th

Two Worlds Trophy, Heat 1

Maserati Eldorado Special

29 June 1958, Monza (I)

Race distance 63 laps of 2.65-mile circuit **Race time**
1h 0m 35.1s (62 laps) **Car no** 10 **Entrant** Zanetti

When the Monza circuit authorities decided to organise the Two Worlds Trophy in 1958, bringing Indianapolis cars to compete against supposedly the best that Europe had to offer on the banked circuit, the financial temptations were just too much for many people to resist.

One such was Mr Zanetti, owner of the Eldorado ice cream concern, who specially commissioned Maserati to build him a USAC-style track racing car based on a 250F chassis and powered by the 4.2-litre V8 engine. At one point in practice it started to rain – the USAC Indianapolis drivers never raced if it was wet – so I told the Maserati chief mechanic, Guerrino Bertocchi, to get the car out and I would take it out for a few laps.

I could drive it 'hands off' on the banking at around 140mph, but when I came past the pits I made it weave slightly to make it look as though it was a real handful. The USAC officials black-flagged me and, when I asked what was wrong, they told me that in their view the whole thing was too dangerous in the wet. I replied that a few little puddles did not worry me and they countered by saying that they did not race in the wet. So I replied that this was fine and that we three non-Americans – Luigi Musso, Jack Fairman and me – would therefore split the prize money. In the event it was dry for race day, so my bluff did not work.

In the first heat I made a poor start, but recovered from ninth to fifth, then fourth and then third, before dropping back to fourth at the chequered flag.

409 — 5th

Two Worlds Trophy, Heat 2

Maserati Eldorado Special

29 June 1958, Monza (I)

Race distance 63 laps of 2.65-mile circuit **Race time** N/A
Car no 10 **Entrant** Zanetti

In the second heat I really felt I was getting the hang of this oval racing business, dicing hard with former Indy 500 winner Troy Ruttman and Jimmy Bryan, who would go on to win the event on aggregate. Towards the end my tyres began to lose grip and I dropped to fifth.

BELOW *The Eldorado Special – my first taste of what we would today call Indycar racing.* (LAT)

410   Retired

Two Worlds Trophy, Heat 3

Maserati Eldorado Special

29 June 1958, Monza (I)

Race distance 63 laps of 2.65-mile circuit
Reason for retirement Crash **Car no** 10 **Entrant** Zanetti

M y clutch failed on the line at the start of the day's third heat and I could not make up such a big deficit, although I got up to fourth and was chasing young A.J. Foyt hard for third.

Suddenly I knew something was wrong

ABOVE *The Eldorado Maserati gave me one of the closest calls in my career when the steering broke on the Monza banking at 175mph and I hit the barrier very hard.* (Klemantaski Collection)

because my arms crossed. I was doing 175mph with the bloody Maser a metre below the top of the banking – and the steering had sheared. I hit the barrier at the top of the banking with a tremendous thump, ripped out three of the supporting posts, and bent a fair section of the barrier itself. The sports car brakes fitted to the car were absolutely useless. Two tyres burst, I lost a wheel, and the car spun into the infield. I closed my eyes and thought that I was going to die. Eventually I spun down to a halt in a cloud of dust and I remember thinking, "If this is hell, it's a bit hot and very dusty."

411   Retired

Reims, Coupe de Vitesse

Cooper-Climax T45

6 July 1958, Reims (F)

Race distance 30 laps of 5.1-mile circuit **Reason for retirement** Oil pressure after 10 laps **Fastest lap** 2m 36.7s, 118.5mph (record) **Car no** 6 **Entrant** R.R.C Walker

T his race marked the start of a frustrating day. I took pole in Rob Walker's Cooper, but Jean Behra's Porsche had the edge on straight-line speed and I was over 18 seconds behind by the time I had to retire with fading oil pressure after 10 laps.

412   2nd

French Grand Prix

Vanwall

6 July 1958, Reims (F)

F1 World Championship, round 6

Race distance 50 laps of 5.159-mile circuit
Race time 2h 3m 45.9s **Car no** 8 **Entrant** Works

The Vanwall was never in the same class as the Ferrari Dino 246s at this event and Mike Hawthorn totally dominated the race. Sadly, his team-mate Luigi Musso crashed heavily trying to keep up with Mike and died from his injuries.

My Vanwall had dropped a valve in practice, with the result that it was fitted with an overly high rear axle ratio in order to reduce stress on the rebuilt engine. In the race, I had slight gear-change problems that slowed me in the early stages and then I inherited second place after Behra's BRM suffered engine failure in the closing stages. It was a most unsatisfactory race for me.

413   1st

Vila Real, Sports Car Race

Maserati 300S

13 July 1958, Vila Real (P)

Race distance 35 laps of 3.3-mile circuit **Race time** 1h 47m 20s **Race speed** 84.169mph **Fastest lap** 88.28mph **Car no** 2 **Entrant** Works

This was very much in the nature of a Portuguese domestic sports car race with a few overseas entries, including Jean Behra and I in a couple of Maserati 300S roadsters that had been invited to give the proceedings a vaguely international flavour.

The opposition was not particularly strong, so Behra and I made a race of it and swapped places regularly throughout, with me winning under team orders by just a second at the end.

414   1st

Silverstone, *Daily Express* Sports Car Race

Lister-Jaguar

19 July 1958, Silverstone (GB)

Race distance 25 laps of 2.9-mile circuit **Race time** 44m 50.8s **Race speed** 97.92mph **Fastest lap** 1m 46s, 99.41mph (shared with Cliff Allison) **Car no** 29 **Entrant** Works

My opportunity to drive the works 3.8-litre Lister-Jaguar came because owner Brian Lister wanted to put privateers Ecurie Ecosse in their place after Masten Gregory had driven one of its cars to victory over that great little one-armed driver Archie Scott-Brown at the International Trophy meeting earlier in the year.

Incidentally, Archie had sadly died in May in a sports car race at Spa.

Since Lister and I were both contracted to BP, there was no problem reaching an agreement, but after Masten crashed the Ecosse entry during practice my biggest challenge came from the other works Lister driven by the American driver Walt Hansgen. In the event I led from start to finish quite comfortably.

OPPOSITE TOP *Chatting to one of the Vanwall mechanics in the paddock at Reims alongside the very smart Leyland Royal Tiger transporter used to take the cars around Europe.* (Klemantaski Collection)

OPPOSITE BOTTOM *Winning for Maserati at Vila Real after Jean Behra and I put on a show for the locals.* (Ludvigsen Library)

BELOW *Applying a touch of opposite-lock through Copse Corner at Silverstone on my way to a clear sports car win in the Lister-Jaguar.* (LAT)

415   Retired

British Grand Prix

Vanwall

19 July 1958, Silverstone (GB)

F1 World Championship, round 7

Race distance 75 laps of 2.927-mile circuit
Reason for retirement Engine **Car no** 7 **Entrant** Works

416   1st

Caen Grand Prix

Cooper-Climax T43

20 July 1958, Caen (F)

Race distance 86 laps of 2.19-mile circuit
Race time 2h 0m 9.7s **Race speed** 93.92mph
Car no 13 **Entrant** R.R.C. Walker

Just as Mike Hawthorn had had a runaway win at Reims, so Pete Collins duplicated that achievement in the Ferrari Dino 246 at Silverstone. The fact that I had managed to qualify on pole position did not count for much when it came to the race and I was 7 seconds behind him after only 10 laps. I managed to trim back some of the deficit by the 20-lap mark but five laps later a connecting rod in my engine broke coming round Woodcote and that was the end of my home *grande épreuve* that year.

On reflection, I have to say that the Vanwall four-cylinder engine was not a particularly nice power unit. We did have quite a lot of problems with it, and I think a significant factor was that a four-cylinder engine has more inherent vibration than a multi-cylinder engine such as the Ferrari V6 or V12, which were extremely smooth.

Immediately after the British Grand Prix, I nipped across the channel for the following day's non-championship race at the Caen circuit in northern France. My Cooper shared the front row with Behra's BRM and we had a good dice in the early stages, although I was beginning to edge away from him when his engine failed at half distance. From then on I led comfortably to the finish.

RIGHT *Sweeping through Copse at Silverstone while holding second place behind Peter Collins's Ferrari during the British Grand Prix. My Vanwall's engine broke a con-rod.* (Klemantaski Collection)

BELOW *The day after Silverstone I went some way towards making up for my disappointment by winning at Caen in Rob Walker's Cooper.* (LAT)

German Grand Prix

Vanwall

3 August 1958, Nürburgring (D)

F1 World Championship, round 8

Race distance 15 laps of 14.17-mile circuit
Reason for retirement Ignition **Fastest lap** 9m 9.2s, 92.9mph
(record) **Car no** 7 **Entrant** Works

At the Nürburgring I was happy to find that the Vanwall was handling much better than it had done there the previous year and, although I lost out to Mike Hawthorn's Ferrari in the battle for pole position, I was on the front row, with my team-mate Tony Brooks ahead of Peter Collins in the other Dino 246.

I jumped into the lead at the start and by the end of the second lap I was 18 seconds ahead of the Ferraris, with Tony Brooks running fourth in the other Vanwall. I was using little more than 7,000rpm and the car felt very good indeed, even on a full load of fuel.

Suddenly the engine cut out, abruptly and immediately, as if someone had switched off the ignition. That was the end of my race. On subsequent examination it appeared that a tiny screw in the magneto had vibrated loose and caused a short circuit.

Tony came through to win, although the day was immeasurably saddened by the death of Peter Collins, who was thrown out of his Ferrari against a tree at the Pflantzgarten right-hander as he tried to keep up with Tony's Vanwall. I always took a philosophical view about fatal accidents, reasoning that we were all competing voluntarily and accepted all the risks of our calling, but Pete's death affected me more than usual.

Peter Collins was a very competent driver. If I had to liken him to a contemporary Formula 1 driver, I would say that he was the Rubens Barrichello of his time. Rubens has won a lot of races and shaped up very well against Michael Schumacher at Ferrari when he was permitted to do so. In the 1955 Targa Florio Peter really did a tremendous job, so really Barrichello is as close as I can come to a comparable modern-day driver. Pete was good.

Kannonloppet

Maserati 300S

10 August 1958, Karlskoga (S)

Race distance 50 laps of 1.86-mile circuit **Race time** 1h 25m
21.3s **Car no** 1 **Entrant** Works

This Swedish event was supposed to replace the Kristianstad fixture on the calendar. Although I was beaten off the line by local driver Gunnar Carlsson in a Ferrari and Carel de Beaufort in a Porsche, I led from the fourth lap onwards and had a fairly easy victory.

RIGHT *Tony Vandervell bends down to have a word with me in the Vanwall cockpit in front of the pits at the Nürburgring.* (Klemantaski Collection)

LEFT *Glum group! Tony Vandervell (left), team manager David Yorke (centre) and myself seem unable to raise a smile between us as the mechanics work on the car at the Nürburgring.* (LAT)

419-424 · 2nd

Copenhagen Grand Prix (Six Heats)

Maserati 300S & JBW-Maserati

15/16 August 1958, Roskilde (DEN)

Reason for retirement Engine **Car no** 1 **Entrant** Works/Naylor

425 · 1st

Portuguese Grand Prix

Vanwall

24 August 1958, Porto (P)

F1 World Championship, round 9

Race distance 50 laps of 4.6-mile circuit **Race time** 2h 11m 27.8s **Race speed** 105.03mph **Fastest lap** 2m 32.58s **Car no** 2 **Entrant** Works

This unusual event comprised six heats and ran over two days. The Roskilde circuit was an amazing place that seemed to me to be about the size of Wembley Stadium, needing only second and third gears.

My Maserati 300S suffered a major engine failure in the first heat, but I was counted as the last finisher. For the second race, Brian Naylor kindly loaned me his JBW-Maserati and I won easily by 11.8 seconds. In the third heat, I scored another win in the JBW-Maserati, which I thought was quite a nice little car, this time by 19 seconds.

I had a fresh engine installed in the 300S for the heats on Sunday and started the day from the back of the grid, losing out on victory by 2.2 seconds in the fourth heat. Things improved through the day, however, and I managed to win the fifth heat by 0.6 seconds.

In the final heat, Gunnar Carlsson's Ferrari proved extremely wide and every time I attempted to get by he would come swooping across my bows. The crowds were booing him and shaking their fists to show their disapproval. After eight of the 16 laps he again pulled the same stunt, but this time I kept coming and simply nudged him out of the way. I won the heat by about 6 seconds, but the aggregate result for all six heats put Carlsson ahead of me by three-fifths of a second.

LEFT *Rear shot of my Vanwall hurtling through a long left-hander at Porto on my way to one of the most satisfying wins of the season.* (LAT)

The World Championship battle was still very tight as we headed for the Porto street circuit. Using widely spaced gear ratios, I successfully won the battle for pole position and, even though the track was initially a little damp, led away from the start.

On the second lap Mike Hawthorn surged past me and he was a second ahead with five laps completed, but I repassed him quite easily and by half distance I was a minute ahead with the fastest lap under my belt. Then came the mistake that would cost me the World Championship.

In the closing stages, Mike was battling with Jean Behra's sick BRM and posted the fastest lap, which in those days earned an extra point for the drivers' championship. In the Vanwall pits they signalled me 'HAW-REC' ('Hawthorn Record'), meaning that Mike had set the fastest lap, but I misread it as 'HAW-REG' ('Hawthorn Regular'), which suggested that he was lapping steadily but not particularly quickly.

I lapped Mike before the finish but he looked so aghast at the experience that I slowed up and permitted him to unlap himself. This meant that as I took the chequered flag he still had another lap to complete, but he promptly spun the Ferrari and when I came upon him he was trying to push-start the car uphill in the direction of the race.

I slowed right down and shouted to him that he would never manage the task and instead should push the car down the hill on the pavement rather than the track. He took my advice, and in doing so avoided the risk of disqualification. Although he was duly hauled up in front of the stewards, I correctly testified that his car was on the pavement and not on the circuit at the time, and consequently his second place – with the crucial point for that fastest lap – was confirmed.

426 · 2nd

Brands Hatch, Kentish 100, Heat 1

Cooper-Climax

30 August 1958, Brands Hatch, Kent (GB)

Race distance 42 laps of 1.24-mile circuit **Race time** 41m 5s **Fastest lap** 57.8s, 77.23mph **Car no** 7 **Entrant** R.R.C. Walker

In this national Formula 2 event, my first race at Brands Hatch for four years, I was up against Jack Brabham in the works Cooper and there was simply no way I could find a gap to pass him in the first heat.

427 · 1st

Brands Hatch, Kentish 100, Heat 2

Cooper-Climax

30 August 1958, Brands Hatch, Kent (GB)

Race distance 42 laps of 1.24-mile circuit **Race time** 41m 12s **Race speed** 75.84mph **Fastest lap** 57.4s, 77.77mph **Car no** 7 **Entrant** R.R.C. Walker

This must have been my lucky day! In the second heat, I beat Brabham. I was carrying my favourite race number, seven, and just look at the speed I posted for the fastest lap!

428   Retired

Italian Grand Prix

Vanwall

7 September 1958, Monza (I)

F1 World Championship, round 10

Race distance 70 laps of 3.573-mile circuit **Reason for retirement** Gearbox after 17 laps **Car no** 26 **Entrant** Works

Just as in 1957, there were three Vanwalls on the front row of the grid, but this time it was Mike Hawthorn's Ferrari that provided the Italian interest in third place between Tony Brooks and Stuart Lewis-Evans. I took pole position and in the race I was embroiled in a wheel-to-wheel slipstreaming battle for the first dozen or so laps, but my hopes of adding to my points tally were spoiled again, this time when the gearbox broke after 17 laps.

Tony won for Vanwall, enhancing a successful season in which he had also been victorious at Spa-Francorchamps and the Nürburgring, and underlining my belief that he was one of the best drivers in the world – even if he was never really well known to the general public. He was a very easy-going, quiet man, but without being subservient in any way. I think he was very good – excellent, in fact.

429   1st

RAC Tourist Trophy

Aston Martin DBR1

13 September 1958, Goodwood (GB)

World Sports Car Championship, round 6

Race distance 4 hours of 2.4-mile circuit (148 laps)
Race speed 88.33mph **Fastest lap** 1m 32.6s, 93.3mph (record)
Co-driver Tony Brooks **Car no** 7 **Entrant** Works

As I have often said, I always looked forward to any race at Goodwood simply because of the excellent mood and atmosphere that always prevailed there, and my final British race of the 1958 season was no exception.

The RAC Tourist Trophy, run to a four-hour format, was always going to be a very suitable event for the excellent Aston Martin DBR1s, and from the start of practice I was very much setting the pace, along with my co-driver Tony Brooks. Just as the 2pm start time approached,

ABOVE *Taking the chequered flag to win the Goodwood Tourist Trophy ahead of the sister Aston Martin DBR1 shared by Jack Brabham and Roy Salvadori.* (LAT)

OPPOSITE *Triumph and tragedy: winning the Moroccan Grand Prix was not enough to take the World Championship and the race was saddened by the fatal accident to my team-mate Stuart Lewis-Evans.* (LAT)

some 29 drivers lined up opposite the cars for the traditional Le Mans-style start. I made good use of the fact that I had set the fastest practice time by being first away, into an immediate lead.

After an hour I came into the pits to hand the car over to Tony and he soon had the DBR1 back into the lead, driving really well and getting nearly a lap ahead of Stuart Lewis-Evans's sister car. I took over just before 5pm for the final run to the flag, and at the finish the DBR1 of Roy Salvadori and Jack Brabham was the only other car on the same lap as Tony and me.

It was perhaps not the most exciting race of the year, but as the Astons crossed the line in one-two-three formation the Feltham marque moved up to second place behind Ferrari in the World Sports Car Championship.

430 — 1st

Moroccan Grand Prix

Vanwall

19 October 1958, Ain Diab, Casablanca (MO)

F1 World Championship, round 11

Race distance 53 laps of 4.734-mile circuit **Race time** 2h 9m 15s **Race speed** 116.462mph **Fastest lap** 2m 22.55s, 117.8mph **Car no** 26 **Entrant** Works

431 — 1st

Melbourne Grand Prix, Heat 1

Cooper-Climax T43

29 November 1958, Albert Park, Melbourne (AUS)

Race distance 8 laps of c3-mile circuit **Race time** 15m 32s **Race speed** 96.57mph **Fastest lap** 99.6mph **Car no** 7 **Entrant** R.R.C. Walker

432 — 1st

Melbourne Grand Prix, Final

Cooper-Climax T43

29 November 1958, Albert Park, Melbourne (AUS)

Race distance 32 laps of c3-mile circuit **Race time** 1h 0m 41.2s **Race speed** 98.86mph **Fastest lap** 1m 50s, 102.26mph **Car no** 7 **Entrant** R.R.C. Walker

This was the day on which I lost the Formula 1 World Championship. The situation I faced was a little like Felipe Massa's in the 2008 Brazilian Grand Prix: all I could do was the best job possible and the outcome of the title battle depended on what other people achieved.

I led in my Vanwall from start to finish, but in the closing stages of the race Ferrari signalled Phil Hill to relinquish second place to Mike Hawthorn, giving him the result he needed to become Britain's first World Champion, by a single point. Actually, thinking about it, I suspect that Phil did not need to be told. He was a good team player and knew the mathematics of the situation as the race unfolded.

People have often asked me whether I approve of team orders and I always say that I do. I was brought up as one of a generation of racing drivers to whom team orders were part of the business. We all knew that, I am sure. As far as Phil was concerned, it did not matter whether he was second or third – he backed off and gave it to Mike.

Of course, the race was tinged with great sadness because Stuart Lewis-Evans crashed his Vanwall, suffering serious burns from which he later died. There was no doubt that he was an enormous talent, even though he was not terribly strong. I think he was probably the bravest of the three of us driving for Vanwall. If anyone was going to try and go flat out through a corner that was not quite flat out, I think it would have been Stuart.

To round off the year I had a whistle-stop trip Down Under. Rob Walker's 2.5-litre Cooper performed to good effect in the first heat at Albert Park and I won comfortably by just under a minute from the Maserati 250F of local racer Bib Stilwell.

In the final I had a lucky win by 39 seconds from Jack Brabham's similar Cooper in torrid conditions that caused my car, in the closing stages, to use up all its coolant and overheat dramatically, with the temperature gauge right off the clock.

1959

A VINTAGE YEAR

This was a varied and busy year, both in terms of cars and events, and, once again, I was in with a chance of becoming World Champion.

As Tony Vandervell had decided at the end of the 1958 season to withdraw the Vanwall team from serious front-line competition, I suppose I had my eye out for a fresh contract with a full works team. Of course, in no way should this be taken as any sort of criticism of dear old Rob Walker, who had done such a brilliant job fielding Formula 1 cars built by other people, and in fact I decided to commit to him again for the whole season, once more operating on the informal basis of a gentleman's agreement. In addition to driving Formula 1 for him, I was also to drive his impressive, new Borgward-engined Cooper in Formula 2 events.

You will see how the story unfolds over the following narrative pages, but, suffice to say, our efforts were comprehensively thwarted by the unreliability of the Colotti gearboxes that Rob and Alf Francis had commissioned specially for the cars. At least two crucial retirements – at Monaco and Zandvoort – were down to gearbox problems. Otherwise the standard of preparation delivered by Alf Francis and his fellow mechanics was of a consistently high order.

As it turned out, I did not drive for Rob in all the *grandes épreuves* as I drove a BRM in the British and French Grands Prix. Whether this was wise, in the great scheme of things, I do not know but I did come second on my home turf.

I also drove my own Cooper-Monaco sports car during the year, when possible, and later in the season we switched to using Climax engines in Rob's Formula 1 Cooper.

In the sports car racing world, I continued to drive for Aston Martin and took another victory in the Nürburgring 1,000kms, but success at Le Mans continued to elude me. As it was, I had to sit and watch as Carroll Shelby and Roy Salvadori, also driving for Aston Martin, completed the job to score a memorable victory for the team, ahead of team-mates Maurice Trintignant and Paul Frère.

As for becoming World Champion, this again went down to the wire and again it was not to be. Even so, I was proud to have had a hand in Aston Martin's efforts in winning the World Sports Car Championship ahead of Ferrari – a minor consolation prize.

LEFT *The 1959 season left me facing up to a life without Vanwall, so I committed to drive for Rob Walker for the entire season. That said, I also had three exploratory outings in the front-engined BRM P25, my best result with it being this second place in the British Grand Prix at Aintree.* (Tom March Collection)

433   Retired

New Zealand Grand Prix, Heat 2

Cooper-Climax F1

10 January 1959, Ardmore, Auckland (NZ)

Race distance 15 laps of 2-mile circuit
Reason for retirement Driveshaft spider failure on last lap
Fastest lap 1m 24.2s (shared with R. Flockhart)
Entrant R.R.C. Walker

Practice took place on Thursday in preparation for the Saturday race and, although the track surface seemed slippery, the Cooper's acceleration was excellent. I set the fastest time ahead of Jack Brabham, Ron Flockhart and Bruce McLaren. On race morning there was a huge crowd, with the organisers estimating that one in three of the entire Auckland population had come out to see the race. To judge by the traffic queues that had been building up since dawn, they could well have been right.

I was leading the first heat easily when a driveshaft spider broke on the last lap, but I

was fortunate enough to be very kindly loaned a spare by Jack Brabham and it was fitted to the Cooper in time for me to start in the final.

434   1st

New Zealand Grand Prix, Final

Cooper-Climax F1

10 January 1959, Ardmore, Auckland (NZ)

Race distance 75 laps of 2-mile circuit **Race time** 1h 48m 24.4s
Race speed 82.8mph **Fastest lap** 1m 24.8s, 85mph (record)
Car no 7 **Entrant** R.R.C. Walker

After my problems in the heat, I had to start the final from the back of the grid, but I was up to second by the second corner and led from lap two to the end.

BELOW *My success in the New Zealand Grand Prix at Ardmore as recorded by the daily press.* (Stirling Moss Collection)

435   Disqualified

Sebring 12 Hours

Lister-Jaguar

21 March 1959, Sebring, Florida (USA)

World Sports Car Championship, round 1

Race distance 12 hours of 5.2-mile circuit
Reason for disqualification Not walking to and from car
Co-drivers Ivor Bueb, Lake Underwood, Briggs Cunningham
Car no 2 **Entrant** Cunningham

Ivor Bueb did the first stint at the wheel of the aerodynamic Costin-bodied Lister-Jaguar entered by Briggs Cunningham and I took over from him after about two and a half hours, by which time the car was in fifth place, two laps behind the leading Ferrari. I made up those lost laps and led as the five-hour mark was reached.

At this point it began to rain and in these conditions I extended my lead, but the car suddenly ran out of fuel. On reflection, it was clear that the final churn of fuel had not been tipped into the Lister's tank at the previous stop. I hitched a lift on a marshal's motorbike to get some more fuel, but after 16 more laps in the rain I was disqualified for 'not walking' to and from my car. I later switched to Lake Underwood's Cunningham Lister but this was 16 laps down at the time and so there was no prospect of a decent result.

436   1st

Goodwood, Glover Trophy

Cooper-Climax F1

30 March 1959, Goodwood, West Sussex (GB)

Race distance 42 laps of 2.4-mile circuit **Race time** 1h 6m 58s
Race speed 90.31mph **Fastest lap** 1m 31.8s, 91.42mph
Car no 7 **Entrant** R.R.C. Walker

This was my début outing in the Formula 1 Cooper fitted with the full 2.5-litre Climax engine, which had been built up by our team of mechanics under Alf Francis's direction. It was equipped from the outset with the 'normal' Cooper gearbox, but that would change as the season unfolded. In practice for this race, I encountered an unusual problem when the steering column briefly came adrift, due to a loose bolt, which sent me into the wattle fencing at Fordwater.

The outcome of the race was fine. I started from the second row and tailed Harry Schell's BRM for 10 laps before squeezing ahead at St Mary's. I won by over 12 seconds from Jack Brabham.

437   1st

Grand Prix d'Europe des Micromills

Micromill

8 April 1959, Paris (F)

Car no 24 Entrant Organisers

This was something of a stunt event with 10 little French dirt-track cars running on an indoor track in the Palais des Sports in Paris. I won two heats but in the third the back axle snapped. I ended up first overall after a selection of spins and shunts among the competitors, although I am not really quite sure how.

BELOW *My outing in the little Micromill was certainly a great deal of fun, but not the most serious event in which I have competed!* (LAT)

Aintree 200

F1 Cooper-BRM

18 April 1959, Aintree, Liverpool (GB)

Race distance 67 laps of 3-mile circuit
Reason for retirement Gearbox **Fastest lap**
1m 58.8s, 90.91mph (record) **Car no** 7 **Entrant** R.R.C. Walker

I suppose you could say that the Cooper-BRM was Rob Walker's secret weapon in the sense that we thought we might end up with the best of both worlds – the nimble-handling Cooper chassis paired with the powerful BRM 2.5-litre four-cylinder engine, which, we felt, was probably not being harnessed to best effect in the P25 front-engined chassis.

The loan of an engine to Rob was duly arranged and it was installed in a specially adapted Cooper chassis, but the problem again was the gearbox and we approached Valerio Colotti to do the job for us. I tested the completed car and its new gearbox at Modena before driving it at Aintree, where it shuddered violently under heavy braking in practice and was really difficult to drive.

I made a decent start from the third row and tailed Masten Gregory's works Cooper until its clutch broke and I inherited the lead. I was 27 seconds ahead when a tab washer locating a nut in the gearbox broke and put me out of the race.

BELOW *On the grid for the Aintree 200 with Rob Walker's Cooper now fitted with a BRM engine. The Colotti gearbox broke while I was well in the lead.* (LAT)

Syracuse Grand Prix

F2 Cooper-Borgward

25 April 1959, Sicily (I)

Race distance 55 laps of 3.47-mile circuit **Race time** 1h 53m 6s
Race speed 101.48mph **Fastest lap** 2m 0.8s, 101.88mph
Car no 12 **Entrant** R.R.C. Walker

You could say the idea of using the powerful Borgward 16-valve, four-cylinder, fuel-injected engine as an alternative to the customary Coventry-Climax was one of the more inspired decisions taken by Rob Walker and me during our time together. After initial contact made by Ken Gregory through the Borgward concessionaire in London, the deal was given the green light by company

ABOVE *Winning the Silverstone GT race in the good-looking Aston Martin DB4 GT.* (Tom March Collection)

founder Carl Borgward on the strict condition that I would be driving the car with the Borgward engine in it.

Rob was to run one car for me with the British Racing Partnership (BRP) fielding a couple for Ivor Bueb and George Wicken, although the latter was soon replaced by an impressively quick new boy called Chris Bristow. I made my début in the Cooper-Borgward at Syracuse, where I was embroiled in a close battle with Jean Behra's Formula 2 Ferrari for many laps until he spun, trying to counter-attack in the closing stages, leaving me to consolidate my lead to the chequered flag.

440	1st

Silverstone, GT Race

Aston Martin DB4 GT

2 May 1959, Silverstone (GB)

Organising club British Racing Drivers' Club **Race distance** 12 laps of 2.92-mile circuit **Race time** 24m 14.4s **Race speed** 86.94mph **Fastest lap** 1m 58.8s, 88.7mph **Car no** 54 **Entrant** Works

This was an easy win for the Aston Martin, beating Roy Salvadori's Jaguar 3.4 into second place. Jaguar were ticking on a bit about the short-wheelbase DB4 GT I was driving, suggesting there were question marks over its eligibility.

441	2nd

Silverstone, Sports Car Race

Aston Martin DBR1

2 May 1959, Silverstone (GB)

Organising club British Racing Drivers' Club **Race distance** 25 laps of 2.92-mile circuit **Race time** 44m 41.8s **Car no** 30 **Entrant** Works

I had to drive very hard to finish second in the big Aston Martin DBR1 in this second supporting race of the day at Silverstone. Frankly, my car simply was not quite quick enough in this sort of company and I could not catch Roy Salvadori's Cooper-Maserati.

442 Retired

Silverstone, BRDC *Daily Express* International Trophy

BRM P25

2 May 1959, Silverstone (GB)

Organising club British Racing Drivers' Club
Race distance 50 laps of 2.92-mile circuit
Reason for retirement Brake failure **Car no** 3
Entrant British Racing Partnership

With all the problems we had been experiencing with the Colotti gearbox on the Cooper, we decided to talk seriously with BRM about the possibility of using one of its front-engined P25 Formula 1 cars for a limited number of races, just to see how the team was progressing with its development and perhaps put down some sort of marker for the future.

Raymond Mays and Peter Berthon were very supportive about the idea of my driving a BRM. However, my father and Ken Gregory rather went over their heads, going directly to Alfred Owen, the boss of the Rubery Owen industrial group, to negotiate the terms on which I would drive it. We wanted Tony Robinson to prepare and run the car out of the British Racing Partnership's base in Highgate in north London. I think Mays and Berthon were rather put out but Alfred Owen had got to the stage where he just wanted the BRM to be performing well and was not particularly concerned how he achieved that aim.

BRP was established by Ken and my father as a fully fledged F1 team. I drove for it from time to time but never on a regular basis, in part because a privateer team was always at some disadvantage – it was the same for Rob Walker – in being unable to get Lotus or Cooper to sell them their latest cars.

The other thing that I would like to point out about BRP is that the choice of lime-green paintwork – criticised by many – was intended to make the cars stand out from a distance, particularly in photographs. In that connection, one should always remember that although green is Britain's national racing colour, there is no such thing as 'British Racing Green', as the dark green used by Jaguar was so often called. It could be any shade of green you chose.

The day after I had won the Easter Monday Glover Trophy at Goodwood, I stayed on to test Harry Schell's BRM. All in all, I came to the conclusion that the chassis was excellent and the engine fair. Then I switched to Jo Bonnier's car, which had a better engine but its chassis did not feel quite as good. We eventually concluded a deal for me to drive the car in the International Trophy at Silverstone, the French Grand Prix at Reims and the British Grand Prix at Aintree under the BRP banner and with Rob Walker's blessing.

I took pole position at Silverstone and led quite convincingly after getting past Jack Brabham's Cooper after a couple of laps, but I sensed there was something funny with the brakes so I eased back early for Copse corner – thank goodness. No front brakes! I held the car on the track until I realised that I would not make it through the corner, so I deliberately spun the car, finishing a few feet from the bank. I was very cross about it and left the circuit before the race was over.

LEFT *In the BRM prior to the start of the Silverstone International Trophy race. I led the race before the brakes failed and I had to spin the car deliberately to avoid a huge shunt.* (Tom March Collection)

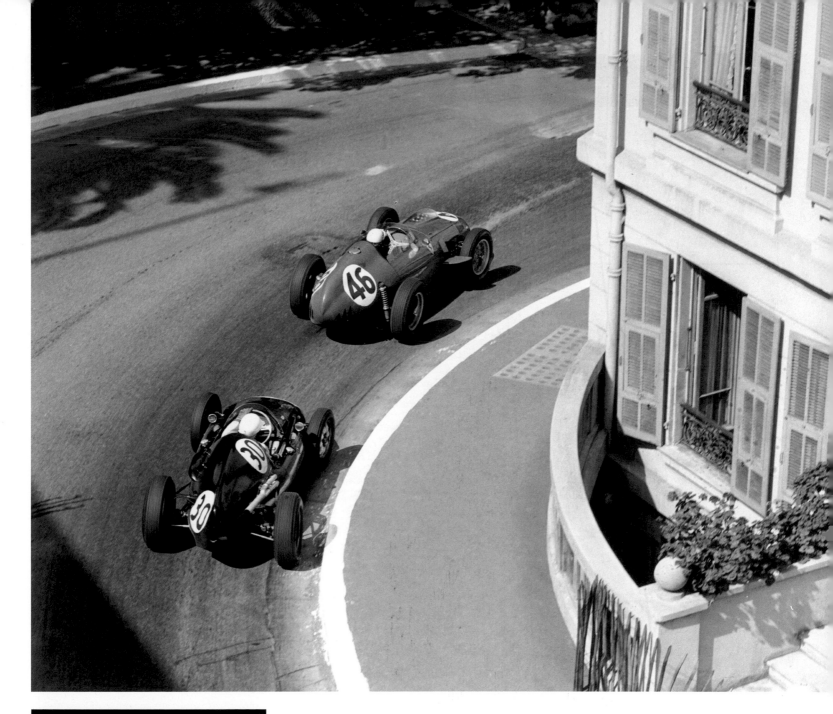

443 Retired

Monaco Grand Prix

F1 Cooper-Climax

10 May, 1959, Monte Carlo (MON)

F1 World Championship, round 1

Race distance 100 laps of 1.95-mile circuit

Reason for retirement Gearbox after 81 laps **Car no** 30

Entrant R.R.C. Walker

Unsurprisingly, I opted to drive the Climax-engined car at Monaco. I qualified on pole, 0.4 seconds faster than Behra's Ferrari Dino 246, with Brabham's works Cooper completing the front row. Behra made a perfect getaway and, with Brabham latching on behind, we formed a high-speed trio, steadily pulling away from the rest of the field.

On lap 20, Behra suddenly slowed as his Ferrari's engine began to tighten up and it appeared that he had dropped quite a lot of oil at the Gasworks hairpin, which made conditions there extremely slippery for a few laps. I took a run at him through Ste Devote and overtook the Ferrari going up the hill towards Casino Square. From that point on I was out on my own and, once my lead over Brabham had expanded to about 40 seconds, I eased back to conserve the machinery.

Then with 19 laps to go it all went wrong. My Cooper's Colotti gearbox broke and I had to sit and watch Brabham's works car go through to an easy win.

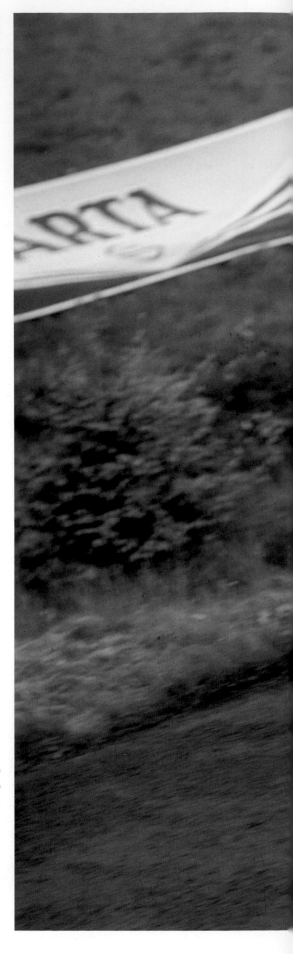

444   Retired

Dutch Grand Prix

F1 Cooper-Climax

31 May 1959, Zandvoort, Haarlem (NL)

F1 World Championship, round 3

Race distance 75 laps of 2.605-mile circuit
Reason for retirement Gearbox after 63 laps **Fastest lap** 1m 36.7s, 96.996mph **Car no** 11 **Entrant** R.R.C. Walker

I t was as blustery as usual during practice at Zandvoort but my Cooper was still pulling 6,750rpm, about 150mph, down the main straight and the car felt good as I lined up on the outside of the front row, beaten only by Jo Bonnier's BRM P25 and Jack Brabham's ever-present works Cooper.

I made a poor start. On reflection, I wonder if I was trying to take things too easy in the interests of preserving the fragile Colotti gearbox. Either way, I was down in eighth place by the end of the opening lap and it took me 24 of the race's 75 laps to pull through to third place behind Bonnier and Brabham. My car was running well and on lap 49 I passed Brabham for second place and then took the lead from Bonnier on lap 60.

Three laps later the wretched gearbox failed again and I was out, leaving Bonnier to inherit a fortuitous and timely win for the BRM team, which had struggled for so many years trying to realise this precious ambition. But now I had retired with gearbox failure from two consecutive Grands Prix and some people were labelling me a car breaker. It was an unfair accusation and those who levelled it were ignoring all the evidence to the contrary.

RIGHT *A great win for Aston Martin at the Nürburgring was only made possible by my co-driver Jack Fairman's determination in salvaging the DBR1 from a ditch into which he had spun while lapping a slower car.* (Klemantaski Collection)

445   1st

Nürburgring, ADAC 1,000kms

Aston Martin DBR1

7 June 1959, Nürburgring (D)

World Sports Car Championship, round 3

Race distance 44 laps of 14.15-mile circuit **Race time** 7h 33m 18.0s Race speed 82.5mph **Fastest lap** 9m 32s, 89.16mph (record) **Co-driver** Jack Fairman **Car no** 1 **Entrant** Works

T his was one of my most memorable sports car races, although there was an unexpected twist to the tale that caught me unawares and might have cost us the victory had it not been for the great determination of my co-driver Jack Fairman. I qualified fastest in the DBR1, got away to a clean start, and was leading Dan Gurney in the best-placed Ferrari by 16 seconds at the end of the opening 14-mile lap. All was going smoothly, or so it seemed, and I extended my lead progressively so that when I handed the car over to Jack at the three-hour mark I was five minutes ahead of the Ferraris. Jack kept up a respectable pace, as was his wont, and lost only a small amount of time to our rivals, but then he got caught out lapping one of the little Alfa Romeo Giuliettas and spun into a ditch.

Back in the pits, I received the message that my car was off the road, and presumably out of the race, so I changed out of my overalls and was chatting with colleagues at the end of the pit lane when the cry went up: "Jack is coming in!" To my amazement, he had heaved the Aston out of the ditch with his backside and was back on the track, so I made a lightning change back into my overalls and took over the car. Now I was 75 seconds behind Olivier Gendebien's Ferrari and 70 seconds behind Jean Behra's similar car, but in three laps I managed to regain the lead. I built up a three-minute advantage before handing the car back to Fairman for two laps, after which I took over for the run to the finish.

At the final handover, the Ferraris of Phil Hill and Tony Brooks were both well over a minute ahead of me. It took me another three laps to get back into the lead and eventually I won by 31 seconds from Hill and Gendebien.

446 Retired

Le Mans 24 Hours

Aston Martin DBR1

20/21 June 1959, Sarthe (F)

World Sports Car Championship, round 4

Race distance 24 hours of 8.38-mile circuit (2,701.65 miles, 323 laps) **Reason for retirement** Engine **Co-driver** Jack Fairman **Car no** 4 **Entrant** Works

---

Success at Le Mans continued to prove elusive for me in 1959, even though the Aston Martin DBR1's performance at the Nürburgring raised my expectations by reminding me just what an excellent overall package it actually was. The cars were superbly prepared for Le Mans and the team made the trip to France with high hopes for a good result.

The Ferraris were again a bit quicker on the Mulsanne straight, but I made a strong start and led for the first hour. Then Jean Behra slipstreamed past me on the Mulsanne straight, towing my Aston up to just over 6,000rpm in his slipstream, which was over 300rpm more than I had seen while I was running alone.

I did the first 38 laps, then handed the car over to Jack Fairman for another 35, but in the first lap of my second stint the engine dropped a valve and that was the end of another abortive Le Mans effort. However, I was glad that the Astons of Salvadori/Shelby and Trintignant/Frère finished first and second.

447 Retired

French Grand Prix

BRM P25

5 July 1959, Reims (F)

F1 World Championship, round 4

Race distance 50 laps of 5.15-mile circuit **Reason for retirement** Spin after 42 laps **Fastest lap** 2m 22.8s, 130.049mph **Car no** 2 **Entrant** BRP

This was the second of three races in which I had agreed to drive the BRM P25 under the BRP banner. In many ways, despite its unreliability, this car represented the ultimate development of the front-engined 2.5-litre Formula 1 concept and it triggered a succession of questions about how difficult it was to make the transition from a front-engined machine to the new generation of rear-engined cars.

I firmly believed that the switch was neither too difficult nor too big. I think that a rear-engined car is inherently easier to drive than a front-engined one. But at that time the front-engined cars were fully developed and sorted, and the incoming rear-engined ones were only beginning.

Yet there were exceptions to that rule, most notably the four-wheel-drive Ferguson P99 in which I won the 1961 Oulton Park Gold Cup. As I will discuss later, the Ferguson was difficult because you could not set it up and throw it around in the same way as you could a Cooper, for example. You could hold a Cooper beautifully balanced in a sideways drift, but you could not do that with the Ferguson. You had to be much more accurate and precise.

I must confess that the BRM felt absolutely superb during practice at Reims. I thought it might be quick enough for the front row of the grid but eventually it was Tony Brooks who took pole in the Fantuzzi-bodied Ferrari Dino 246 ahead of Jack Brabham in the works Cooper and Phil Hill in the other Ferrari. I lined up on the second row alongside Jean Behra's Ferrari.

Race day was punishingly hot and Tony simply ran away with the race in as unflustered a demonstration of disciplined car control as you could wish to see. The rest of us could not get close to him. I ran second from the start, then dropped to fifth and, despite driving as hard as I could, I found myself making virtually no impression at all on the leading bunch. Eventually I caught Brabham for third place and set off after Phil Hill's Ferrari.

Then I spun on melted tar at the Thillois hairpin and, because the clutch had packed up, I exhausted myself by fruitlessly attempting to push-start the car while it was in gear. There was simply no chance of achieving that and I was out of the race.

BELOW *On an exceedingly hot day, here I am trying to push-start the BRM P25 after spinning on melted tar at the Thillois hairpin in the French Grand Prix – but to no avail.* (LAT)

---

448   1st

Reims, Coupe de Vitesse

F2 Cooper-Borgward

5 July 1959, Reims (F)

Race distance 25 laps of 5.15-mile circuit **Race time** 1h 4m 54.2s **Race speed** 119.22mph **Fastest lap** 2m 33.1s, 121.22mph (record, shared with Hans Herrmann) **Car no** 8 **Entrant** R.R.C. Walker

Makes you think, doesn't it? After wrestling the BRM in the French Grand Prix, I had a short break before it was time to line up for the Formula 2 supporting race, still with the temperature nudging the wrong side of 100 degrees Fahrenheit. I had a good start and went straight into the lead, ahead of Hans Herrmann in the Behra Porsche Special, which was a bit quicker than my Cooper. But Herrmann overdid his braking and slid off, so I came home to win, feeling exceedingly tired in that terrific heat.

449   1st

Rouen, Coupe Delamere Deboutteville

Maserati Tipo 60

12 July 1959, Rouen-les-Essarts (F)

Race distance 35 laps of 4.05-mile circuit **Race time** 1h 29m 40.9s **Race speed** 95.18mph **Car no** 2 **Entrant** Works

Maserati's racing programme may have been all but wiped out the previous year after the big crash in Venezuela, but the team still had high-octane fuel coursing through its veins and, after the Monaco Grand Prix, I had been invited to Modena to test its new 2-litre sports car.

It was built around a chassis composed of an incredibly complicated latticework of tubing and clad in what I can only describe as a skimpy aluminium bodyshell.

My first impression of this distinctive little machine was that it was absolutely fantastic – responsive and agile in equal measure. I briefly tested it again during practice for the Nürburgring 1,000kms, in which I was driving an Aston Martin, but the engine seized before I could complete a lap.

I persuaded Maserati to let me drive the car at Rouen in the supporting race to the Formula 2 international, in which I was racing Rob Walker's Cooper-Borgward. I started from pole position and led all the way. What a great little car it was.

450   1st

Rouen Grand Prix

F2 Cooper-Borgward

12 July 1959, Rouen-les-Essarts (F)

Race distance 35 laps of 4.05-mile circuit **Race time** 1h 28 5.8s **Race speed** 96.9mph **Fastest lap** 2m 24.9s, 100.98mph (record) **Car no** 2 **Entrant** R.R.C. Walker

ABOVE *My efforts to win the Aintree sports car race supporting the British Grand Prix were frustrated when I was rammed from behind at the start after my Cooper Monaco jumped out of gear.* (Tom March Collection)

LEFT *Sampling the glorious 2-litre Maserati Tipo 60 with a good sports car victory at Rouen.* (Edward Eves, Ludvigsen Library)

There was an unwelcome glitch with the timing system during practice, with the result that Hans Herrmann, driving the Behra Porsche Special, was credited with pole position, although we were convinced that I had done the fastest time in Rob Walker's Cooper-Borgward.

As events transpired, this mattered precious little because I took the lead from the start and held it throughout to score my second victory of the day at this excellent circuit. I won by half a minute from Harry Schell.

451   Retired

Aintree, Sports Car Race

Cooper-Monaco

18 July 1959, Aintree, Liverpool (GB)

Race distance 17 laps of 3-mile circuit
Reason for retirement Burst oil pipe **Fastest lap** 87.66mph (record) **Car no** 1 **Entrant** Stirling Moss Ltd

This really was not too good a start to the day of the British Grand Prix. I qualified on the front row of the grid but the car jumped out of gear at the start and I was hit from behind by the Hon Edward Greenall. After a precautionary stop to check for damage, I flew through the field until an oil pipe burst and started a small fire in the cockpit. The fire soon went out, but my race was over.

452 — 2nd

British Grand Prix

BRM P25

18 July 1959, Aintree, Liverpool (GB)

F1 World Championship, round 5

Race distance 75 laps of 3-mile circuit **Race time** 2h 30m 33.8s
Fastest lap 1m 57s, 92.308mph (shared with Bruce McLaren)
Car no 6 **Entrant** BRP

453 — 1st

Trophée d'Auvergne

F1 Cooper-Borgward

26 July 1959, Clermont-Ferrand (F)

Race distance 26 laps of 5-mile circuit **Race time** 1h 41m 46.1s
Race speed 76.72mph **Fastest lap** 3m 48.8s, 78.73mph (record)
Car no 14 **Entrant** R.R.C. Walker

After that unfortunate spin at Reims, I was looking forward to trying the P25 at Aintree, where I had guarded hopes that I might do reasonably well. I took the short flight from Heathrow to Manchester on the Wednesday evening and was soon comfortably ensconced at the Adelphi Hotel in Liverpool.

Unfortunately, Thursday dawned grey and rainy, which did not bode well for first practice, although I managed to end up setting the quickest time on 2m 8.4s, ahead of Carroll Shelby in the Aston Martin (2m 9.2s), Jack Brabham in the Cooper-Climax (2m 9.4s) and Tony Brooks in one of the old Vanwalls (2m 10.2s), which had been dusted down for the team's home Grand Prix and, frankly, looked as though it had seen better days.

On the Friday, the weather was patchy, both wet and dry, and I spent a lot of time battling with clutch slip on the BRM. I was disappointed that I had to settle for seventh place on the grid in the middle of the third row. Brabham took pole by a full second from Roy Salvadori's Aston, with the other BRM P25 driven by Harry Schell on the outside of the front row. I made a good start but lost quite a bit of ground on the opening lap as the damned clutch slipped again.

After about 10 laps I had moved through to second place behind Jack and I pressed on hard until I had reduced his lead to about nine seconds. Then I had to make a pit stop to change worn tyres, followed by another to top up with fuel due to a fuel-feed problem. By the chequered flag, though, I was back up to second place, just ahead of Bruce McLaren's Cooper.

The thing I remember most about this race was that the start was given by the legendary French official Raymond 'Toto' Roche, who usually presided over events at Reims and whose antics on the starting grid in front of the assembled field, seconds before the start, were matched only by the infamous Louis Chiron's similar behaviour at Monaco through the 1950s and '60s when he would fumble with the flag and jump about, getting in everyone's way.

On this occasion, Roche elected to stand right in front of my Cooper-Borgward, then dropped the flag and ran for his life. That allowed Chris Bristow's BRP Cooper-Borgward to take an immediate lead from the outside of the front row. Bristow was looking very ragged and I passed him on the sixth lap, leading all the way to the finish to win ahead of Henry Taylor's Parnell-entered Cooper. Sadly, poor Ivor Bueb crashed heavily and was thrown out of his BRP Cooper, sustaining very serious injuries from which he died a week later.

LEFT *Seventh on the grid with the BRM for the British Grand Prix at Aintree. Ahead of me are Harry Schell's BRM (8), Roy Salvadori's Aston Martin (2) and the Coopers of Masten Gregory (14) and Maurice Trintignant (18), while Carroll Shelby's Aston Martin (4) is to my left.* (Ludvigsen Library)

German Grand Prix, Heat 1

Cooper-Climax

2 August 1959, AVUS (D)

F1 World Championship, round 6

Race distance 30 laps of 5.16-mile circuit
Reason for retirement Gearbox after 1 lap **Car no** 7
Entrant R.R.C. Walker

This was all a bit of a fiasco because I somehow got myself involved in the controversy surrounding the transfer of this race from the Nürburgring to what you would have to say, in all honesty, was a pretty damned stupid circuit at the AVUS.

I was asked what I thought of the place, particularly its banking. I think I said something to the effect that the track was unsafe, unsatisfactory and uninteresting, and proved absolutely nothing in terms of a challenge to driver skill and ability. This questioning took place before the sad death of Jean Behra, who skidded over the banking in his Porsche sports car on the Saturday, the day before the race, and hit one of the flag poles before being thrown out.

I also said I thought that moving the race here was almost certainly down to political considerations. I finished an interview with the local newspaper *B.Z. Berlin* by commenting, "I am in with all the other drivers who agree with me that this is a very bad, unsatisfactory and untesting course as far as the drivers are concerned, and not worthy of a World Championship race." Then I concentrated on going about my business for the weekend.

I flew direct from Gatwick on the Wednesday before the race and was up and ready to go the following morning by 9am,

had a bit of a snack and headed off out to the circuit. I did only a small amount of practice in the Cooper but on the long straights I still managed to pull 196mph at 7,000rpm – which I thought was pretty impressive. Even so, it was clear that the front-engined Ferrari Dino 246s would be the cars to beat on this high-speed circuit, so I was satisfied to qualify between Tony Brooks and Dan Gurney in the middle of the front row.

The race was hardly memorable for me, although Hans Herrmann miraculously walked away from a terrifying accident that was captured in a very dramatic photograph showing driver and car suspended vertically

in the air. Two laps into the first heat, the ball race broke again in the wretched Colotti transmission and wrecked the input gears. So that was that – back to the hotel, a quick bath, and then the flight back to Gatwick, arriving there about 9.30pm.

It later transpired that the Berlin newspaper took a pop at me for my remarks, commenting, 'The organisers paid very heavily for this man [Moss], considering he did no more than a few training laps for this AVUS race.' I suppose at moments like this it is best to smile sweetly. But I was grateful to Gregor Grant for fighting my corner in the following week's issue of *Autosport*.

455   1st

Kannonloppet

Cooper-Monaco

9 August 1959, Karlskoga (S)

Race distance 30 laps of 1.86-mile circuit **Race time** 50m 2.8s
Race speed 67.37mph **Fastest lap** 1m 38.1s, 68.37mph (record)
Car no 1 **Entrant** Stirling Moss Ltd

This win was not a bad result considering what I noted in my diary: 'Bad brakes, jumping [out of] second gear. Duff clutch, broken rollbar connector. Good start and led to finish. Car goes well, left front brake locks and I was very careful with the gearbox.'

456-461   1st

Copenhagen Grand Prix (Six Heats)

Cooper-Monaco

15/16 August 1959, Roskilde (DEN)

Fastest lap 46.2s (record, shared with David Piper)
Car no 1 **Entrant** Stirling Moss Ltd

As in the previous year, this was a curious six-heat affair spread out over two days. Driving my Cooper-Monaco, I won four of the heats, which gave me overall victory on aggregate, and put on a bit of a show racing against Jack Brabham's similar car and David Piper's Lotus.

This was only my third event in the Cooper-Monaco, which was prepared for me by Mike Keele, the man behind Keele karts and whose son Roger would later race in 1-litre Formula 3 more than a decade later.

462   1st

Portuguese Grand Prix

Cooper-Climax

23 August 1959, Monsanto, Lisbon (P)

F1 World Championship, round 7

Race distance 62 laps of 3.38-mile circuit **Race time** 2h 11m 55.410s **Race speed** 95.317mph **Fastest lap** 2m 5.07s, 97.297mph **Car no** 4 **Entrant** R.R.C. Walker

I took pole on the challenging Monsanto street circuit, but made another slow start before working my way through into the lead by the end of the first lap, passing the works Coopers of Jack Brabham and Masten Gregory in the process.

I pulled away quite easily, but when Jack crashed heavily – although, happily, without injury – I eased back even more, treating my car with kid gloves and keeping my fingers firmly crossed.

At last the Colotti gearbox held together and five laps from the end I was even able to lap Masten, in second place, meaning that I had lapped the entire field. It was my first Grand Prix win of the season – and about time too! I was also pleased for Rob, whose faith in me never diminished.

LEFT *At last the Colotti gearbox held together long enough for me to win the Portuguese Grand Prix at the picturesque seaside Monsanto circuit in Lisbon.* (LAT)

463   3rd

Brands Hatch, Kentish 100, Heat 1

F2 Cooper-Borgward

29 August 1959, Brands Hatch, Kent (GB)

Race distance 42 laps of 1.24-mile circuit **Race time** 40m 43.3s
Car no 2 **Entrant** R.R.C. Walker

---

464   4th

Brands Hatch, Kentish 100, Heat 2

F2 Cooper-Borgward

29 August 1959, Brands Hatch, Kent (GB)

Race distance 42 laps of 1.24-mile circuit **Race time** 40m 58s
Car no 2 **Entrant** R.R.C. Walker

---

465   1st

RAC Tourist Trophy

Aston Martin DBR1

5 September 1959, Goodwood (GB)

World Sports Car Championship, round 5

Race distance 224 laps of 2.4-mile circuit **Race time** 6h 46.8s
Race speed 89.41mph **Co-drivers** Tony Brooks, Carroll Shelby
and Jack Fairman **Car no** 1 & 2 **Entrant** Works

This was a particularly interesting race because it marked the British début of the impressive Porsche 718 in the hands of Jo Bonnier and would set both Rob Walker and the German company thinking in terms of my racing one of these cars the following year.

I was fastest in practice, but my car's handling in the race was just awful due to our adopting the wrong suspension set-up. I could do no better than third behind Jack Brabham's works car and Graham Hill's Lotus 16.

There was more of the same story, unfortunately, in the second heat of the Kentish 100 at Brands Hatch. I finished fourth in the Cooper-Borgward behind Brabham, Hill and Bonnier. A very disappointing day, indeed.

Winning at Le Mans had put Aston Martin ahead of Ferrari in the battle for the World Sports Car Championship and we fielded a full three-car team for the Tourist Trophy at Goodwood, which was the final round of the series.

This event was also a turning point from a technical standpoint. Throughout the DBR1's career to date, most of the drivers had spared no criticism of its dreadful gearbox, but in practice at Goodwood I drove one equipped with a Maserati transaxle and this transformed it beyond belief into a really excellent car.

I led the race for the first hour and a quarter before coming in to change tyres because the canvas was beginning to show through. Roy Salvadori took over, but when he came in for his second stop some fuel was spilled on to the exhaust pipe and the Aston erupted in flame. Thankfully the conflagration was doused before it threatened to burn down the entire pit complex, but it was the end of the race for our DBR1. I was immediately drafted in to take over the DBR1 being shared by Carroll Shelby and Jack Fairman, who were in second place.

I drove flat out for the rest of the afternoon, just as I had at the Nürburgring. The leader at this stage was the Porsche of Jo Bonnier and Wolfgang von Trips, which, although slower in absolute terms, was much easier on its tyres than the Aston. We were ahead going into our final tyre stop, whereupon the Porsche went back into the lead, but I piled on the pressure and repassed to win by half a minute, with Tony Brooks only a few lengths behind the Porsche in third place at the finish.

I had driven just over four and a half hours of this six-hour race. I must have forgotten what I had promised myself after the Nürburgring 1,000kms the previous year!

LEFT TOP *Struggling with the wrong suspension settings with the Cooper-Borgward Formula 2 car at Brands Hatch.* (LAT)

LEFT BOTTOM *Easing through the Goodwood chicane with the Aston Martin DBR1 on my way to another Tourist Trophy victory.* (LAT)

466   1st

Italian Grand Prix

Cooper-Climax

13 September 1959, Monza (I)

F1 World Championship, round 8

Race distance 72 laps of 3.57-miles **Race time** 2h 4m 5.4s
Race speed 124.384mph **Car no** 14 **Entrant** R.R.C. Walker

467   1st

Oulton Park, Gold Cup

Cooper-Climax

26 September 1959, Oulton Park, Cheshire (GB)

Race distance 55 laps of 2.76-mile circuit **Race time** 1h 34m 37.2s **Race speed** 96.29mph **Fastest lap** 1m 41.8s, 97.64mph (record) **Car no** 7 **Entrant** R.R.C. Walker

Although Alf Francis had fitted 'knock-off' rear wheels to Rob Walker's Cooper for the Italian Grand Prix, the real concern was front tyre wear. Wily old Jack Brabham identified this early, fitting a Dunlop tyre of sports car specification to his left-front wheel in the hope that it would offer enhanced durability. Thanks to some quick thinking and good contacts, we did the same.

Although I started from pole position, I allowed Phil Hill to set the early pace in his front-engined Ferrari Dino 246. As in Argentina the previous year, I judged that it was crucially important to conserve my tyres in the early stages of the race. The outcome of the race was ultimately decided between laps 33 and 36, when all three Ferraris pitted for tyres. That left me comfortably ahead and I eventually won by just over 45 seconds from Phil, with Jack trailing home third.

Now there just remained the US Grand Prix at Sebring, with Tony Brooks, Jack Brabham and me all in with a chance of the title, having won two races apiece up to that point in the season. It was going to be a long wait: this was the beginning of September and the American race was not going to take place until the second week of December.

To round off my European racing programme for 1959, I drove Rob Walker's Cooper in the Gold Cup at Oulton Park. I trailed Jack Brabham in the opening stages because he had jumped the start. He was penalised one minute, which would be added later, so after I had overtaken him I was satisfied to keep him at bay by a couple of seconds on the road, secure in the knowledge that I had that additional minute's cushion in hand on corrected times.

However, the stewards changed their minds and Rob's pit signals were suddenly showing me I *really* was only a couple of seconds in front. I took that as my cue to speed up and won by just over 5 seconds.

468   Retired

Los Angeles Times Grand Prix

Aston Martin DBR2

10 October 1959, Riverside, California (USA)

Reason for retirement Oil pressure **Car no** 28
Entrant E. Walker

Fitted with a 4.2-litre engine, this locally owned Aston DBR2 was wildly outclassed by the Ferrari opposition in this domestic sports car event, which ended with my spinning off and eventually retiring with no oil pressure.

RIGHT *At Monza in Rob Walker's Cooper, running between the Ferraris of Phil Hill and Dan Gurney during the opening stages of the Italian Grand Prix, which I went on to win.* (LAT)

469 **1st**

Watkins Glen Grand Prix

Cooper-Climax

18 October 1959, Watkins Glen, New York (USA)

Race distance 98 laps of 2.35-mile circuit (230 miles)
Race speed 82.27mph **Fastest lap** 1m 24s, 97.1mph
Car no 1 **Entrant** Yeoman Credit

This outing was at the wheel of a Cooper-Climax fielded by my father and Ken Gregory under the Yeoman Credit banner. It was a *Formule Libre* race, pure and simple, although we would be back at 'The Glen', as this upstate New York circuit was affectionately named, two years later for a World Championship round.

I missed the first practice session, I am ashamed to say, because I was watching television, and then it rained during the second. The result was that I started at the back of the grid on a rolling start but I came through to win.

BELOW *On the way to victory at Watkins Glen and lapping Rodger Ward, whose USAC Midget racer was totally outclassed. Whose idea was it to enter a Midget in a Formula 1 race and for Rodger to drive it? (Pete Lyons)*

470 — 1st

Governors' Trophy, Heat

Aston Martin DB4 GT

27 November 1959, Oakes Field, Nassau (BA)

Race distance 16 laps of 3.5-mile circuit
Race speed 89.91mph **Car no** 5
Entrant F. de Arellano

Back in pleasantly sunny surroundings for the Bahamas Speed Week, this was an enjoyable outing in a privately owned Aston Martin DB4 GT.

I really enjoyed my visits to the Bahamas, so much so that I built a two-bedroom house there – although I wasn't able to stay there as often as I would have liked because I was racing around the world. Its most striking feature was a sunken bath alongside a plate-glass window looking out over an enclosed miniature garden. I called the house 'Blue Cloud', as I had spent a happy childhood in our family home 'Long White Cloud' at Bray-on-Thames.

471 — Retired

Governors' Trophy, Final

Aston Martin DB4 GT

27 November 1959, Oakes Field, Nassau (BA)

Race distance 16 laps of 3.5-mile circuit
Reason for retirement Brakes **Fastest lap** 82.78mph
Car no 5 **Entrant** F. de Arellano

After my victory in the heat, it was a shame that brake problems put my privately entered Aston Martin DB4 GT out of the final.

472 — 1st

Nassau Trophy, Heat

Aston Martin DBR2

2 December 1959, Oakes Field, Nassau (BA)

Race distance 5 laps of 3.5-mile circuit **Car no** 3
Entrant E. Walker

The old Aston Martin DBR2 ran rather better than it had done during our previous acquaintance at Riverside, but that was probably not saying much. Anyway, I won this heat.

473 — 1st

Nassau Trophy, Final

Aston Martin DBR2

2 December 1959, Oakes Field, Nassau (BA)

Race distance 12 laps of 3.5-mile circuit **Car no** 3
Entrant E. Walker

Although the final for the Nassau Trophy was an unmemorable race, it gave me another victory, bringing my tally for the Bahamas Speed Week to three wins in four races.

474 — Retired

United States Grand Prix

Cooper-Climax

12 December 1959, Sebring, Florida (USA)

F1 World Championship, round 9

Race distance 42 laps of 5.2-mile circuit **Reason for retirement** Gearbox after 5 laps **Car no** 7 **Entrant** R.R.C. Walker

---

This was to be the clincher in the World Championship. Would I or wouldn't I be World Champion this year?

As it turned out, my part in the 1959 World Championship finale, and the first *grande épreuve* to be held in North America, was fleeting to say the least. To beat Jack Brabham for the title, I needed to win and set the fastest lap.

Tony Brooks's chances flopped on the opening lap when he was rammed by Ferrari team-mate Wolfgang von Trips and had to pit to check for damage. I was in the lead from the start, confident that I had the measure of both works Coopers behind me.

Then the gearbox broke after only five laps…

It was an all-too-familiar story.

1960

ANOTHER GOOD SEASON

The 1960 season delivered another memorable milestone for me as it turned out to be the first year during which I raced a Lotus Formula 1 car.

I first set eyes on the Lotus 18 in the paddock at Buenos Aires in February, on the occasion of the Argentine Grand Prix, the opening round of the World Championship. This very straightforward, mid-engined Formula 1 challenger was as far removed from its predecessor – the Lotus 16 or 'Mini Vanwall' as some called it – as it was possible to be.

I had first-hand experience of Colin Chapman's design talents, of course, from the time he reworked the chassis on the Vanwalls and I knew that the new Lotus would certainly be a promising performer. Unreliability and frailty, however, were underlying concerns but, after Innes Ireland ran away from the field in Argentina – before the car started to fall to pieces around him – it was clear that I was going to have a hard time matching up to such a Lotus at the wheel of my Cooper.

Once we were back from South America, I found myself beaten by Innes in non-championship races at both Goodwood and Silverstone. From my vantage point, a few lengths behind the new Lotus, I could see that it had better grip and could corner faster. For his part, Rob Walker hardly needed to be told by me what we were up against. Immediately after Goodwood, he ordered a Lotus 18. It was delivered just before the Monaco Grand Prix, where I used it to score the first *grande épreuve* win for Lotus, just as I had done with Cooper in Argentina two years earlier.

I also became unwelcomely acquainted with the inherent frailty of the Lotus, spending six weeks out of the racing season following a suspension failure in practice for the Belgian Grand Prix at Spa-Francorchamps. That accident left me quite badly injured, with three of my vertebrae cracked and both legs broken.

This was also the season in which I became acquainted with the excellent Lotus 19 sports racing car as well as the fabulous Ferrari 250 GT SWB Berlinetta, which was owned by Dick Wilkins – a jobber/stockbroker and, I believe, a director of the Savoy Hotel – but fielded in Rob Walker's distinctive dark-blue-and-white livery. With the Ferrari, I won the 1960 Tourist Trophy, my sixth victory in that classic event. Other highlights included drives in the superb Porsche Formula 2 car and in the Camoradi team's splendid Maserati Tipo 61 'Birdcage', the latter giving me my third consecutive victory in the Nürburgring 1,000kms, this time sharing the car with Dan Gurney, who drove absolutely superbly and without whom I really doubt I could have won the race on this occasion.

As for the World Championship...

LEFT *In Rob Walker's new Lotus 18 leading through Tarzan on the opening lap of the Dutch Grand Prix at Zandvoort ahead of the works cars of Innes Ireland and John Surtees. The frailty of Colin Chapman's Lotus engineering was to be a defining factor in another troubled year for me.* (LAT)

475   2nd

South African Grand Prix

F2 Cooper-Borgward

1 January 1960, East London (SA)

Race distance 60 laps of 2.4-mile circuit **Race speed** 84.4mph
Fastest lap 1m 39s, 88.57mph **Car no** 7 **Entrant** Yeoman Credit

Borgward had decided not to continue developing its Formula 2 engines into the 1960 season but I had one final outing in the Borgward-engined Cooper at the East London circuit in South Africa, where Graham Hill would clinch his first World Championship two years later. I qualified on pole and led for 50 laps. Then a fuel-injection pipe split and I limped home with the engine misfiring, 36 seconds behind Paul Frère's Equipe Nationale Belge Cooper-Climax.

476   1st

New Zealand Grand Prix, Heat 1

F1 Cooper-Climax

9 January 1960, Ardmore (NZ)

Race distance 15 laps of 2-mile circuit **Race time** 20m 45.9s
Car no 7 **Entrant** Yeoman Credit

I was unable to take part in first practice on the Wednesday because a fresh engine for my Cooper, the car that I had raced at Watkins Glen, was late arriving by air freight, with the result that there was insufficient time to install it for that day's session.

When I went out for practice on the Thursday, I could not match Jack Brabham's pole-winning time due to the windy conditions. I contested the first heat and Jack ran in the second, and then we met up in the final. I won this first heat by just over a second from Bruce McLaren's works Cooper and David Piper's Lotus 16.

BELOW *I used the Cooper to finish third in the Buenos Aires race. Here I am ahead of Graham Hill's BRM P25 and the Cooper of local driver Carlos Menditéguy.* (LAT)

477 Retired

New Zealand Grand Prix, Final

F1 Cooper-Climax

9 January 1960, Ardmore (NZ)

Race distance 75 laps of 2-mile circuit
Reason for retirement Transmission **Fastest lap** 1m 21.2s
(record) **Car no** 7 **Entrant** Yeoman Credit

For the final, Bruce McLaren was first away at the start, with me almost alongside him, but Jack Brabham came rocketing up the inside going into the first corner and just managed to take third place. I was still second at the end of the opening lap, but Jack had the bit between

his teeth and was really getting on with the job. On lap two he tore past me and then overtook Bruce for the lead. I overtook Bruce a couple of laps later but took until lap 27 to get past Jack and into the lead. It was a short-lived success, however, because almost immediately my transmission failed and I was out.

478 3rd

Argentine Grand Prix

F1 Cooper-Climax

7 February 1960, Buenos Aires (ARG)

F1 World Championship, round 1

Race distance 80 laps of 2.43-mile circuit **Race time** 2h 18m 26.4s **Fastest lap** 1m 38.9s, 88.482mph **Car no** 36 & 38
Entrant R.R.C. Walker

I managed to grasp pole position at Buenos Aires but it was clear from the speed demonstrated by Innes Ireland in the new factory Lotus 18 that this was a machine we would all have to watch closely. Innes qualified alongside me on the front row of the grid, an amazing effort with a brand new car, and then surged into the lead at the start. I ran third behind Graham Hill's BRM in the early stages, but eventually retired with a rear coil spring failure.

I then took over Maurice Trintignant's car and together we finished third overall, with Bruce McLaren winning his second straight World Championship Grand Prix victory to add to his success at Sebring at the end of the previous year. Cliff Allison's Ferrari Dino 246 finished second.

479 1st

Cuban Grand Prix

Maserati Tipo 61

28 February 1960, Havana (CU)

Race distance 50 laps of 3.23-mile circuit **Race time** 1h 57m 31.5s **Fastest lap** 2m 16s, 81.97mph (record) **Car no** 7
Entrant Camoradi

As I said earlier, I was most impressed with the performance of the 2-litre Maserati Tipo 60 'Birdcage' in that sports car race at Rouen in the summer of 1959, and for the 1960 season Maserati increased the engine size to 2.8 litres. There was no question of the team fielding a works effort, however, because the Maserati business was in receivership, but it was prepared to support any customer who might be prepared to write cheques for parts and engines.

At this point Lloyd Casner – 'Lucky' to his friends – entered the equation. I am not sure if he actually had money, or, because of his innate charm, managed to get backers. Anyway, he successfully persuaded Goodyear to, in effect, sponsor his sports car team. The team would be called 'Camoradi', an acronym for 'Casner Motor Racing Division'. It had fielded its first entry in the Buenos Aires 1,000kms race, where Dan Gurney and Masten Gregory had dominated until the chassis cracked.

I was invited to drive for the team in the Cuban Grand Prix, which took place on a new circuit made up of parts of a military aerodrome and a road past the Havana golf club. I qualified on pole position and led from the start, although we had all been rather confused by the fact that the organisers chose to announce that the race distance had been trimmed back from 61 to 50 laps when we were actually lined up on the starting grid.

I led the opening lap from Pedro Rodriguez in a NART Ferrari and his younger brother Ricardo in a Porsche. For the first 10 laps or so, Pedro hung on closely and I had to bang in a couple of really quick laps to break his challenge. I later discovered that for some reason Casner had fitted harder rear Goodyears to the car without telling me so, although I encountered no wear problems, there was precious little grip.

Oh, yes, and the driver's seat broke and the exhaust system fell apart, but otherwise I had a fairly easy win. I could see that the big 'Birdcage' had huge potential, despite the problems I had experienced.

LEFT *The Porsche 718 was an excellent Formula 2 machine, but on my debut outing at Syracuse I lost a commanding lead when the engine failed.* (Porsche)

BELOW *I had an enjoyable run to finish second in the Sebring 4 Hours in the agile little Austin-Healey Sprite.* (LAT)

480 Retired

Syracuse Grand Prix

F2 Porsche 718

19 March 1960, Syracuse, Sicily (I)

Race distance 56 laps of 3.47-mile circuit
Reason for retirement Engine after 25 laps **Fastest lap** 1m
58.8s, 103.49mph **Car no** 20 **Entrant** R.R.C. Walker

As part of Porsche's preparations for the forthcoming 1.5-litre Formula 1 regulations, which would come into force at the start of the 1961 season, it arranged to loan Rob Walker one of its excellent type 718 Formula 2 cars for me to drive in various races throughout the 1960 season.

I had my first drive in the car at Syracuse, that challenging road circuit in Sicily where, the previous year, I had won in the Cooper-Borgward. I qualified on pole with a lap in 1m 57.6s, which was 1.3 seconds quicker than the lap record, set by Jean Behra in a Ferrari the previous year. Innes was again alongside me on the front row, in an F2-specification Lotus 18,

and again he made the best start, although I quickly overtook him for the lead going into the hairpin on the opening lap.

I managed to pull away from the field at about a second a lap, but on lap 26, right in front of the main grandstands, the Porsche engine dropped a valve and that was that.

481 2nd

Sebring 4 Hours

Austin-Healey Sprite

26 March 1960, Sebring, Florida (USA)

Race distance 57 laps of 5.2-mile circuit **Race time** 56 laps,
71.5mph **Car no** 2 **Entrant** Works

It was Donald Healey who asked me to drive one of his Sprites in the small-capacity sports car race that preceded the 12-hour event on the Florida aerodrome circuit. I was ranged against the Fiat-Abarths, which were just too quick for me, but I had an enjoyable drive to finish second behind a guy named Paul Richards, who was driving one of the little Italian machines.

482 Retired

Sebring 12 Hours

Maserati Tipo 61

26 March 1960, Sebring, Florida (USA)

World Sports Car Championship, round 2

Race distance 200 laps of 5.2-mile circuit **Reason for retirement** Final drive unit **Car no** 23 **Entrant** Camoradi

I was paired with Dan Gurney for this race and I took the lead on the third lap after a busy time cutting my way through traffic away from the starting line-up. After two hours I came in to hand over to Dan with a 50-second lead, but unfortunately he had not been warned of my imminent arrival and was not ready. Can you believe that? Camoradi efficiency!

That lost us a lot of time, but Dan showed himself to be an absolutely first-rate driver and quickly regained the deficit, to the point at which we had built up a two-lap lead by half distance. With four hours to run, Dan came in to refuel and reported that the gearbox was playing up. I took over and a pinion shaft in the final drive unit broke a couple of laps later. We were out.

483 1st

Brussels Grand Prix, Heat 1

F2 Porsche 718

10 April 1960, Heysel, Brussels (B)

Race time 1h 13m 25.6s, 80.89mph **Race distance** 35 laps of 2.80-mile circuit **Fastest lap** 2m 4s, 82.11mph **Car no** 10 **Entrant** R.R.C Walker

The Heysel circuit was a makeshift road circuit on the fringes of Brussels, quite tricky in places but unmemorable. I was beaten to pole position in the first heat by Jo Bonnier's works Porsche, but overtook him only three laps into the race and won quite comfortably.

BELOW *Working hard on the bumpy Heysel road circuit in the Formula 2 Porsche. I finished second on aggregate.* (Porsche)

484 3rd

Brussels Grand Prix, Heat 2

F2 Porsche 718

10 April 1960, Heysel, Brussels (B)

Race distance 35 laps of 2.80-mile circuit **Race time** 1h 23m 51.6s **Fastest lap** 2m 17.1s, 119.52mph **Car no** 10 **Entrant** R.R.C Walker

Jack Brabham's Cooper had finished second in the first heat, so all I had to do in the second race was finish within 51 seconds of him to secure the aggregate victory. Unfortunately my Porsche jumped out of gear at the start, so I had to stagger away from the line in third gear. I got to within 14 seconds of Jack, only to spin on the now-wet track when the car jumped out of gear with a couple of laps to go. I recovered to finish third, good enough only for second on aggregate.

485 2nd

Goodwood, Glover Trophy

F1 Cooper-Climax

18 April 1960, Goodwood, West Sussex (GB)

Race distance 42 laps of 2.4-mile circuit **Race time** 1h 0m 17.6s **Fastest lap** 1m 24.6s, 102.13mph (record, shared with Innes Ireland) **Car no** 7 **Entrant** R.R.C Walker

This turned out to be just my first pasting of the day at the hands of Innes Ireland and his Team Lotus 18, which demonstrated a high-speed stability and poise through the long corners at Goodwood that my Walker-team Cooper simply could not match. I qualified third behind Innes, sandwiched between Innes and the Yeoman Credit Cooper of Harry Schell, and gave it everything I had got off the line as we sprinted towards Madgwick for the first time.

Chris Bristow was away first, ahead of me, then came Roy Salvadori and Ireland was in fourth. I managed to take the lead by the end of lap one and pressed on as hard as I could, but eventually Innes got up to second place and I could not hold him off. We raced neck and neck to the finish and in the end Innes won.

486 2nd

Goodwood, Lavant Cup

F2 Porsche 718

18 April 1960, Goodwood, West Sussex (GB)

Race distance 15 laps of 2.4-mile circuit **Race time** 22m 30.6s **Fastest lap** 97.3mph (record) **Car no** 21 **Entrant** R.R.C Walker

There was just nothing I could do about Innes and the Lotus 18 in the Formula 2 race, either. Simple as that. I drove as hard as I could, and I think the Porsche had a slight edge under braking, but the Lotus had traction and cornering that were in another league.

487   1st

Goodwood, Fordwater Trophy

Aston Martin DB4 GT

18 April 1960, Goodwood, West Sussex (GB)

Race distance 10 laps of 2.4-mile circuit **Race time** 17m 20.6s
Race speed 83.03mph **Car no** 102 **Entrant** R.R.C Walker

This was my third outing and my third win in the Aston Martin DB4 GT, a short race in which I comfortably saw off the Jaguar 3.8-litre Mk2 saloons of Roy Salvadori and Jack Sears.

ABOVE *My Cooper could not match the pace of Innes Ireland's Lotus 18 in the Glover Trophy and I had to settle for second place.* (LAT)

RIGHT *Back in an Aston Martin, winning the Fordwater Trophy in a DB4 GT.* (LAT)

488   1st

Aintree 200

F2 Porsche 718

30 April 1960, Aintree, Liverpool (GB)

Race distance 50 laps of 3-mile circuit **Race time** 1h 41m 47.6s
Race speed 88.41mph **Car no** 7 **Entrant** R.R.C. Walker

I was determined at least to interrupt the run of Lotus domination and qualified on pole position at Aintree, but I messed up the start, changing from second gear back into first, rather than third, as I accelerated away from the grid. That momentarily 'buzzed' the engine to 9,000rpm, which it did not seem to mind in the slightest, but it dropped me down into the midfield mess and so I spent the first half of the race clawing my way back up to third. Then Brabham and Salvadori retired in front of me and I led home a Porsche one-two-three ahead of the factory cars of Jo Bonnier and Graham Hill.

489   Retired

Silverstone, BRDC International Trophy

F1 Cooper-Climax

14 May 1960, Silverstone (GB)

Organising club British Racing Drivers' Club **Race distance** 50 laps of 2.9-mile circuit **Reason for retirement** Suspension failure after 33 laps **Car no** 20 **Entrant** R.R.C. Walker

This meeting was considerably saddened by the death of Harry Schell, who was thrown out of his Yeoman Credit Cooper after he crashed at Abbey Curve during a rain-soaked practice session.

I qualified Rob Walker's Cooper on pole, ahead of the BRMs of Jo Bonnier and Dan Gurney, but it was Innes Ireland's Lotus that again proved to be the toughest competitor in the race. I made a good start and pulled away in the early stages, but by lap 15 Innes was in second place and starting to catch me.

He overtook me for the lead on lap 25 and, eight laps later, my Cooper's right-front suspension wishbone broke as I was going into Copse and I was out.

OPPOSITE TOP *Working really hard in the Cooper to keep ahead of Innes Ireland's Lotus 18 in the International Trophy race. My right front suspension eventually broke.* (LAT)

OPPOSITE BOTTOM *In Tommy Sopwith's Equipe Endeavour Jaguar 3.8 chasing Roy Salvadori's similar car.* (Tom March Collection)

BELOW *Standing on the grid alongside the Walker Porsche 718 prior to my victory in the Aintree 200.* (Porsche)

490   2nd

Silverstone, Touring Car Race

Jaguar 3.8 Mk2

14 May 1960, Silverstone (GB)

Race distance 12 laps of 2.92-mile circuit **Car no** 42
Entrant Equipe Endeavour

I accepted an invitation to drive this Jaguar Mk2 saloon from Tommy Sopwith's Equipe Endeavour organisation. Roy Salvadori, in a similar car, made a better start than me, but I soon got through into the lead, only for Roy to repass after I was baulked on the Hangar Straight. I finished second.

491   1st

Nürburgring, ADAC 1,000kms

Maserati Tipo 61

22 May 1960, Nürburgring (D)

World Sports Car Championship, round 4

Race distance 44 laps of 14.15-mile circuit **Race time** 7h 31m 40.5s **Race speed** 82.77mph **Fastest lap** 9m 37s, 88.48mph **Co-driver** Dan Gurney **Car no** 5 **Entrant** Camoradi

After the fiasco at Sebring, the Camoradi team was much better organised at the Nürburgring for my next outing in the Maserati Tipo 61, but I was shocked when I drove it for the first time during practice. Its handling and normally excellent brakes were terrible, and it was over-geared. On the Saturday, Dan Gurney suffered a broken oil pipe, which meant I got no mileage in the car at all that day.

We were saved by the weather. The 1,000kms was held in continuous rain and low mist, which played to our strengths. I led from the start and when I pitted after 15 laps was able to hand Dan a lead of two minutes 30 seconds over Phil Hill's Ferrari, only for Dan to lose a lap and a half having another broken oil pipe repaired in the pits. But Dan's recovery after that setback was simply amazing.

On lap 24 he was one minute 35 seconds behind third-placed Phil Hill. Next time around Dan had pared the gap to Hill down to 47 seconds. And then on lap 28 he came through in the lead.

The stop for me to take over for the final stint dropped us down to third, so now it was my turn to go on the offensive. With eight laps left I went back into the lead, cementing victory in my third straight 1,000kms race on this uniquely demanding circuit.

I was truly exhilarated.

LEFT *Mist and rain helped the Maserati Tipo 61 Birdcage to be just what Dan Gurney and I needed to win the Nürburgring 1,000kms race.* (Klemantaski Collection)

BELOW *On the way to a really memorable victory.* (LAT)

492 1st

Monaco Grand Prix

Lotus 18

29 May 1960, Monte Carlo (MON)

F1 World Championship, round 2

Race distance 100 laps of 1.95-mile circuit **Race time** 2h 53m 45.5s **Race speed** 67.48mph **Car no** 28 **Entrant** R.R.C. Walker

This race was another turning point in my career. The Walker team's Lotus 18 was finally completed just seven days before the Monaco Grand Prix and I took the opportunity to give it a preliminary run at Goodwood before we set off for the Cote d'Azur.

My first impression was that it was an extremely sensitive car, less forgiving than the Cooper when it came to taking outrageous liberties but ultimately superbly responsive – a real driver's car *par excellence*. I used to joke and say that when following a driver with great car control, such as John Surtees, you would see as much of the front of his car as the back because it was always sliding around. The Lotus was not at all like that. It rewarded meticulous precision and subtle chassis adjustments.

After trying both the Lotus and the Cooper in practice, I eventually opted to drive our new car. I qualified on pole, but also accepted an invitation to do a few laps in the Scarab Formula 1 car, which had been sponsored and developed by Lance Reventlow, the millionaire son of the Woolworths heiress Barbara Hutton. It was beautifully built, but this front-engined challenger was already outdated and my best time was 9 seconds slower than my pole time in the Lotus – a dramatic reminder of just how quickly things progress in the split-second world of Formula 1.

At the start of the race, Jo Bonnier went straight into the lead and I was content to let him set the pace during the opening stages. On lap 17, I moved ahead and built up enough of an advantage that I was able to ease back when a rain shower brushed the circuit. With 40 laps to go, I made a quick pit stop to have a loose plug lead replaced, but still had plenty of time to repass Bonnier, who had slipped back into the lead while I was delayed.

First race in the Lotus – and my first win. Things were looking up!

RIGHT *Making history at Monaco, where I scored Lotus's first* grande épreuve *victory, albeit in Rob Walker's private entry.* (LAT)

BELOW *Savouring the moment. Waving to the crowd with my garland on the victory lap after the race.* (LAT)

493   4th

Dutch Grand Prix

Lotus 18

6 June 1960, Zandvoort, Haarlem (NL)

F1 World Championship, round 4

Race distance 75 laps of 2.61-mile circuit **Race time** 2h 2m 44.9s
Fastest lap 1m 33.8s, 99.99mph **Car no** 7 **Entrant** R.R.C. Walker

The Lotus continued to display its impressive form at the famous circuit through the Dutch sand dunes and I qualified comfortably on pole position ahead of Jack Brabham's Cooper, with Innes Ireland completing the outside of the front row in the factory Lotus 18.

Brabham got away first at the start, with me following tight in his wheel tracks, and the pair of us quickly pulled away from the remainder of the pack, which was headed by Ireland and Alan Stacey in their Lotus 18s. I was quietly confident that I could eventually find a way past Jack, but on lap 17 one of his Cooper's rear wheels kicked up a huge stone slab, which landed on one of my front tyres, bursting it and bending the wheel rim.

I had no choice but to come straight into the pits, where I lost three minutes while the mechanics fitted a replacement wheel and tyre, their task made longer by the fact that the car was not fitted with 'knock-off' hubs.

I went back into the race in 12th place, got my head down, and hauled my way back to fourth place by the chequered flag, crossing the line only a few lengths behind Graham Hill's third-placed BRM. It was a disappointing race in many ways, but satisfying in others because it had underlined the versatility offered by our new car.

494 Did not start

Belgian Grand Prix

Lotus 18

18 June 1960, Spa-Francorchamps, Liège (B)

F1 World Championship, round 5

Reason did not start Crash in practice **Car no** 12
Entrant R.R.C. Walker

My season suffered a major setback during practice at Spa-Francorchamps when I crashed heavily coming through the long Burnenville right-hander, which leads on to the Masta straight. I was doing around 140mph in fifth gear when I suddenly felt the rear of the car go dramatically loose and snap into a wildly oversteering slide.

I knew immediately that the Lotus had suffered a major structural breakage. In fact, the left rear had come off and shot ahead. I braced myself hard between the steering wheel and seat back as I smashed into the left-hand bank at about 90mph. I came to where I ended up, crouched on all fours by the side of the track, having been thrown from the car.

RIGHT *I spun off and was disqualified from the Portuguese Grand Prix for precisely the offence I had tried to defend Mike Hawthorn from two years earlier – pushing the car against the direction of the race!* (Klemantaski Collection)

BELOW *Winning the Kannonloppet in the Lotus 19. I think this must have been the first time that I used a helmet with a 'bubble' visor in rainy conditions.* (LAT)

I was gasping for breath, but fortunately Bruce McLaren, the first driver on the scene, correctly refused my request that he give me artificial respiration on the basis that if I had sustained broken ribs, then this was the last thing I needed. My diary entry for 18 June 1960 reads thus: 'Shunt. Nose. Back. Legs. Bruises. Bugger!'

I was taken to hospital in Malmédy and was flown back to London that evening, where I was admitted to St Thomas's hospital. I was very lucky because Mr Urquhart was on duty and he immediately cut me out of the head-to-feet plaster that I was in. He explained to me that because my legs were broken, but not impacted, I would not need plaster as long as my muscles were kept strong, and the next day he had me standing for a few seconds. My back was technically broken because I had crushed three vertebrae, but it required only strapping. Later, I was confined to bed during daytime, but allowed to go dancing in the evenings!

The race was won by Jack Brabham, but tragically the talented Chris Bristow and Lotus driver Alan Stacey both crashed fatally.

celebrated my return to the cockpit by winning after a dice with Jo Bonnier's Maserati.

495   1st

Kannonloppet

Lotus-Climax 19

7 August 1960, Karlskoga (S)

Race distance 25 laps of 1.86-mile circuit **Race time** 41m 8.8s **Race speed** 67.971mph **Fastest lap** 1m 33.3s, 69.457mph (record) **Car no** 1 **Entrant** Yeoman Credit

After a rigorous programme of physiotherapy, combined with my unwillingness to be in a hospital bed for a minute longer than was absolutely necessary, only six weeks after my big shunt at Spa I was off to Sweden for my annual visit to Karlskoga. This time I was having my first outing in the new Lotus 19 sports car that had been acquired by the Yeoman Credit team. I

496   Disqualified

Portuguese Grand Prix

Lotus 18

14 August 1960, Porto (P)

F1 World Championship, round 8

Race distance 55 laps of 4.6-mile circuit **Reason for disqualification** Pushing the car against the race direction **Car no** 12 **Entrant** R.R.C. Walker

My return to the Formula 1 front-line after my Spa accident was inauspicious, to say the least. Rob Walker's team had a brand-new Lotus 18 built up for me in time for the Portuguese Grand Prix at Porto. I qualified on the second row and followed spectacular new boy John Surtees's works Lotus in the opening stages, but later lost time with two pit stops for fresh plugs, dropping to 10th.

I had a front brake lock only four laps from the finish and spun off. But I was disqualified for pushing the car on the pavement against the direction of the race. It was precisely the charge that I had helped Mike Hawthorn to escape without penalty in 1958. Times change.

497   1st

RAC Tourist Trophy

Ferrari 250 GT SWB

20 August 1960, Goodwood (GB)

Race distance 3 hours of 2.4-mile circuit (108 laps)
Race speed 85.58mph **Fastest lap** 1m 36.6s, 89.44mph
(record) **Car no** 7 **Entrant** R.R.C. Walker

The Tourist Trophy was reduced in 1960 to a three-hour affair for GT cars and the Dick Wilkins-owned Ferrari 250 GT SWB Berlinetta, run by Rob Walker, was the ideal tool for the job. The biggest problem at Goodwood was rear-tyre wear and I faced quite a challenge from Roy Salvadori's Aston Martin DB4 GT. I was unable to build up enough of a lead before my first tyre change, so the Aston went ahead, but when Roy stopped to change all four tyres a few laps later I went back ahead and stayed there until the finish.

498   11th

Brands Hatch, Kentish 100

F2 Porsche 718

27 August 1960, Brands Hatch, Kent (GB)

Race distance 40 laps of 2.65-mile circuit **Car no** 6
Entrant R.R.C. Walker

This was the second international meeting to take place on the newly extended Brands Hatch circuit, but I was out of luck with carburation problems that put me out of the running from the outset because I had to pit at the end of the opening lap. I finished near the back of the field.

499   1st

Brands Hatch, Redex Trophy

Ferrari 250 GT SWB

27 August 1960, Brands Hatch, Kent (GB)

Race distance 10 laps of 2.65-mile circuit **Race time** 19m 47.4s
Race speed 80.35mph **Entrant** R.R.C. Walker

A nice, routine and very short sprint race in the Wilkins/Walker Ferrari 250 GT SWB Berlinetta at least put another win in my personal record book.

500   4th

Copenhagen Grand Prix

F2 Porsche 718

10/11 September 1960, Roskilde (DK)

Race time 54m 50.3s **Car no** 7

The Porsche seemed to be off-form for most of the weekend and I spent a lot of time battling gear-selection problems. I eventually finished fourth on a day saddened by the death of the young New Zealand driver George Lawton, who crashed his Cooper right in front of me.

RIGHT *Winning the now-shortened Tourist Trophy in the superb Ferrari 250 GT SWB Berlinetta owned by City businessman Dick Wilkins and fielded by Rob Walker.* (LAT)

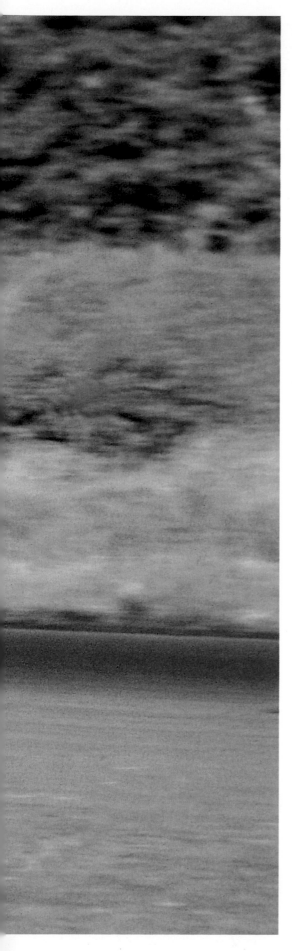

501 — 1st

Austrian Grand Prix

F2 Porsche 718

18 September 1960, Zeltweg, Knittelfeld (OST)

Race distance 59 laps of 1.98-mile circuit **Race time** 1h 20m 13.2s **Race speed** 87.6mph **Fastest lap** 1m 16s, 94.19mph **Car no** 7 **Entrant** R.R.C. Walker

This was the first Austrian Grand Prix for single-seaters, held on the Zeltweg military aerodrome circuit near Knittelfeld, where the country's maiden World Championship event would be staged four years later. It was basically an L-shaped track delineated by straw bales, very rough and ready, and with an exceedingly bumpy track surface. The Walker Porsche stood up to the pummelling very well and I scored quite an easy win.

502 — 1st

Oulton Park, Gold Cup

Lotus 18

24 September 1960, Oulton Park, Cheshire (GB)

Race distance 60 laps of 2.76-mile circuit **Race time** 1h 45m 54s **Race speed** 93.85mph **Fastest lap** 1m 45.4s, 94.3mph (shared with Bruce McLaren) **Car no** 7 **Entrant** R.R.C. Walker

This was certainly an extremely satisfying note on which to round off the British domestic F1 season. I qualified on pole, but alongside me on the front row was the works Lotus 18 of Jim Clark, who I could already tell was emerging as possibly the most outstanding member of the new generation of rising stars.

Jack Brabham was first away in the works Cooper, followed by Innes Ireland's Lotus. I sat back in the early stages watching Clark, Brabham and Ireland battling at the front, but by lap 32 Innes had been eliminated with gear-change problems and Jimmy had been put out in a collision with Brian Naylor's JBW-Maserati. I was left with pretty much a clear run to win from Brabham.

503 — Retired

Modena Grand Prix

Lotus 18

2 October 1960, Monza (I)

Race distance 100 laps of 1.46-mile circuit **Reason for retirement** Broken tappet **Entrant** Parnell

For this race I used a Lotus 18 fielded by Reg Parnell, but it was an unsuccessful outing. At first, I ran quite near the front of the field, although my car was no match for the factory Porsches on this occasion. I made a pit stop to see if a plug change would correct a misfire, but on close inspection we found that a tappet had broken so I was out of the race.

LEFT *Sweeping to victory in the Oulton Park Gold Cup. Clearly nobody had told us about the value of roll-over bars at this stage!* (Tom March Collection)

504 1st

Watkins Glen Grand Prix

Lotus 18

9 October 1960, Watkins Glen, New York (USA)

Race distance 100 laps of 2.3-mile circuit **Race time** 2h 10m 2.2s **Race speed** 105.8mph **Fastest lap** 1m 16s, 109mph (shared with Jack Brabham) **Car no** 7 **Entrant** R.R.C. Walker

This was my second outing at Watkins Glen in as many years, this time with rather more in the way of contemporary Formula 1 opposition in this *Formule Libre* event. In the end I beat Jack Brabham's Cooper by just over 6 seconds.

505 Retired

Los Angeles Times Grand Prix

Lotus-Climax 19

16 October 1960, Riverside, California (USA)

Race distance 61 laps of 3.27-mile circuit **Reason for retirement** Stripped crown wheel **Entrant** Yeoman Credit

Another outing in the superb so-called 'Monte Carlo.' I had the quickest car on the grid, but a stripped crown wheel caused my retirement from the race.

506 1st

Pacific Grand Prix, Heat 1

Lotus-Climax 19

23 October 1960, Laguna Seca, California (USA)

Race distance 100 miles **Race speed** 86.4mph **Car no** 1 **Entrant** Yeoman Credit

I had a relatively easy run to victory in the first race of this two-heat event.

507 1st

Pacific Grand Prix, Heat 2

Lotus-Climax 19

23 October 1960, Laguna Seca, California (USA)

Race distance 100 miles **Race speed** 87.8mph **Fastest lap** 1m 17.2s (record) **Car no** 1 **Entrant** Yeoman Credit

The second heat nicely rounded off my day with another routine win at the wheel of one of my favourite cars.

508 1st

United States Grand Prix

Lotus 18

20 November 1960, Riverside, California (USA)

F1 World Championship, round 10

Race distance 75 laps of 3.27-mile circuit **Race time** 2h 28m 52.2s **Race speed** 98.996mph **Car no** 5 **Entrant** R.R.C. Walker

This was a really satisfying drive to victory in the first of the Formula 1 World Championship events to be held on the West Coast of the USA. Jack Brabham led initially but suffered a brief fire, so I was ahead from lap five onwards and had the satisfaction of beating Innes Ireland in the works Lotus 18 by almost 40 seconds.

RIGHT *Rounding off the World Championship season with victory in the inaugural US Grand Prix at Riverside.* (LAT)

509 — 13th

Nassau Go-Kart Race

Bultaco go-kart

25 November 1960, Oakes Field (BA)

Race distance 5 laps **Car no** 191

When putting this book together I was uncertain whether or not to include this go-kart race in Nassau as it was something of a fun event and not terribly serious. Of course, in the 1960s karting would really take off all over the world and by 2009 just about every driver on the Formula 1 starting grid had come up using this route.

510 — 1st

Nassau Tourist Trophy

Ferrari 250 GT SWB

27 November 1960, Oakes Field (BA)

Race distance 25 laps of 4.5-mile circuit **Race time** 1h 20m 46.85s **Race speed** 83.559mph **Car no** 5 **Entrant** R.R.C. Walker

Back to the welcome winter sunshine and a good run to another victory in Rob Walker's Goodwood TT-winning Ferrari.

511 — Retired

Governor's Trophy

Lotus-Climax 19

3 December 1960, Oakes Field (BA)

Race distance 26 laps of 4.5-mile circuit **Reason for retirement** Front suspension **Fastest lap** 92.045mph **Entrant** Yeoman Credit

The front suspension of the Lotus-Climax 19 broke on lap 12, thwarting my ambitions.

512 — Retired

Nassau International Trophy

Lotus-Climax 19

4 December 1960, Oakes Field (BA)

Race distance 54 laps of 4.5-mile circuit **Reason for retirement** Bonnet mechanism **Car no** 2 **Entrant** Yeoman Credit

513 — 1st

Cape Grand Prix

F2 Porsche 718

17 December 1960, Killarney (SA)

Race distance 75 laps of 1.98-mile circuit **Race time** 1h 57m 40.8s **Race speed** 78mph **Car no** 7 **Entrant** R.R.C. Walker

514 — 1st

South African Grand Prix

F2 Porsche 718

27 December 1960, East London (SA)

Race distance 80 laps of 2.444-mile circuit **Race time** 2h 11m 2s **Race speed** 89.24mph **Car no** 7 **Entrant** R.R.C. Walker

Starting from pole position, I had an easy run to victory in Rob Walker's excellent Porsche.

I was denied another win at Nassau when the Lotus 19's bonnet mechanism broke while I was leading.

This was my second South African GP of the year, because the previous winter's event had been on New Year's Day! I rounded off 1960 with another comfortable win in this non-championship race.

1961

TWO OF MY BEST WINS

If you look in the motor racing history books, you will find that my 1961 season – my final full season as a professional racing driver – was highlighted by two of my most satisfying drives to victory, in the Monaco and German Grands Prix. Yet, those two notable successes were set against a backdrop of a year in which Rob Walker's team again found itself in the position of being unable to obtain a fully up-to-date car from any of the established manufacturers. This is one of the reasons why success in those two Grands Prix was so sweet. I had managed to win against the toughest opposition and in an inferior car.

Obviously, our first choice would have been to acquire one of the latest Lotus 21s, which were being fielded by Team Lotus for Jim Clark and Innes Ireland, but this was simply not possible because Lotus was contracted to Esso and Rob Walker and myself were with BP. The oil companies paid a lot of money to get the best teams they could, and Esso would not have wanted me, on BP fuel and oil, beating them. The fact that Lotus's sole Grand Prix victory thus far was my win in 1960 at Monaco, on BP, must have really rubbed salt into the wounds!

Frustrated by all the difficulties the team was facing, we decided that all we could do was to work with our existing Lotus 18 – and so it was painstakingly updated. Alf modified the rear suspension set-up and adopted a slightly sleeker body profile that owed a lot to the style of the 21. There was also no question of using the planned new 1.5-litre Coventry-Climax engine because it was clear that this would not be available to any team before mid-season and, when it was ready, Cooper would be the first to use it, thanks to its status as reigning World Champion constructor. Independent teams, such as Rob Walker's, would be much further down the pecking order.

This season was even richer than usual in variety. I started in no fewer than 55 races, from the New Zealand Grand Prix at the beginning of January through to the South African Grand Prix on Boxing Day. The schedule also included some races run to the new 'intercontinental' formula, which was, in effect, a short-lived UK-led 2.5-litre alternative to the new 1.5-litre regulations that were disapproved of by so many of the British teams.

After all the animosity through the years between Ferrari and myself, I was amazed when Enzo Ferrari approached me once more, towards the end of the year, about the possibility of my driving for Ferrari in 1962. We had a secret meeting and I decided to let bygones be bygones and compromise. The idea was that I would drive a Formula 1 works car – run under the Rob Walker banner and colours – and also a 250 GTO sports car, and the British Racing Parnership (BRP) would also be given a 246 sports car for me to drive.

It was a dream that perished in the wreckage of my car at Goodwood on Easter Monday in 1962. Ferrari had stuck to his promise to build a Formula 1 car for me, and, if only it had been ready in time for Goodwood, perhaps events would have turned out differently and I could have continued racing for many more years, rather than having to find a job of work at the age of 32! As I had no experience of anything other than racing, very few other occupations were open to me – estate agent and Member of Parliament come to mind.

LEFT *With its side body panels removed for additional driver cooling, some observers wrongly concluded that my Walker team Lotus 18 was 'falling to bits' during my drive to the third Monaco Grand Prix victory of my career!* (Klemantaski Collection)

515 — 1st

New Zealand Grand Prix, Heat 1

2.5 Lotus 18 'Intercontinental'
7 January 1961, Ardmore (NZ)

Race distance 15 laps of 2-mile circuit **Race time** 90.1mph
Fastest lap 1m 19.9s, 90.1mph (record) **Car no** 7
Entrant R.R.C. Walker

I opened the season by taking on the locals in New Zealand, as this had become an almost traditional fixture for me over recent years. Rob's Lotus 18 was equipped with a 2.5-litre Climax FPF four-cylinder engine for this event, competing under the newly initiated 'intercontinental formula' regulations, and I won the first heat quite easily.

516 — Retired

New Zealand Grand Prix, Final

2.5 Lotus 18 'Intercontinental'
7 January 1961, Ardmore (NZ)

Race distance 75 laps of 2-mile circuit
Reason for retirement Driveshaft after 29 laps
Fastest lap 1m 20.6s (record) **Car no** 7 **Entrant** R.R.C. Walker

In the final, later that day, I had a frustrating time because I was leading quite comfortably when a driveshaft cracked on lap 30 and I had to retire.

517 — 2nd

Lady Wigram Trophy

2.5 Lotus 18 'Intercontinental'
21 January 1961, Christchurch (NZ)

Race distance 47 laps of 2.12-mile circuit **Entrant** R.R.C. Walker

This was a particularly busy event for me because not only was I beaten by Jack Brabham's Cooper, but my Lotus was shunted a couple of times, the carburettors virtually knocked off the engine, and the race distance was reduced by 50 miles due to a heavy rainstorm. I was glad when this one was over.

518 — 1st

Australian Grand Prix

2.5 Lotus 18 'Intercontinental'
29 January 1961, Warwick Farm, Sydney (AUS)

Race distance 45 laps of 2.25-mile circuit **Race time** 76m 33.9s **Race speed** 79.6mph **Fastest lap** 1m 40.3s, 80.68mph **Car no** 7 **Entrant** R.R.C. Walker

Australia can be a punishingly hot country in which to contest a motor race, but this year's Grand Prix at Warwick Farm had track temperatures of 148 degrees, approaching the sort of torrid levels experienced these days at venues such as Sepang in Malaysia. I managed to post another win at record speed, though.

519 — 5th

Sebring 4 Hours

Austin-Healey Sprite
24 March 1961, Sebring, Florida (USA)

Race distance 4 hours of 5.2-mile circuit (59 laps)
Race time 1 lap behind **Car no** 2 **Entrant** Works

This time in the Sebring 4 Hours BMC tried even harder to beat the Fiat-Abarths and fielded four cars in total, for me, Bruce McLaren, Walt Hansgen and my sister Pat, who shared hers with the Australian Paul Hawkins. I was surprised how well the Sprites handled, but we just did not have the speed. I got up to second place, but then the clutch began slipping and I dropped to fifth.

BELOW *Sprinting across to my Austin-Healey Sprite (2) at the start of the Sebring 4 Hours, with my sister Pat heading for her car (1).* (LAT)

520   Retired

Sebring 12 Hours

Maserati Tipo 61

25 March 1961, Sebring, Florida (USA)

World Sports Car Championship, round 1

Race distance 12 hours of 5.2-mile circuit
Reason for retirement Broken exhaust **Fastest lap** 3m 13.2s
(record) **Co-driver** Graham Hill **Car no** 23 **Entrant** Camoradi

For the Sebring 12 Hours I found myself back in the Camoradi ranks, this time in the new rear-engined Maserati Tipo 63 that 'Lucky' Casner's team, by now short of cash, was running on the proverbial shoe-string. I was sharing the car with Graham Hill, but by the time the corrugated track surface had pretty much beaten its rear suspension to death during practice, we switched to the back-up Tipo 61 'Birdcage', which seemed marginally better, although I had mounting concerns about the team's rather sloppy level of preparation.

Before the Le Mans-style start, I asked very specifically whether the car's battery was fully charged. Oh yes, they assured me, no problem. At the start I ran and got into the car, and what should happen? The battery was as flat as a pancake! It took six minutes or so to coax the car into life.

I see from my diary that I had the tyres at 45lb at the front and 50lb at the rear. I drove for two hours flat out and then, in second place, passed the car to Graham

ABOVE *Sharing the Camoradi 'Birdcage' in the Sebring 12 Hours with Graham Hill: sadly we were unable to repeat the sort of form that we had demonstrated at the Nürburgring the previous year.* (Pete Lyons)

Hill, but we had to call it a day at three hours because the exhaust system fell apart. I then switched to the rear-engined Tipo 63, being driven by Casner and Masten Gregory, climbing from ninth to seventh before its rear suspension gave out. Interestingly, I managed a 3m 12.5s lap in the front-engined car and only 3m 16s in the rear-engined one.

---

521   1st

Goodwood, Lavant Cup

2.5 Cooper 'Intercontinental'

3 April 1961, Goodwood, West Sussex (GB)

Race distance 21 laps of 2.4-mile circuit **Race time** 33m 25.6s
Race time 90.47mph **Car no** 6 **Entrant** R.R.C. Walker

Rob purchased a brand-new Cooper for the Intercontinental formula at the start of the 1961 season and, powered by the 2.5-litre Climax four-cylinder, it really was a terrific car to drive. I gave the 'Intercontinental', officially designated the T53P, its début race at Goodwood, starting from pole position, but I fumbled my start because the car jumped out of gear when I dropped the clutch. It took me until lap three to recover to third place and soon afterwards I was through into the lead, where I stayed all the way to the chequered flag.

---

522   4th

Goodwood, Glover Trophy

Lotus 18

3 April 1961, Goodwood, West Sussex (GB)

Race distance 42 laps of 2.4-mile circuit
Race time 1h 4m 43.6s **Car no** 7 **Entrant** R.R.C. Walker

I started from pole, but my engine was not running properly from the outset and there was no way I could stick with John Surtees in the Yeoman Credit Cooper, which started alongside me on the front row of the grid. The rough-running eventually got worse and I slipped back to fourth at the chequered flag.

523 1st

Goodwood, Sussex Trophy

Lotus 19 'Monte Carlo'

3 April 1961, Goodwood, West Sussex (GB)

Race distance 10 laps of 2.4-mile circuit **Race time** 26m 29s
Race speed 81.57mph **Car no** 78 **Entrant** UDT Laystall

524 3rd

Goodwood, Fordwater Trophy

Aston Martin DB4 GT Zagato

3 April 1961, Goodwood, West Sussex (GB)

Race distance 10 laps of 2.4-mile circuit **Race time** 17m 26.6s
Entrant Essex Racing

Three Lotus 19s were fielded by UDT Laystall in this event for Cliff Allison, Henry Taylor and me, and I won quite easily.

BELOW *Starting from pole in the Goodwood Glover Trophy ahead of John Surtees, Roy Salvadori and Graham Hill.* (LAT)

Taking on Mike Parkes and his Equipe Endeavour Ferrari 250 GT was always going to be a tall order, even with the latest Zagato version of the Aston DB4 GT, which was lighter and more powerful than the regular DB4 GTs. Innes Ireland, in a similar car, beat me to second place behind Parkes, who won in his Ferrari.

525 Unclassified

Brussels Grand Prix, Heat 1

Lotus 18

9 April 1961, Heysel (B)

Race distance 22 laps of 4.06-mile circuit
Reason for being unclassified Carburation problems
Car no 18 **Entrant** R.R.C. Walker

526 8th

Brussels Grand Prix, Heat 2

Lotus 18

9 April 1961, Heysel (B)

Race distance 22 laps of 4.06-mile circuit **Race time** 21 laps
Car no 18 **Entrant** R.R.C. Walker

527 2nd

Brussels Grand Prix, Heat 3

Lotus 18

9 April 1961, Heysel (B)

Race distance 22 laps of 4.06-mile circuit **Race time** 46m 17s
Fastest lap 2m 4.7s, 81.8mph **Car no** 18 **Entrant** R.R.C. Walker

This was an extremely frustrating meeting because my Lotus was beset by apparent carburation problems, which prevented it from running smoothly all weekend. As a result, in the first of the event's three heats, from which an aggregate result would be produced, I was actually unclassified even though I was still circulating at the finish in 15th place.

More of the same, I'm afraid, in the second heat, when I could only trail home eighth.

ABOVE *Tailing Jack Brabham's Cooper in what for me was a deeply disappointing and frustrating Brussels Grand Prix.* (LAT)

The carburation problems seemed to be less severe for this third heat and the Lotus ran much better than it had earlier in the day, although by no means perfectly.

I was able to finish the heat in second place, which gave me seventh place on aggregate after a troubled and deeply disappointing weekend.

528   1st

Preis von Wien

Lotus 18

16 April 1961, Aspern (OS)

Race distance 55 laps of 1.69-mile circuit 1h 10m 1.6s
Race speed 80.15mph **Fastest lap** 1m 12.2s, 84.57mph
(record) **Car no** 17 **Entrant** R.R.C. Walker

530   Retired

Aintree 200

F1 Cooper-Climax

22 April 1961, Aintree, Liverpool (GB)

Race distance 50 laps of 2-mile circuit
Reason for retirement bearings after 2 laps **Car no** 7
Entrant R.R.C Walker

531   8th

Syracuse Grand Prix

Lotus 18

25 April 1961, Sicily (I)

Race distance 56 laps of 3.47-mile circuit **Car no** 18
Entrant R.R.C. Walker

O n the way down to Syracuse, the team stopped off to contest this minor-league event on a bumpy airfield circuit near Vienna. I won quite easily from albeit a small field, although I was impressed by a young British driver called Shane Summers, who qualified his Cooper alongside me on the front row.

T he Lotus 18 was making its long journey down to Syracuse, via Aspern, so the Walker team pressed into service its old Cooper for the Aintree 200, but it hardly seemed worth all that effort when the bearings went on the third lap and I had to retire.

T his was another frustrating outing, caused by carburation problems. I ended up four laps down on newcomer Giancarlo Baghetti's winning Ferrari and was classified eighth after a race in which I ended up wondering whether we would ever solve the problem that had dogged us so much over the past few races.

529   1st

Aintree, Sports Car Race

Lotus 19 'Monte Carlo'

22 April 1961, Aintree, Liverpool (GB)

Race distance 17 laps of 2-mile circuit **Race time** 35m 5.6s
Race speed 87.19mph **Fastest lap** 2m, 90mph **Car no** 93
Entrant UDT Laystall

W hile the Lotus 18 continued its journey to Syracuse, I enjoyed another fairly routine victory with the excellent Lotus 19 in this British domestic sports car event, supporting the Aintree 200.

RIGHT *Taking the chequered flag in the Aintree 200 supporting sports car race at the wheel of the Lotus 19 'Monte Carlo'.* (LAT)

532 Retired

Targa Florio

Porsche RS60

30 April 1961, Piccolo Madonie, Sicily (I)

World Sports Car Championship, round 2

Race distance 10 laps of 45-mile circuit
Reason for retirement Differential **Co-driver** Graham Hill
Car no 136 **Entrant** Camoradi/Works

With a 2-litre engine that offered enhanced torque compared with the smaller 1.7-litre power units, this Porsche was pretty much the perfect car for the Targa Florio.

I led the first four laps by a minute and a half from Jo Bonnier's Porsche and then handed over to Graham Hill, who did two laps, after which I took it over again for the run to the finish.

When I got back behind the wheel, I was 76 seconds behind the leading Ferrari. I managed to haul back the deficit and went into the final lap 65 seconds ahead. Then just five miles from the finish, the Porsche differential failed and all that effort had been for nothing.

533 1st

Silverstone, BRDC International Trophy

2.5 Cooper 'Intercontinental'

6 May 1961, Silverstone (GB)

Organising club British Racing Drivers' Club **Race distance** 80 laps of 2.9-mile circuit **Race time** 2h 41m 36.6s **Race speed** 87.09mph **Fastest lap** 1m 52.4s, 93.75mph **Car no** 4 **Entrant** R.R.C. Walker

OPPOSITE *I came tantalisingly close to winning the Targa Florio in the Porsche RS60 but its differential failed just before the finish.* (LAT)

ABOVE *Splashing to victory in the rain-soaked International Trophy race. I lapped the entire, high-quality field.* (Tom March Collection)

I have to say that I was quite proud of this performance. Although Rob entered me in the Lotus, this would be one of four races in which I drove the excellent 'Intercontinental' Cooper T53P against one of the best non-championship grids of the season. This may have been no *grande épreuve*, but I roundly defeated a grid that included the reigning World Champion Jack Brabham and future title-holders Graham Hill, Jim Clark and John Surtees.

I always relished racing in the wet because I found I could beat the others in these conditions if I had a competitive car, although sometimes I could beat them even when my car was not particularly competitive. Rain is a great equaliser.

This was probably the most satisfying race of my career and I finished a lap ahead of the whole field.

534 1st

Silverstone, Sports Car Race

Lotus 19 'Monte Carlo'

6 May 1961, Silverstone (GB)

Organising club British Racing Drivers' Club
Race distance 25 laps of 2.9-mile circuit **Race time** 42m 53.6s
Race speed 102.36mph **Fastest lap** 1m 39.2s, 106.22mph (record) **Car no** 12 **Entrant** UDT Laystall

This was quite a closely fought event, which I eventually won by just over 4 seconds from Roy Salvadori's Cooper, with Cliff Allison following home third in his Cooper.

Monaco Grand Prix

Lotus 18

14 May 1961, Monte Carlo (MON)

F1 World Championship, round 1

Race distance 100 laps of 1.95-mile circuit **Race time** 2h 45m 50.1s **Race speed** 70.704mph **Fastest lap** 1m 36.3s, 73.055mph (shared with R. Ginther) **Car no** 20 **Entrant** R.R.C. Walker

Dutch Grand Prix

Lotus 18

22 May 1961, Zandvoort, Haarlem (NL)

F1 World Championship, round 2

Race distance 75 laps of 2.61-mile circuit **Race time** 2h 2m 14.3s **Car no** 14 **Entrant** R.R.C. Walker

I qualified on pole for Monaco, extracting every ounce of potential from the Walker Lotus 18 to post a time quicker than both Richie Ginther's Ferrari and Jim Clark's Team Lotus 21, which shared the front row with me.

Just as I was preparing to take my place on the grid, I noticed that one of the Lotus's chassis tubes had developed a slight crack, so with no further ado Alf Francis produced his welding equipment and went to work repairing the problem on the starting grid, his torch flame just a few inches from the brim-full 30-gallon fuel tank. Looking back on it, I can quite see how some people might have concluded that we had gone raving mad to take such a risk, but it had to be done.

The conditions that day were simply sweltering and the team removed the car's lower side body panels to provide some welcome extra cooling for the driver. Ginther led for the first 13 laps, but I quickly concluded that I should give it all I could and try to take the lead and move away from him and Phil Hill. They were not going to give up hounding me and, although I led for the remaining 83 laps, I never got more than a paltry 3.6 seconds ahead. All credit to Richie, who fought like a tiger the whole way, and we both finished up sharing the fastest lap of the race.

I think this was probably my greatest drive in a Formula 1 race. With my old Climax 'four', I managed to hold off the Ferraris despite the fact that they had 30bhp more from their V6 engines.

A surprising fact is that if I had driven my car at my pole position time for all 100 laps, it would only have taken 40 seconds less than the actual race time.

The euphoria generated by that Monaco victory certainly did not last long. Eight days later I was contesting the Dutch Grand Prix at Zandvoort, where the fast corners and long straights played to the strength of the Ferraris. I qualified fourth and finished in the same position, with Jim Clark's Lotus 21 about 7 seconds ahead of me in third place. The Ferraris might have been the most immediate problem during the 1961 season, but it was becoming very clear that I was not going to be able to handle Jimmy if I was to be handicapped by a year-old car that was less competitive than his. I was still confident I could beat him, but not with one arm tied behind my back!

LEFT *Braking for Station Hairpin on my way to victory in the Monaco Grand Prix in Rob Walker's Lotus 18. I judge this race to have been my finest drive in Formula 1.* (Klemantaski Collection)

537   8th

Nürburgring, ADAC 1,000kms

Porsche RS61

28 May 1961, Nürburgring (D)

World Sports Car Championship, round 3

Race distance 44 laps of 14.17-mile circuit **Race time** 8h 2m 7.5s **Car no** 20 & 22 **Co-driver** Graham Hill **Entrant** Works

---

After our unlucky outing in the Targa Florio, Porsche invited me to share its 1.7-litre RS61 with Graham Hill in the Nürburgring 1,000kms race, an event in which I had done rather well over the years. With its enlarged engine – actually only 5cc over 1.6 litres, tipping it just inside the 2-litre class – it was a very nice little machine, although the fact that it was open made it a little on the damp side in the early wet stages of what proved to be a very long race.

I started the race on Dunlop's excellent D12 rain tyres, which enabled me to take the lead on the second lap from Jim Clark's old Aston DBR1, but as the circuit dried the more powerful Ferraris overtook me. After 12 laps Graham took over and we dropped to fifth, shortly before it began to snow. That swung the advantage back into our favour and I was back up to second place, but then the car broke. We took over a Carrera coupé from Herbie Linge and Sepp Greger, and brought it through to victory in the 2-litre class.

538   1st

Brands Hatch, Silver City Trophy

Lotus 18/21

3 June 1961, Brands Hatch, Kent (GB)

Race distance 76 laps of 2.65-mile circuit **Race time** 2h 11m 40.6s **Race speed** 84.70 mph **Fastest lap** 1m 42s, 93.52mph (record) **Car no** 26 **Entrant** UDT Laystall

---

I used one of the UDT Laystall Lotus 18/21s for this non-title race, winning comfortably after John Surtees crashed and Jim Clark over-revved his engine. Shane Summers crashed fatally in practice.

539   Retired

Le Mans 24 Hours

Ferrari 250 GT SWB

10/11 June 1961, Sarthe (F)

World Sports Car Championship, round 4

Race distance 24 hours of 8.38-mile circuit (2,781.61 miles, 333 laps) **Reason for retirement** Sliced radiator hose **Car no** 18 **Co-driver** Graham Hill **Entrant** R.R.C Walker/NART

After my success during 1960 with the 250 GT SWB fielded by Rob Walker and Dick Wilkins, they ordered one of the new 1961 Competizione versions to replace it. This car had bigger valves, different carburettors and a lighter bodyshell than its predecessors. It was delivered to us at Le Mans, where it was run by

Luigi Chinetti's North American Racing Team, which made a first-rate mess of operating it on its début outing.

I was sharing the car with Graham Hill again and we were up to third place overall late on Saturday evening, and leading the GT class by miles, when the car suddenly boiled away all its water. For some utterly incomprehensible reason NART had left in the road-going cooling fan, which had flown apart because of the engine's sustained high-speed revving and had sliced clean through a radiator hose. It was an unbelievable lapse of preparation for a supposedly professional racing team.

540   8th

Belgian Grand Prix

Lotus 18/21

June 18 1961, Spa-Francorchamps, Liège (B)

F1 World Championship, round 3

Race distance 30 laps of 8.76-mile circuit **Race time** 2h 6m 59.4s **Car no** 14 **Entrant** R.R.C. Walker

The Walker team had started the updating process for our Lotus 18 for this race, equipping the car with the more streamlined 21-style upper bodywork and modified rear suspension, but the car was still bog slow on the long straights. Eighth place was a pretty average result, but considering how I ended up at Spa the previous year, I suppose it was a relief to finish with all the wheels on.

LEFT *Leaning into the Karussell with the Porsche RS61 during the Nürburgring 1,000kms.* (LAT)

ABOVE RIGHT *With Colin Chapman, celebrating after winning the Silver City Trophy race at Brands Hatch.* (LAT)

RIGHT *In the new Dick Wilkins-owned, NART-entered Ferrari 250 GT SWB Competizione ahead of one of the Aston Martins at Le Mans. NART's teamwork was always chaotic and the race turned out to be a fiasco.* (LAT)

541 · 1st

Players 200, Heat 1

Lotus 19 'Monte Carlo'
24 June 1961, Mosport Park, Toronto (CAN)

Race distance 40 laps of 2.46-mile circuit **Race time** 1h 8m 4s
Fastest lap 1m 40s, 86.4mph (record) **Car no** 1
Entrant UDT Laystall

A quick trip across the Atlantic during a rare spare weekend during the course of an intensive European season yielded the first of two heat wins, which were included for the inaugural meeting at the challenging Mosport Park circuit close to Toronto.

BELOW *Back behind the wheel of an excellent Lotus 19 on my way to one of two wins at Mosport Park.* (Klemantaski Collection)

OPPOSITE *Another troubled French Grand Prix at Reims ended with my Lotus colliding with Phil Hill's Ferrari.* (LAT)

542 · 1st

Players 200, Heat 2

Lotus 19 'Monte Carlo'
24 June 1961, Mosport Park, Toronto (CAN)

Race distance 40 laps of 2.46-mile circuit
Race time 1h 7m 50s **Car no** 1 **Entrant** UDT Laystall

The second heat win gave me overall victory on aggregate at an average speed of 84.7mph.

543 · Retired

French Grand Prix

Lotus 18/21
2 July 1961, Reims (F)

F1 World Championship, round 4

Race distance 52 laps of 5.16-mile circuit
Reason for retirement Collision **Fastest lap** 2m 30.4s, 123.48mph **Car no** 26 **Entrant** R.R.C Walker

I think I drove even better at Reims than I had at Spa. Even though the venue for the French Grand Prix was a very quick circuit indeed, I started the weekend on a satisfying note by getting my Lotus into the slipstream of Wolfgang von Trips's Ferrari, which towed me around to qualify fourth on the inside of the second row. I was the first non-Ferrari in the field.

In the opening stages I ran as high as third, but gradually I became aware that the Lotus's braking performance was gradually deteriorating. Eventually I pitted for attention and the mechanics discovered that a rear brake pipe was slowly leaking away all its fluid. This problem was attended to, but, unbeknown to any of us, a lump of molten tar from the deteriorating track surface had lodged around the inside edge of the wheel rim.

As soon as I returned to the race I realised that something was wrong; the car was vibrating so much that I was convinced the wheel had not been re-fitted properly. Finally the problem was resolved at a second pit stop and I went back into the race again. Then Phil Hill spun his Ferrari at Thillois, I slid into him, and struggled into the pits to retire.

544 — 1st

Silverstone, British Empire Trophy

2.5 Cooper 'Intercontinental'
8 July 1961, Silverstone (GB)

Race distance 52 laps of 2.9-mile circuit **Race time** 1h 27m 19.2s **Race speed** 104.58mph **Fastest lap** 1m 35.4s, 109.31mph **Car no** 7 **Entrant** R.R.C. Walker

545 — 1st

Silverstone, GT Race

Ferrari 250 GT SWB
8 July 1961, Silverstone (GB)

Race distance 25 laps of 2.9-mile circuit **Race time** 46m 25.4s **Race speed** 94.58mph **Fastest lap** 1m 49.8s, 95.97mph (record) **Car no** 32 **Entrant** R.R.C. Walker

546 — Retired

British Grand Prix

Lotus 18/21 & Ferguson P99
15 July 1961, Aintree, Liverpool (GB)

Race distance 75 laps of 3-mile circuit **Reason for retirement** Brakes after 44 laps & push-start in pit lane **Car no** 28 & 26 Race **Entrant** R.R.C. Walker

This was my third so-called intercontinental race in Rob Walker's super Cooper T53P and I ended up lapping everybody but the second-placed John Surtees, in a similar car, who had beaten me to pole position.

This was another satisfying win in the Rob Walker Ferrari 250 Competizione.

The British Grand Prix took place at Aintree in absolutely torrential conditions in which, to be fair, Wolfgang von Trips drove extremely well to lead the lion's share of the distance after overtaking his Ferrari team-mate Phil Hill as early as lap seven.

I had no complaints about the conditions at all because I had the Walker Lotus in among the Ferraris and was holding second place in the early stages. Then, on lap 24, I spun wildly on a huge puddle at Melling Crossing, recovering after losing only 10 seconds to von Trips. As the track dried out, so I developed a rear-brake problem and eventually brought the car in to retire.

For the remainder of the race I took over the four-wheel-drive Ferguson P99 that Rob was also running for Jack Fairman, although the car was later disqualified as a result of Fairman having benefited from a push-start in the pits earlier in the race. The P99 was an extraordinary piece of Formula 1 engineering developed by Tony Rolt at Harry Ferguson's company to showcase the potential of four-wheel drive in a motor racing application. As you will see when we come to the 1961 Oulton Park Gold Cup, it achieved its target rather well.

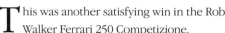

LEFT *In company with two fine rivals, Innes Ireland (left) and Jim Clark.* (LAT)

OPPOSITE *A rain-soaked British Grand Prix at Aintree began for me in the Rob Walker Lotus 18/21 (top) and finished in the four-wheel-drive Ferguson P99 (bottom), which I took over from Jack Fairman. The Ferguson was a stunning car in the wet.* (LAT)

547 Retired

Solitude Grand Prix

Lotus 18/21

23 July 1961, Solitude, Stuttgart (D)

Race distance 25 laps of 7.09-miles **Reason for retirement**
Gearbox **Car no** 17 **Entrant** UDT Laystall

This excellent road circuit close to Stuttgart was the scene of several closely fought non-championship races over the years, including the 1961 event, which was won in spectacular style by Innes Ireland in the factory Lotus 21 after a ferocious battle with the works Porsches. Unfortunately, I was destined to take no part in this contest because the gearbox on my Lotus wilted and I had to retire.

548 1st

German Grand Prix

Lotus 18/21

6 August 1961, Nürburgring (D)

F1 World Championship, round 6

Race distance 15 laps of 14.17-miles **Race time** 2h 18m 12.4s
Race speed 92.297mph **Car no** 7 **Entrant** R.R.C. Walker

The Nürburgring was another circuit on which our elderly Lotus might be in with a chance. In practice I was very impressed with the high-hysteresis Dunlop D12 rain tyres and I decided to run them in the race, even though Dunlop's man Vic Barlow was appalled when I made the suggestion. "You can't use those," he said. "I've got to," I replied to him. He said, "They will fail at high speed," but I told him

that was a risk that I had to take. All in all, it looked like a bit of a re-run of Argentina 1958.

I also pointed to the fact that Innes had used them to win at Solitude on a quick circuit in hot conditions. He had judged that these so-called 'green spots' were worth risking because of the high levels of additional grip they afforded and I was going to take the same risk. I qualified third behind Phil Hill and Wolfgang von Trips, but my biggest worry was Jack Brabham, who had the new Climax V8 installed in his works Cooper. Jack had managed to convince his team that it would be ideal to start with hard tyres on the rear wheels of his car, so I reasoned that, although he might make a quick start, I absolutely had to get ahead of him before we plunged down through the Hatzenbach section beyond the North Curve.

My conclusions came true. Jack went ahead of me at the start and, the first time I tried to pass him, chopped across me quite firmly. But then he went off the road, so I was left in the lead with the track surface reassuringly damp, which enabled me to get the best performance and durability out of my 'marginal' tyres. I really drove hard, flat out the whole way. In the closing stages, the rain started to fall again, which helped me ease away to beat von Trips into second place by 22 seconds. The most traffic I saw on that day was on the autobahn when I was driving back to Düsseldorf after the race, when I was stationary in a queue for 40 minutes.

LEFT Chasing Jack Brabham's Cooper in the pale green UDT Laystall Lotus 18/21 in the non-championship Solitude Grand Prix. (LAT)

BELOW With runner-up Wolfgang von Trips framed in the winners' garland after winning the German Grand Prix at the Nürburgring. Little could I have imagined that this would be my last grande épreuve victory. (LAT)

549   1st

Brands Hatch, Peco Trophy

Ferrari 250 GT SWB

7 August 1961, Brands Hatch, Kent (GB)

Race distance 20 laps of 2.65-mile circuit **Race time** 38m 33.6s
Race speed 82.47mph **Fastest lap** 1m 54.2s, 82.53mph (record)
Car no 97 **Entrant** R.R.C. Walker

This was another routine victory with Rob Walker's Ferrari in the main supporting race to the Guards Trophy at Brands Hatch.

550   Retired

Brands Hatch, Guards Trophy

2.5 Cooper 'Intercontinental'

7 August 1961, Brands Hatch, Kent (GB)

Race distance 76 laps of 2.65-mile circuit
Reason for retirement Gearbox **Car no** 12
Entrant R.R.C. Walker

I was going for my fourth win out of four races with Rob Walker's Cooper T53P. John Surtees led, but crashed, and I was then comfortably ahead when the gearbox broke.

551   1st

RAC Tourist Trophy

Ferrari 250 GT SWB

19 August 1961, Goodwood, West Sussex (GB)

Race distance 109 laps of 2.4-mile circuit **Race time** 3h 1m 12s
Race speed 86.62mph **Car no** 7 **Entrant** R.R.C. Walker

I went to Goodwood aiming for my seventh TT victory and my fifth consecutive win in this prestigious race, only to find that I had my hands full with a challenge from Michael Parkes driving a similar 1961-spec GT for the Maranello Concessionaires/Equipe Endeavour combine. Mike may not have been a full-time professional driver, but he certainly impressed me with his application, precision, and consistency.

The race was a battle between the two of us, but Mike, with his more flamboyant driving style, wore out his Ferrari's rear tyres more quickly than I did. Eventually, I won quite comfortably, and afterwards Mike graciously said that he had learned more about driving a racing car during the time he spent following me at Goodwood than at any other point in his career.

552   1st

Kannonloppet

Lotus 18-21

20 August 1961, Karlskoga (S)

Race time 46m 15.8s, 69.26mph **Race distance** 30 laps of 1.86-mile circuit **Fastest lap** 1m 30.4s, 74.23mph (shared with John Surtees) **Car no** 1 **Entrant** UDT Laystall

There was a special extra practice session laid on by the Karlskoga organisers for those competitors who had raced at Goodwood the previous day, but I somehow managed to arrive too late even for that. As a result I started my now-regular 'Scandinavian tour' by starting from the back of the grid in the UDT-Laystall Lotus we had borrowed. At the end of the first lap I was third, then on the second lap I went into the lead and stayed there until the finish.

553 — 1st

Copenhagen Grand Prix, Heat 1

Lotus 18-21

26 August 1961, Roskilde (DEN)

Race distance 20 laps of 0.75-mile circuit **Race time** 15m 47.7s **Race speed** 57.14mph **Fastest lap** 47s, 58.23mph **Car no** 7 **Entrant** UDT Laystall

A 15-minute Formula 1 race? Hard to believe it! In this little event I beat Jack Brabham by less than a second. A good dice.

554 — 1st

Copenhagen Grand Prix, Heat 2

Lotus 18-21

27 August 1961, Roskilde (DK)

Race distance 30 laps of 0.75-mile circuit **Race time** 21m 36.8s **Race speed** 61mph **Fastest lap** 42.8s, 63.02mph **Car no** 7 **Entrant** UDT Laystall

In this race, 30 laps instead of the first heat's 20, I beat Innes Ireland by a bit more…

555 — 1st

Copenhagen Grand Prix, Heat 3

Lotus 18-21

27 August 1961, Roskilde (DK)

Race distance 30 laps of 0.75-mile circuit **Fastest lap** 43.1s, 62.14mph **Car no** 7 **Entrant** UDT Laystall

ABOVE *Battling for victory in number 7 during the Copenhagen Grand Prix at Roskilde.* (LAT)

OPPOSITE *Manhandling fuel churns in the Goodwood pits during another victorious run in the Tourist Trophy.* (Sutton Motorsport Images)

And then, in the third heat, again of 30 laps, I beat Innes Ireland into second place yet again. That meant I took a decisive victory on aggregate.

556 — 1st

Modena Grand Prix

Lotus 18/21

3 September 1961, Modena aerautodromo (I)

Race distance 100 laps of 2.36-mile circuit **Race time** 1h 40m 8.1s **Race speed** 88.1mph **Fastest lap** 59.2s, 89.4mph **Car no** 26 **Entrant** R.R.C. Walker

I was repatriated to the cockpit of my more familiar Walker team Lotus 18/21 for this race, in which I managed to post another quite

comfortable victory on the bumpy airfield perimeter road circuit, which had become such a regular testing venue for most of the local Italian teams.

557 Rtd

Italian Grand Prix

Lotus 21

10 September 1961, Monza (I)

F1 World Championship, round 7

Race distance 43 laps of 6.214-mile circuit **Reason for retirement** Wheel bearing after 36 laps **Car no** 28 **Entrant** Works

I started this unfortunately tragic weekend on a disappointing note when my Lotus 18/21 refused to cool properly, so Innes

Ireland made the very generous suggestion that Team Lotus loan me his Lotus 21, provided Esso and BP gave their approval. With hindsight, I think Innes's gesture reflected the fact that he was a Lotus man through and through at that time.

This was very much a Ferrari circuit, and, despite the slight aerodynamic advantage gained by running the more slippery Lotus 21, I was only able to qualify 11th. In the race, I gradually progressed through the field – thanks to a lot of other cars breaking down – and ended up battling for second place with Dan Gurney's Porsche, some way behind Phil Hill's leading Ferrari. But then the Lotus succumbed to a failed wheel bearing, the legacy of the punishment that it had received on the banking.

Only after I had come in did I hear the dreadful news that Wolfgang von Trips had been killed, and more than a dozen

ABOVE *On the banking at Monza during the Italian Grand Prix in the Lotus 21 that the works team were generous enough to loan to the Rob Walker team.* (LAT)

OPPOSITE *Winning the Oulton Park Gold Cup race in the remarkable four-wheel-drive Ferguson P99, to which the newspaper cutting refers.* (Tom March Collection)

spectators, in a collision with Jim Clark's Lotus on the second lap. That placed the other disappointments of the day into their correct perspective.

558   1st

Oulton Park, Gold Cup

Ferguson P99

23 September 1961, Oulton Park, Cheshire (GB)

Race distance 60 laps of 2-mile circuit **Race time** 1h 51m 53.8s
Race speed 88.83mph **Fastest lap** 1m 46.4s, 93.42mph (record)
Car no 7 **Entrant** R.R.C. Walker

The thing that made the four-wheel-drive Ferguson so very special was the driving style one had to adopt to get the very best out of the machine. Most significantly, if one backed off the throttle going through a corner, the car would not tighten its line. It would simply slow down. Its traction and brakes were outstanding.

I was a little on the lucky side in winning this non-championship race, as the intermittently wet weather played to the P99's inherent strengths. The conditions also masked its downside, especially the considerable additional weight of the four-wheel-drive transmission. It was certainly an interesting experience, although I never raced the Ferguson again – primarily because this was an experimental car but also because my retirement came six months later.

Moss's car can win on the corners

By DENYS AINSWORTH

Boldness needed

You can leave your braking

559   3rd

Canadian Grand Prix

Lotus 19 'Monte Carlo'

30 September 1961, Mosport Park, Toronto (CAN)

Race distance 100 laps of 2.459-mile circuit **Race time** 2h 47m 29s (99 laps) **Fastest lap** 1m 34.2s, 91.71mph (record) **Car no** 7 **Entrant** Works

By this stage in the season, UDT Laystall's Lotus 19 had been sold to a private owner in the USA and, although I continued to be invited to drive it, there was no doubt that its previously high standards of preparation had been allowed to slip. I should have won on this second outing of the year at Mosport Park, but irritating and relatively minor problems such as jamming gears dropped me to a lapped third at the chequered flag.

DEX BP SUP

560 — Retired

United States Grand Prix

Lotus 18/21

8 October 1961, Watkins Glen, New York (USA)

F1 World Championship, round 8

Race distance 100 laps of 2.3-mile circuit **Reason for retirement** Bearing failure after 58 laps **Car no** 7

I qualified a respectable third for this final World Championship Formula 1 race of the season, lining up on the front row of the grid alongside Masten Gregory's Cooper, on pole position, and Graham Hill's BRM-Climax.

I led from the start and spent much of the first half of the race locked in a battle with Jack Brabham, who was using the new Climax V8 again in his works Cooper, but his engine overheated and my Climax four-cylinder suffered bearing failure just before the 60-lap mark. That handed the lead to dear old Innes Ireland, who duly kept everything together to win by just under 5 seconds from Dan Gurney's Porsche, thereby scoring the first *grande épreuve* victory for Colin Chapman's Team Lotus.

BELOW *The start of the US Grand Prix at Watkins Glen with Jim Clark's works Lotus 21 (14) trying to squeeze past me as we accelerate away from the grid.* (LAT)

OPPOSITE *With Jack Brabham, sitting in the Sunbeam Alpine we drove in the production car race at Riverside. Next to us is Rootes competition boss Norman Garrad.* (LAT)

561 — 16th

Los Angeles Times Grand Prix

Lotus 19 'Monte Carlo'

13 October 1961, Riverside, California (USA)

Race distance 61 laps of 3.27-mile circuit **Entrant** ex-UDT Laystall

Another great run in the ex-UDT Laystall Lotus 19, but again it was ruined by poor preparation. I led commandingly until a brake seal failed, causing me to drop right down the finishing order to be classified 16th.

562   3rd

3-Hour Production Car Race

Sunbeam Alpine

15 October 1961, Riverside, California (USA)

Race distance 3 hours of 3.27-mile circuit
Co-driver Jack Brabham **Entrant** Works

I was asked by the Rootes Group to drive at Riverside, California, with Jack Brabham in this Sunbeam Alpine and, because Jack himself had a Rootes agency – in Woking, Surrey – I agreed to do so. The car suffered big-end failure after a couple of laps of practice.

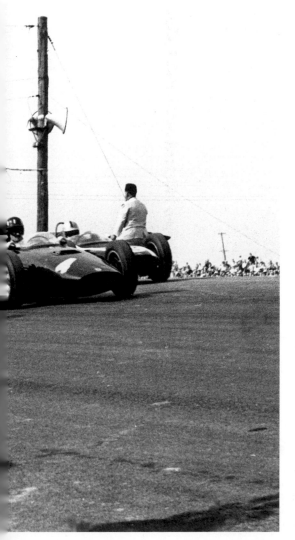

The temperature on race day was in excess of 110 degrees Fahrenheit. In what was a distinctly unmemorable event, run over three hours, we won our class and finished third overall despite the car suffering a rear brake seal failure and a gearbox breakage.

563   1st

Pacific Grand Prix, Heat 1

Lotus 19 'Monte Carlo'

22 October 1961, Laguna Seca (USA)

Race distance 100 miles **Race time** 1h 9m 15.8s
Race speed 90.3mph **Car no** 7 **Entrant** UDT Laystall

This was a decent result for me – in one of my favourite cars – after a string of disappointments in North American events.

564   1st

Pacific Grand Prix, Heat 2

Lotus 19 'Monte Carlo'

22 October 1961, Laguna Seca (USA)

Race distance 100 miles **Race time** 1h 8m 15.3s
Race speed 91.9mph **Fastest lap** 1m 15.2s **Car no** 7
Entrant UDT Laystall

I repeated the first-heat victory to give me overall victory on aggregate.

565   1st

Nassau Tourist Trophy, Heat 1

Ferrari 250 GT SWB

3 December 1961, Oakes Field (BA)

Race distance 21 laps of 3.5-mile circuit **Car no** 4
Entrant R.R.C. Walker

More fun in the winter sun at the wheel of Rob Walker's Ferrari. By now I had my holiday home in the Bahamas and I really enjoyed my visits there.

ABOVE *Chasing a Ferrari rival on my way to victory in one of the two heats of the Nassau Tourist Trophy.* (LAT)

BELOW *Leaping into the cockpit of the Lotus 19 at the start of the Nassau Trophy at Oakes Field.* (Tim Hendley, Terry O'Neil Collection)

566   1st

Nassau Tourist Trophy, Heat 2

Ferrari 250 GT SWB

3 December 1961, Oakes Field (BA)

Race distance 21 laps of 3.5-mile circuit **Car no** 4
Entrant R.R.C. Walker

A second win made this a good day in the sun.

567   Retired

Governor's Trophy

Lotus 19 'Monte Carlo'

8 December 1961, Oakes Field (BA)

Race distance 30 laps of 3.5-mile circuit
Reason for retirement Rear upright **Fastest lap** 2m 56s
Car no 4 **Entrant** Rosebud Racing

Another retirement with the Lotus 19, but the precise cause on this occasion is lost in the mists of time.

568   Retired

Nassau Trophy

Lotus 19 'Monte Carlo'

10 December 1961, Oakes Field (BA)

Race distance 56 laps of 3.5-mile circuit
Reason for retirement Rear wishbone after 27 laps **Car no** 4
Entrant UDT Laystall

I retired from this race with a broken rear-suspension wishbone, leaving Dan Gurney to win in a similar Lotus 19. I would not drive one of these cars again until 1963, when I tested one at Goodwood just before making my announcement to retire from racing.

BELOW *Oversteering my way to second place in what was to be the final South African Grand Prix of my career.* (LAT)

569   2nd

Natal Grand Prix

Lotus 18/21

17 December 1961, Westmead (SA)

Race distance 89 laps of 2.24-mile circuit **Race time** 2h 14m 30.3s **Fastest lap** 1m 24.8s, 93.37mph **Car no** 7 **Entrant** UDT Laystall

The two final non-championship Formula 1 races of the season formed part of the so-called Springbok series that rounded off the season in South Africa. Both events served to reaffirm what I had come to realise some time before, namely just what a formidable driver Jim Clark was developing into. At Westmead my engine would not rev above 7,400rpm, so he had a slight edge over me in his works Lotus 21 on the slippery track. I had to settle for second behind him.

570   2nd

South African Grand Prix

Lotus 18/21

26 December 1961, East London (SA)

Race distance 80 laps of 2.43-mile circuit **Race time** 2h 7m 4.9s **Fastest lap** 1m 33.1s, 93.86mph **Car no** 7 **Entrant** UDT Laystall

Having taught Jimmy Clark how to water-ski on Christmas Eve, I was up all night the following day feeling really unwell. In the race I had a good start but Jim and his new Lotus team-mate, Trevor Taylor, out-accelerated me. Jim then spun and handed me a 14-second lead, but he was just too quick and whatever I did I just could not keep him at bay. In the end I had to let him by – second again!

1962

NOW TO WORK FOR A LIVING!

Unfortunately, I never made it to the first *grande épreuve* of the 1962 season, although I competed in 15 races in the first three months of the year. Little could I have known that my win in Rob Walker's little Lotus in the previous year's German Grand Prix would be my last win in a World Chamipionship event – my 16th *grande épreuve* victory.

As I stormed through the winter months into 1962, I was determined to continue competing in as many events as possible.

I was really looking forward to the prospect of racing a dark blue 'works' Formula 1 Ferrari and was grateful that Enzo Ferrari had accepted that the car could be maintained and entered by Rob Walker, and painted in his racing colours. Furthermore, he also agreed that the British Racing Partnership could have a new 250 GTO plus a 246 sports car for me to drive, and that these cars could be painted in the team's rather bilious green colour.

The GTO was delivered to Goodwood direct from Maranello Concessionaires, the Ferrari agent in Britain, for me to race there on Easter Monday. As the day's events turned out, I never had the chance to try it and, I must say, it was rather poignant, later in the year, to watch Innes Ireland driving 'my' GTO to victory in the Tourist Trophy on the very circuit where my racing career ended so abruptly.

Part of my Ferrari deal also involved the prospect of racing one of its rear-engined 250 TR/61 machines, fielded jointly by UDT and NART, and in March I drove one of these excellent cars at Sebring. The experience convinced me that it was a terrific car but, at the same time, reinforced my feelings that NART was one of the most shambolic teams that I had ever driven for! I vowed there and then that the whole organisation would have to improve if I was to go on driving under their banner.

Then came the Easter meeting at Goodwood – and the accident. Although I remember nothing of it, of course. What I can piece together about it is related on pages 348-349.

From the moment I became lucid, it was clear that it would take a great deal longer to get better than after any of my previous serious accidents. It was actually a year later that I went back to Goodwood to test drive one of the UDT Lotus 19 'Monte Carlo' sports racing cars. After lapping the damp circuit for more than an hour, it became fairly obvious to me that my reactions at the wheel were no longer as spontaneous as they had been in the past. Even though my times were not bad, what had been instinctive was no longer there.

I took the decision to announce my retirement.

LEFT *Easter Monday, 1962, Goodwood – where the story almost ended.* (LAT)

571 1st

New Zealand Grand Prix

2.5 Lotus 21

6 January 1962, Ardmore (NZ)

Race distance 50 laps of 2-mile circuit **Race time** 1h 23m 14.38s **Race speed** 72.3mph **Fastest lap** 1m 32.8s **Car no** 7 **Entrant** R.R.C. Walker

Rob Walker had, the previous year, ordered a Lotus 21 for me to drive, but it was clear that it would not be delivered until the end of the 1961 World Championship season and I duly made my race début in the car at the New Zealand Grand Prix, where it was fitted with a 2.5-litre Climax engine. We also took out the team's 'intercontinental' Cooper-Climax.

The Lotus cockpit was cramped in the extreme compared with the Cooper's. Rain hosed down, so I made a tremendous effort to grab the lead from the start so that I would have the best of the visibility. In fact, the Lotus was such a benign-handling and well-balanced car that it would skim across the surface of deep puddles without displaying any directional instability whatsoever. In that respect it was very reassuring indeed.

BELOW *The Lotus 21 proved to be the perfect car for the heavy rain that prevailed throughout the New Zealand Grand Prix at Ardmore.* (LAT)

572 2nd

Vic Hudson Memorial Trophy, Heat 1

2.7 Cooper

13 January 1962, Levin (NZ)

Race distance 28 laps of 1.18-mile circuit **Car no** 7 **Entrant** R.R.C. Walker

I drove the Cooper in this event on the bumpy little Levin circuit, finishing second to Jack Brabham in the first heat.

573   2nd

Vic Hudson Memorial Trophy, Final

2.7 Cooper

13 January 1962, Levin (NZ)

Race distance 28 laps of 1.18-mile circuit, race abandoned after 8 laps **Car no** 7 **Entrant** R.R.C. Walker

ABOVE *Leading the Lady Wigram Trophy, and heading for quite an easy win, on the aerodrome circuit at Christchurch.* (LAT)

The final started in heavy rain and, after eight laps, we were called in. The organisers were not prepared to restart the race, which I found most unfair. If it was safe enough to start the race in such conditions – and in my view they had not worsened – then it was wrong to stop it. Why precisely was it not safe to continue? It seemed most illogical to me.

574   1st

Lady Wigram Trophy

2.5 Lotus 21

20 January 1962, Christchurch (NZ)

Race distance 71 laps of 2.11-mile circuit **Race time** 1h 36m 38.7s **Fastest lap** 1m 20.1s, 95.1mph (record, shared with John Surtees) **Car no** 7 **Entrant** R.R.C. Walker

I used the Lotus for this important event at the Christchurch circuit and won quite easily without too much pressure

<table>
<tr><td>

575   2nd

Teretonga Trophy, Heat 1

2.5 Cooper 'Intercontinental'

27 January 1962, Invercargill (NZ)

Race distance 50 laps of 1.5-mile circuit **Car no** 7
Entrant R.R.C. Walker

</td><td>

576   2nd

Teretonga Trophy, Main Race

2.5 Cooper 'Intercontinental'

27 January 1962, Invercargill (NZ)

Race distance 50 laps of 1.5-mile circuit **Race time** 1h 56.2s
Car no 7 **Entrant** R.R.C. Walker

</td><td>

577   1st

Warwick Farm, 100-Mile Race

2.7 Cooper 'Intercontinental'

4 February 1962, Warwick Farm, Sydney (AUS)

Race distance 45 laps of 2.2-mile circuit **Race time** 1h 14m 36.6s
Race speed 81.49mph **Car no** 7 **Entrant** R.R.C. Walker

</td></tr>
</table>

Back in the Cooper again for the final New Zealand event of the winter, and I finished second.

Another second place, this time to Bruce McLaren's Cooper on his home patch.

When I arrived in Australia everybody was tipping my Lotus 21 as the ideal car for the 100-mile race at Sydney's

Warwick Farm circuit and I must say that this rather irritated me.

Just to prove a point, I opted to race Rob Walker's Cooper instead. I suppose it was a rather juvenile decision, but when you are told that a certain circuit is a Cooper or Lotus circuit it really tees me off, so I got a little bit of pleasure in being childish.

In practice, I actually sliced 4 seconds off my existing lap record to qualify on pole position. In the race, Jack Brabham, Bruce McLaren and I had a great dust-up but at the end of the day I managed to pull off another victory, although Bruce posted a new lap record.

Phew! Thank goodness my gamble in choosing the Cooper paid off!

578 4th

Daytona Continental 3 Hours

Ferrari 250GTB

11 February 1962, Daytona, Florida (USA)

World Sports Car Championship, round 1

Race distance 80 laps of 3.81-mile circuit **Car no** 18 **Entrant** NART

This was my first experience on the combined road circuit and banked oval track at Daytona and, on reflection, this race was part of the process of integrating myself with the Ferrari family in preparation for the main events of the 1962 season. This outing was at the wheel of NART's 1961 Le Mans Berlinetta, which was slightly over-geared in practice, but in the race it ran perfectly to finish only two laps behind Dan Gurney's winning Lotus 19. I did not think that was at all bad.

579 5th

Sandown Park, *Formule Libre*

2.5 Cooper 'Intercontinental'

11 March 1962, Sandown Park (AUS)

Race distance 60 laps of 2-mile circuit **Race time** 1h 10m 20.3s (59 laps) **Entrant** R.R.C. Walker

I travelled back to Australia for my final race Down Under, sadly without achieving a win.

LEFT *Blasting off the front row of the grid at Teretonga, my Rob Walker Cooper flanked by Jack Brabham (4) and Bruce McLaren (47).* (LAT)

580   3rd

Sebring 3 Hours

Austin-Healey Sprite

23 March 1962, Sebring, Florida (USA)

World Sports Car Championship, round 2

Race distance 45 laps of 5.3-mile circuit **Car no** 15
Entrant Works

581   Disqualified

Sebring 12 Hours

Ferrari 250 TR/62

25 March 1962, Sebring, Florida (USA)

World Sports Car Championship, round 3

Race distance 206 laps of 5.2-mile circuit
Reason disqualified Refuelling too soon
Co-driver Innes Ireland **Car no** 26 **Entrant** NART

This race, usually of four hours, was reduced to a three-hour affair in 1962. I had a great time racing with Innes Ireland, Pedro Rodríguez and Steve McQueen – the film star – as my team-mates. It rained at the start of the race and initially I pulled away in the lead, until the circuit began to dry out. I thought I could hold off the Fiat-Abarths of Bruce McLaren and Walt Hansgen, but in the closing stages my car began to misfire due to fuel starvation. I had to stop in the pits for a top-up and dropped down to third place.

The original intention for this race was that Innes Ireland and I should share NART's brand-new rear-engined V8 Ferrari, but, although it handled pretty well, it was surprisingly gutless. Consequently, we opted to race what was basically a three-year-old

Testa Rossa, which we judged would suit the bumpy track surface extremely well, in addition to having plenty of power. In fact, during practice it was 9 seconds a lap faster than the V8.

Innes did the Le Mans start and briefly led the race until Pedro Rodríguez boomed past him in another Ferrari. I took over at the first refuelling stop, by which time I had been reminded yet again what a total shambles the NART pit organisation really was. The team had eight cars competing in this event and nobody was even keeping a lap chart. In fact, Innes had come in for fresh brake pads before covering the minimum 20 laps between refuelling stops, as stipulated in the rules, and the marshal in charge of the filler cap seals mistakenly snipped ours open in the chaos of the pit lane. One of our mechanics put fuel in and we were disqualified. We continued racing, but it was obvious that we were in trouble with officialdom.

First we were told that we were being penalised 15 seconds because Innes had entered the pits too soon. Then somebody protested us, the officials deliberated, and we were eventually disqualified. We were leading by a lap when the penalty was formally announced – four hours after the offence was committed!

Needless to say, we were both furious. But I am happy to relate that Innes told the officials exactly what he thought of them. And, if you knew Innes, you could understand that it was well worth hearing!

BELOW *Chaotic pit organisation by NART cost Innes Ireland and I a possible good result with this Ferrari Testa Rossa in the Sebring 12-hour epic. I came in for attention to the brakes but the mechanics regrettably refuelled the car before the permitted time and we were disqualified.* (Ozzie Lyons, Pete Lyons Collection)

582   2nd

Brussels Grand Prix, Heat 1

Lotus 18/21

1 April 1962, Heysel (B)

Race distance 22 laps of 4.06-mile circuit **Race time** 47m 7s **Fastest lap** 2m 2s, 83.46mph **Car no** 1 **Entrant** R.R.C. Walker

I started the 1962 non-championship Formula 1 season with the Walker team's Lotus 18/21 'special', into which had been shoehorned a Climax V8. It was a pretty makeshift piece of kit that really did not feel very good at all to drive. At Brussels I kicked off by finishing second to Graham Hill's BRM, but could not realistically get close enough to make a race out of it.

583 Retired

Brussels Grand Prix, Heat 2

Lotus 18/21

1 April 1962, Heysel (B)

Race distance 22 laps of 4.06-mile circuit
Reason for retirement Timing gear **Fastest lap** 2m, 84.85mph
Car no 1 **Entrant** R.R.C. Walker

584 7th

Snetterton, Lombank Trophy

Lotus 18/21

14 April 1962, Snetterton, Norwich, Norfolk (GB)

Race distance 50 laps of 2.71-mile circuit **Fastest lap** 1m 33.6s,
104.23mph **Car no** 7 **Entrant** UDT Laystall/R.R.C. Walker

585 Retired

Goodwood, Glover Trophy

Lotus 18/21

23 April 1962, Goodwood, West Sussex (GB)

Race distance 42 laps of 2.4-mile circuit
Reason for retirement Collision **Fastest lap** 1m 22s, 105.37s
(shared with John Surtees) **Car no** 7
Entrant UDT Laystall/R.R.C. Walker

I accidentally managed to change down into second when I was supposed to be changing up into fourth. It buzzed the engine to about 9,000rpm and shortly afterwards a timing gear broke. As a result, I was unable to take part in the third heat.

Rob lent the V8-engined Lotus 18/21 to UDT Laystall for me to drive in the early-season British domestic Formula 1 races. I had just taken the lead at Snetterton from Graham Hill's BRM when my throttle began to stick. I pitted for attention and finished seventh.

And here the story ended…
    The factual sequence of events that led to my being unconscious in hospital for a month and paralysed down one side for six months or so has always been unclear.

Suffice it to say that, in the Glover Trophy on Easter Monday, driving the Rob Walker Lotus 18/21 in the pale green colours of BRP, I had pulled into the pits with throttle or gearbox problems, which lost me a couple of laps. Once I rejoined the race, I was too far back to have any hope of winning but, ever competitive, I decided to go after the lap record.

Approaching the right-hander at St Mary's, I came up behind race leader Graham Hill's BRM, which was a lap ahead of me. Rather naturally, I wanted to unlap myself. Here the forensic trail goes cold. I cannot remember what happened next.

The bare facts are that, having pulled too far to my left, I did not make the corner and went straight on, hitting the bank nearly head-on at about 60mph. I was unconscious and had to be cut out of my car, which,

OPPOSITE *Heading for second place in the first heat of the Brussels Grand Prix at Heysel, just three weeks before my appointment with destiny.* (LAT)

ABOVE RIGHT *The tangled wreckage of my Lotus at the Goodwood trackside.* (Getty Images)

I believe, took over an hour. I was really lucky that the car did not catch fire.

Quite why my accident happened has never been explained to my total satisfaction. I would never normally have taken such a line at St Mary's. What I think *could* have happened, being wise after the event, is that the flag marshals gave Graham the blue flag to let him know that

he was about to be overtaken. He may have acknowledged it with a wave. It was the sort of thing that one did then. Graham's style was to take a wide entry, whereas I always took a narrow one. Anyway, I think he may have moved to his left to get on line. I would have eased to the left and got on the damp grass – and then I would have had very little braking or steering.

POSTSCRIPT

It took another two or three years for me to realise it, but it eventually became clear to me that I had taken the decision to retire extremely prematurely. At the time of my accident, I think I was driving as well as at any time in my career and I believe I could well have raced on into my mid-40s – that is to say well into the 1970s.

But by the time I realised that I really was ready to resume my motor racing career, my life had filled up with so many other business activities that there was just not enough room in my schedule to consider it. In 1979 I did make what I can only describe, on reflection, as an ill-starred return to saloon car racing driving an Audi 80, but I never managed to get fully used to the slick tyres that were being used then, and I very much regretted ever doing it.

The emergence of international historic racing has turned out to be far more attractive to me and for many years this has

proved a great source of satisfaction. I have been reacquainted with many of the cars I drove in their heyday and I have even acquired my own OSCA MT4, a great little car that is identical to the one I drove at Sebring on my first trip to the United States in 1954.

As far as my personal life is concerned, I have gained great happiness and contentment in my third marriage to Susie and our son Elliot, who is now approaching 30, works with me in my property business. I have also remained close to my daughter Alison from my second, albeit brief, marriage to an American lady, Elaine Barbarino.

Susie, who I have known since she was a child, runs my office at our London home with great zest and efficiency. We are a great team and she has been patient and forbearing throughout the 32 years we have been together. I owe her a huge amount.

INDEX